Studies in Race Relations South Africa & USA

(Second Edition)

Frank Cooney
(Principal Teacher of Modern Studies, St Columba's High School Gourock)

Gordon Morton
(Principal Teacher of Modern Studies, Lenzie Academy, Lenzie)

Barry Wright
(Assistant Head Teacher, Gleniffer High School, Paisley)

PULSE PUBLICATIONS

Contents

SOUTH AFRICA

1 Background to South Africa Today 3

2 Structures of Apartheid 6

3 Application of Apartheid 10

4 Modernising Apartheid 15

5 Internal Opposition to Apartheid 1948 - 1988 23

6 External Reaction to Apartheid 28

7 Dismantling Apartheid 36

8 Legacy of Apartheid 46

THE UNITED STATES OF AMERICA

9 The USA - A Nation of Minorities 58

10 Towards Reform 60

11 Civil Rights in Action 66

12 Blacks and the Political Process 73

13 The Impact of the New Right 79

14 Economic Situation of Blacks 83

15 The Hispanics 88

Index 92

Acknowledgements

The authors and publishers would like to thank the following for permission to reproduce copyright material.

The Economist (page 87); Glasgow Herald (page 73); The Guardian (pages 54, 90); Leadership (page 56); Popperfoto (pages 15, 26, 41, 42, 56, 68, 76, 77, 79, 80); South African Consul (page 36); Soviet Weekly (page 18); Time Magazine (page 71); Times Educational Supplement (page 50); Wright (page 82).

Every attempt has been made to contact copyright holders, but we apologise if any have been overlooked.

Published and Typeset by **Pulse Publications**
26 Burnside Gardens, Glasgow G76 7QS

Printed by **Holmes McDougall**, Edinburgh

British Library Cataloguing-in-Publication Data
A Catalogue record for this book is available from the British Library

ISBN 0 948766 14 X

1 Background to South Africa Today

In 1948, South Africa embarked upon the development of a unique political, economic and social structure which became known as apartheid - an Afrikaans word meaning 'separate development'. The policy of apartheid was decided upon by the Whites, one of the groups within South Africa. The other groups were forced to accept it. The reasoning behind apartheid was to allow the distinct peoples of South Africa to control their own destiny and develop within their own traditions and customs. The fact that the Whites, a minority of South Africa's population, could take such a decision and continue to enforce it into the early 1990s tells us where the economic and political power lay by 1948. The development and colonisation of South Africa is a history of white supremacy being established and sustained in a land where non-Whites continuously formed the majority of the population.

BOERS, BRITISH & AFRICANS

White settlers came to Southern Africa because of the needs of Europe's trade with India and the Far East. The sea route rounded the Cape of Good Hope into the Indian Ocean and in 1652 a settlement was established by the Dutch East India Company to supply fresh provisions for their trading ships. Before the appearance of the Dutch, the land had been inhabited by two main tribes, the San and the Khoikhoi - often referred to as Bushmen and Hottentots respectively. The San were mostly hunters leading a nomadic life, whilst the Khoikhoi were herders. Inevitably the Dutch settlers began to expand in numbers with a consequent increase in demand for land. It was not only Dutch who came, but also French Huguenots, Germans and even some Scottish Calvinists.

As the settlement expanded, the subsistence farmers moved inland and competed with the indigenous inhabitants for land. Due to their superior technology and weapons, the settlers were able to push them back and establish their own values and customs in the Cape area. As the Africans were pushed out, some of them were absorbed into the work force of the white farmers. This was the beginning of a social structure which was to develop and deepen over the centuries; the Whites, in the form of the Dutch farmers, were the masters and the Africans the labourers.

By 1806 the British government had decided that control of Cape Colony was the key to controlling the trading routes to India and consequently took it over. The resultant increase in immigration from Britain established two distinct white communities - the Afrikaners (Boers) and English-speaking Whites (Anglos). Their attitudes to the Cape were quite different, with the Anglos viewing it as a colony of the British Empire and the Afrikaners as their home and country. They also differed in their religious beliefs and in their attitude to Blacks. The Afrikaners practised a strict form of Protestantism which saw the hand of God putting Whites over Blacks. The Anglos were mostly Anglicans and were more tolerant of Blacks, accepting that they could be independent traders, farmers and professionals.

The British control of the colony was deeply resented by the Afrikaners and this resentment was fanned by the British decision in 1833 to abolish slavery throughout the Empire. The Afrikaners saw this as an attack on their values, namely that Europeans were intrinsically superior and fitted to be masters.

Between 1836 and 1846, therefore, thousands of Boers left Cape Colony in the Great Trek to establish the independent republics of Transvaal and the Orange Free State, where Whites were to be dominant politically and economically. Piet Retief, an Afrikaner leader, said that the Trek was undertaken in order "to preserve proper relations between masters and servants". According to another Afrikaner, Anne Steenkamp, it was because the British had placed their slaves "on an equal footing with Christians, contrary to the law of God and the natural distinction of race and religion ... in order thus to preserve our doctrine in purity."

The Afrikaners were able to establish these two new republics with less opposition from African tribes than might have been expected. This was due to the rise of the Zulu military leader, Tshaka, in the early nineteenth century. He led a well-trained militarised band of Africans further north. In order to protect themselves, many African tribes had herded together into defensible areas. This substantially reduced the African population in large tracts of Natal, Orange Free State and Transvaal, and when the Afrikaners began the Great Trek north they were able to fill this vacuum which had been temporarily created by the fear of Tshaka and his warriors. This was to prove important as it allowed the Afrikaners to claim, at a later date, that they occupied empty land and therefore the Africans had no right to settle there.

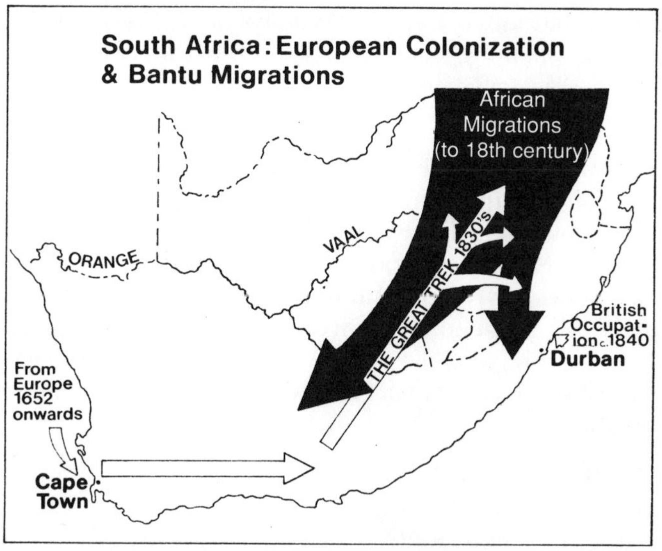

Britain left these Afrikaner Republics alone as they had no strategic or economic value. This changed, however, with the discovery of diamonds in 1867 and gold in 1886 in the Transvaal and the Orange Free State. Britain proceeded to annexe the Afrikaner republics and friction between the two white groups increased for the following reasons:

- Anglos controlled most of the new mining companies and thus gained the wealth from them.
- Conflict over the scarce labour existed between Boer-dominated agriculture and Anglo-dominated industry.
- Anglos/British forced their values and political control on the Boer Republics.

This eventually led to the Boer War 1899-1902 in which Boer hostility towards the Anglos was fuelled by the British use of concentration camps and a scorched earth policy. Alienation continued after the war when the British adopted an Anglicisation policy whereby only English was to be spoken in schools and in economic life. The Afrikaners' humiliation was complete when many of them were forced into waged labour as their farms failed.

During this period of industrialisation, the Whites continued to hold the same attitudes towards Blacks as in the past, thus setting the pattern for their future involvement in the economy. Their labour was essential in mining, but they were only employed in unskilled work, their contracts were for limited periods and they were not expected to have any permanent role within the industry or locality.

THE UNION OF SOUTH AFRICA

In 1910 the four colonies were united under one government elected by the Whites. At first the Whites were divided between two parties - the South Africa Party, which looked for unity between the English and Afrikaners as the ruling class, and the National Party, which was predominantly Afrikaner in composition and support, longing for a Boer Republic which had no English associations.

The eventual implementation of Grand Apartheid from 1948 onwards owes much to two interconnected developments - the establishment of the Broederbond and the rise of the National Party. The Broederbond is a secret society of Afrikaners dedicated to the advancement of Afrikaner values in all spheres of South African life. As a future Prime Minister, Dr VH Verwoerd declared, "The Broederbond must gain control of everything it can in every walk of life." From 1938 onwards it sought to develop and support Afrikaner enterprises with remarkable success. Gaining control of the industrial sector was essential if Afrikanerdom was to dominate in the white-controlled society.

The National Party's base of success was laid down in 1924 when it won the General Election in alliance with the Labour Party which drew its support from white working-class miners. They supported job reservation for Europeans in the mines and extended this to other areas of the economy after 1924. This combination of Afrikaners, mainly based in agriculture, and the white working class in industry, ensured that the National Party was in a dominant position politically.

In 1948 the National Party again won the election and set about establishing Grand Apartheid as its vision for the final settlement of South Africa. In 1961 South Africa cut its ties with Britain and became an independent republic.

SOUTH AFRICA'S ECONOMY

South Africa has the strongest and most developed economy on the continent of Africa. Its strength is based on the natural resources with which it is endowed and the ability to exploit these to the benefit of the dominant white population.

The three sectors which dominate are agriculture, mining and manufacturing industry. Figure 1.1 illustrates the growing dominance of the manufacturing sector and the decline in agriculture.

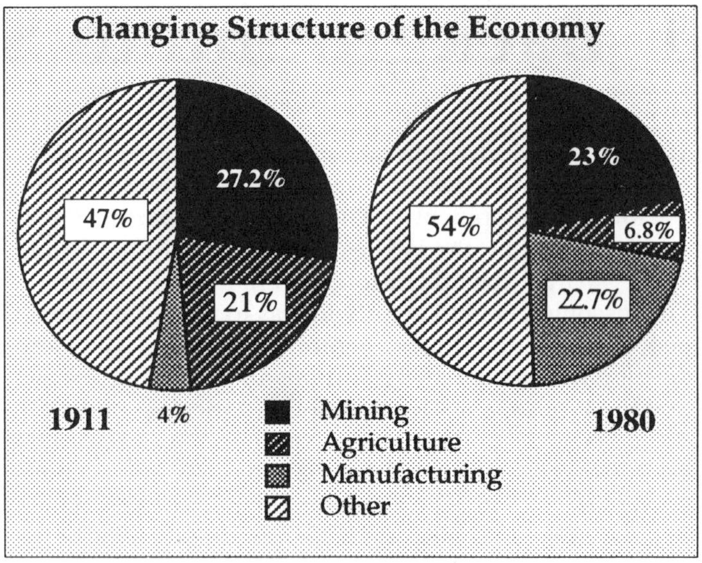

Figure 1.1 Source: Official Yearbook of RSA

Agriculture

Agriculture, once the dominant industry and the basis of Afrikaner strength and tradition, is still a major industry in South Africa. Today, though, it contributes a substantially smaller proportion to the Gross Domestic Product (GDP) than in the past. It accounts for about 7% of GDP compared with about 20% fifty years ago and 15% in 1955. This is mostly due to the growing importance of secondary and tertiary industries in the country. However, agriculture still provides about 18% of all South Africa's exports by value.

The land is by no means perfect for agricultural production. Most of it lies above 3,500 feet and the rainfall is unreliable, with drought a frequent occurrence. On 65% of the total surface area, the annual rainfall is less than 500mm per year. Soils are often poor with only 10% of the land suitable for cultivation. In the less fertile areas pastoral farming dominates, with sheep-rearing and cattle-ranching particularly strong. The trend in farming has moved towards a steady decline in the number of farms as the size of individual farms increases. The climate, however, varying from sub-tropical through Mediterranean to semi-desert, allows almost any crop to be grown. Maize is the most important crop but wheat, sorghum, groundnuts, tobacco, cotton, dry beans, sugar cane, sunflower seeds and fruit are also grown.

Mining

South Africa's industrial prosperity is based on the wealth of her mineral deposits. Although the country has only 0.08% of the world's land surface it is a leading producer of many of the most useful and valuable minerals used by industry and consumers, as shown in Table 1.1. This also shows the potential in these minerals by looking at the known reserves.

In addition to these minerals, South Africa has major reserves of Uranium, Nickel, Phosphates, Coal, Iron Ore, Copper, Tin, Lead, Zinc and Silver. Although the minerals are exported in their raw state, the South Africans have developed large-scale processing plants which increase the value of their minerals. This has helped to establish the secondary industry sector in South Africa upon which economic prosperity and growth are based.

South Africa's Mineral Wealth	WORLD PRODUCTION		WORLD RESERVES	
	Rank	%	Rank	%
Gold	1	55	1	51
Vanadium	1	30	2	34
Chrome Ore	1	34	1	63
Andalusite/Sillimanite	1	38	1	34
Manganese Ore	2	22	1	78
Platinum	3	21	1	66
Vermiculite	2	31	2	28
Antimony	2	20	3	5
Diamonds	3	18	2	21
Fluorspar	2	11	1	34
Titanium	3	20	3	15

Table 1.1 Source: Official Yearbook of RSA

Gold accounts for 60% of South Africa's mining output and 33% of total export earnings. After gold, coal is South Africa's second largest foreign exchange earner. This was a deliberate attempt by the South African government to reduce its dependence on oil, given the possible threat of economic sanctions.

South Africa's mineral resources extend throughout the country but are particularly concentrated in the industrial region based on Johannesburg and Pretoria — known as the PWV area. (See the map below)

SOUTH AFRICA'S MINERALS

Manufacturing Industry

South Africa's industrialisation began around 1900 but proceeded fairly slowly until the end of the Second World War. Industrial growth has been particularly marked since about 1960 and today South Africa has industrial concerns in most fields of production such as food processing, textiles, clothing and footwear, petro-chemicals, and engineering industries.

Electronics is a growth area and was ranked third in importance behind mining and chemicals. This area is heavily dominated by foreign companies, who control 75 per cent of the market in the electronics sector.

This industrial growth has resulted from a number of factors. Firstly, the wealth produced by mining provided the capital required to develop industry. Secondly, South Africa has been able to attract considerable foreign investment to expand its manufacturing base. Thirdly, the government adopted an aggressive import substitution policy to ensure that the country could produce most of the goods which it required.

South Africa, however, has always had a number of difficulties in developing as a trading nation, particularly in industrial goods. Firstly, she is about 5,000 miles from her main trading partners in Europe and the Americas. Secondly, her manufacturing centres are based inland mostly, with half of all her manufactured output produced in the PWV area, which increases transport costs for exporters. Finally, her economy is very sensitive to world fluctuations in trade and in metal prices, particularly gold. This is demonstrated by the fact that total foreign trade accounts for almost half of South Africa's GDP and 30% of foreign exchange earnings are received from gold sales.

The increasing importance of industry after 1960 was viewed with great suspicion by the agriculturally based Afrikaners. They feared that it would merely tempt more Blacks into the 'white' areas and increase the prosperity of the English-speaking Whites who controlled most of the business and industry. A determined drive, therefore, was made to ensure that the Afrikaner community secured a greater proportion of the increasing prosperity. As can be seen from Table 1.2, they succeeded in securing a very large slice of the private sector. Indeed, by the early 1980s the largest gold mining company, Sanlam, was Afrikaner owned, with about 30% of South Africa's gold processing capacity. In the public sector, where the government set up a number of state-owned industries to encourage industrial development, Afrikaners also came to dominate the posts. It is estimated that 35% of all economically active Afrikaners are employed in this sector compared to only 25% of all English-speaking Whites. The Afrikaner success in the industrial and commercial field is also demonstrated by the Afrikaner income per head which was half that of English speakers in 1946, increasing to an equal rate by 1976. It was this victory over the once dominant English-speaking Whites that the Afrikaners were so willing to defend against black advances or demands.

Afrikaner Advances	1948 (%)	1975 (%)
Private Business Ownership by Afrikaners	9.6	20.8
Mine Ownership by Afrikaners	1	18
Professional Posts filled by Afrikaners	16	38

Table 1.2 Source: Official Yearbook of RSA

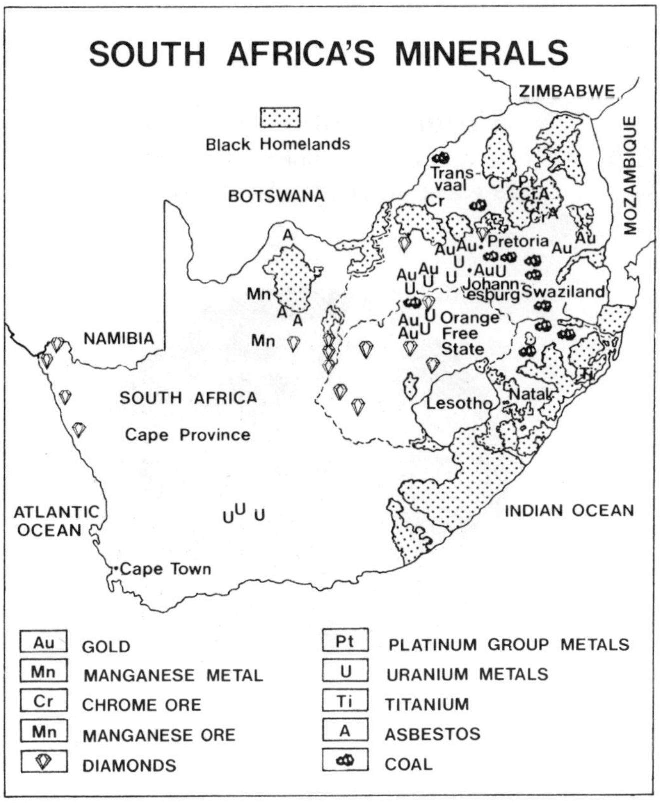

2 STRUCTURES OF APARTHEID

To most Whites in South Africa the solution to their problem of being a minority of the population was to redefine the population into separate groups, each identified by common language, customs and traditions. These groups would then be allocated land to be regarded as their home and country, thus ensuring that the Whites retained economic, social and political control in their section of South Africa. In 1978, a leading government Minister, Connie Mulder, expressed quite simply the aim of the Whites.

> "If our policy is taken to its logical conclusion, as far as the black people are concerned there will be not one black man with South African citizenship."

DIVIDING THE POPULATION

The first step in the National Party's development of apartheid was to define the races or national groups to which people belonged. This was done through the *Population Registration Act* (1950) which decreed that all people were to be racially classified into three main groups with subdivisions. These are shown in Table 2.1.

WHITES	COLOUREDS	AFRICANS
	Asians	Xhosa
	Cape Coloureds	Tswana
	Malay Coloureds	Zulu
		Sotho
		Venda
		Shangaan
		Swazi
		Ndebele

Table 2.1

Population Statistics

The total population of South Africa in 1989 was estimated to be 36.5 million

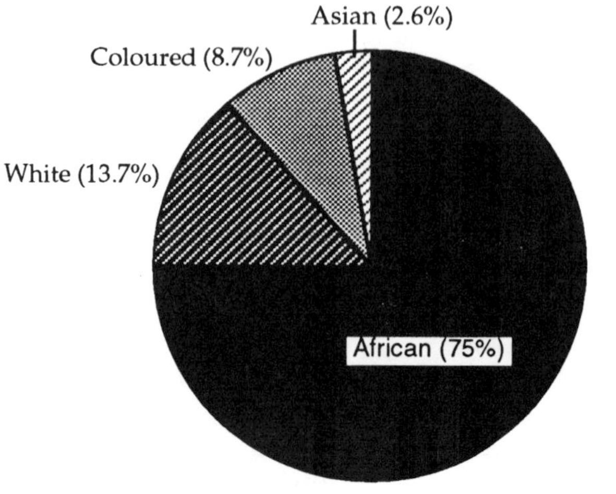

Figure 2.1 **Source: Bureau of Market Research *Regional Population Estimates for 1989***

Thus the majority African population, categorised according to language, features and/or ancestry, is divided into eight tribal groups. The Coloureds are made up of two main groups. Firstly, there are descendants from miscegenation between Whites and the original African inhabitants of the Cape, the San and Khoikhoi. Secondly, there are the Asians, or Indians, descended from Indian workers who were indentured from India to work, especially in Natal, in the nineteenth century.

This piece of legislation was the foundation stone upon which apartheid was built. Having defined the population, the government acted to maintain its 'purity' by passing the *Mixed Marriages Act* (1949). which banned marriage between Europeans and non-Europeans, and the *Immorality Acts* (1950, 1957), which made inter-racial sexual relations illegal.

DIVIDING THE LAND

Having divided the population, the National Party began to divide the land to define where the different groups could live and exercise their individual and political rights. The 1950s saw the creation of the Homelands policy which defined the territory which Whites saw as the traditional land of the Africans living in South Africa. It was in these Homelands that the Africans would be entitled to exercise citizenship rights.

The legislation establishing the Homelands, however, was based on the *Native Lands Acts* passed in 1913 and 1936. The 1913 Act established that all existing African reserves were not to be sold to non-Africans and made it illegal for any African to be on European land unless he or she was a hired servant. This meant that only 7.3% of African land was reserved for Africans, who made up 67% of the population. It also forced many African tenant farmers into the reserves. The resultant overcrowding in the reserves led to the government passing the *Native Trust and Land Act* in 1936 which earmarked about 6% more land to be added to the reserves over a ten-year period. Thus Africans were to be allowed to own only approximately 13% of the land, and it was on this figure that future governments were to construct the Homelands policy.

800 Change Races

Nearly 800 South Africans became, officially, members of a different race group last year, according to figures given to Mr Tian van der Merwe (PFP, Green Point).

They included 518 Coloureds who were officially reclassified as White, 14 Whites who became Coloured, seven Chinese who became White and two Whites who became Chinese.

There were also three Malays who became White, one White who became an Indian, 50 Indians who became Coloured, 54 Coloureds who became Indian, 17 Indians who became Malay, four Coloureds who became Chinese and a Malay who became Chinese. There were 89 Blacks who became Coloured, five Coloureds who became Black.

Source: *Rand Daily Mail*, 8.2..85

THE HOMELANDS POLICY

By the 1950s, the white government was finding it more and more difficult to justify apartheid to the rest of the world. It was a period when white dominance was being questioned and rejected in the Old European Empires, and American Blacks were rejecting the denial of their civil rights in a white-dominated society. To sustain white superiority in the South African economy and society, it was necessary for the Whites to develop a policy which was ostensibly rational in its approach to the different racial groups in South Africa and thus acceptable to other governments, in particular those of Europe and America.

The answer was Grand Apartheid: the National Party vision of South Africa split up between the different racial groups, with the Blacks being accorded full citizenship in their Homelands (or Bantustans). The ultimate aim was to develop these 'reserves' into independent countries with a government elected by those Africans recorded as citizens of the Homeland. The 10 Homelands are shown on the map below.

From the map of the Homelands the main point to note is that most of the Homelands consisted of a number of tracts of land separated from each other by white land. It was appreciated by the white government that this made their policy less viable and more difficult to sell to foreign governments and so in 1975 they introduced consolidation proposals to reduce the number of pieces making up each Homeland. Despite this consolidation exercise, most Homelands remained geographically disunited - Kwazulu, for example, still had 10 pieces of land separated by white land.

The legal framework for the development of the Bantustans was to unfold from the 1950s onwards. In 1951 the *Bantu Authorities Act* established local 'tribal authorities' which were to evolve slowly over the years as the 'legitimate' representative bodies of the Blacks while the final indirect representation which Blacks had in the white political structure was removed. In 1959 the *Promotion of Bantu Self-Government Act* carried the process a stage further by creating white Commissioners-General to act as agents of the Pretoria government in the Homelands and to set up the eight Bantu authorities. A government publication, *Bantu*, said that the Act "gave the Bantu peoples of South Africa a categoric assurance that the South African government had irrevocably set a course on a road that would lead the Homelands to meaningful self-government." Seventeen years later the practical result of this Act was seen when the first Homeland, Transkei, gained its 'independence'. By 1985 four Homelands had become 'independent' - Transkei, Bophuthatswana, Venda and Ciskei, collectively known as the TBVC countries.

In 1970 the *Bantu Homelands Citizenship Act* delivered an essential element in the implementation of Grand Apartheid. Under this Act all Africans were to be allocated a Homeland as their 'country of origin'. They would be regarded as citizens of that Homeland and as foreigners in other parts of South Africa. Thus, when Transkei became 'independent' on 26 October 1976, every African with 'Xhosa' stamped in his or her passbook lost his or her South African citizenship. The same thing happened to those labelled 'Tswana' when Bophuthatswana became 'independent' on 6 December 1977. The 'independence' of those two Homelands led to over 6 million Africans losing their South African citizenship and many of them had never even seen their new 'countries'.

Africans living in the 'white' areas were particularly concerned that this Act would strip them of Section 10 rights to stay in the urban areas (see page 11). Their fears appeared well founded when the Minister for Bantu Affairs said of these rights during the Act's debate in Parliament, "I am going to remove all and every one of them."

POPULATION CONTROL

The development of such a political and social system as apartheid would inevitably lead to considerable alienation among those groups who were oppressed and deprived. Realising this, the National governments have sought to control the population in a number of ways.

By dividing the population it was hoped to foster the differences between the tribal groups and so reduce any

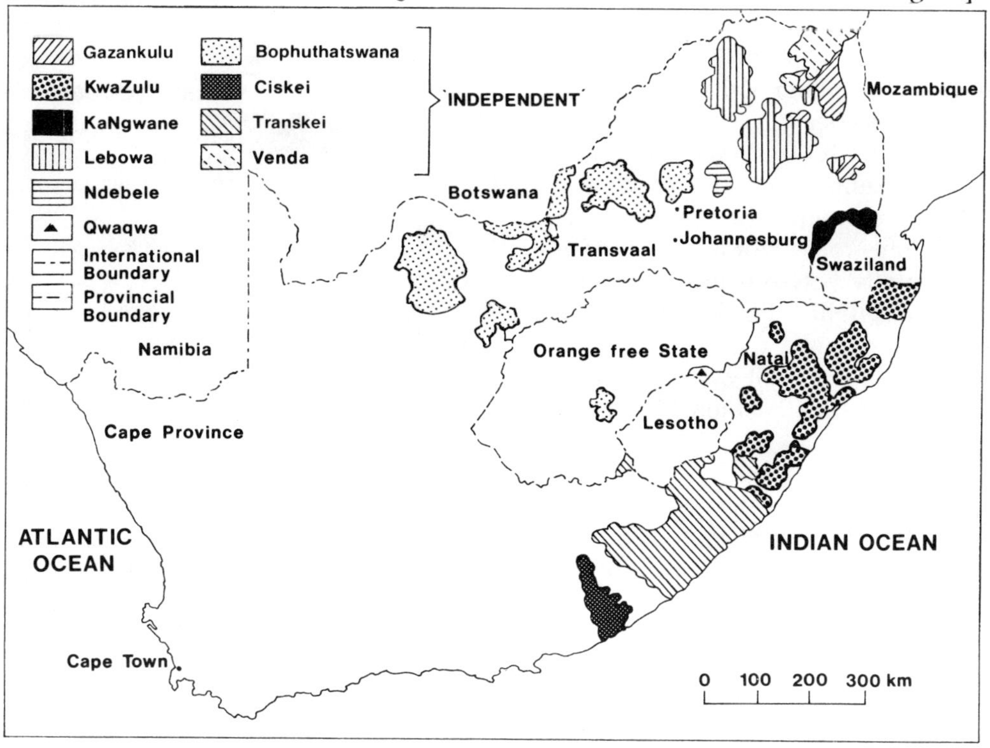

sense of unity they might feel in opposing apartheid. The expulsion of so many Blacks to the scattered Homelands also made organised resistance more difficult to sustain. However, the government relied on harsh and repressive laws to control the movement of Blacks and any organised resistance,violent or nonviolent.

The Pass Laws

The most notorious and widely used regulations for controlling the movements of Blacks were the Pass Laws. These were introduced in 1952 and required all Africans to carry a set of documents which were meant to prove their identity to any representative of white authority and to show whether they were legally entitled to be in the 'white' area.

Every African over 16 had to carry such a pass, or a 'passport' if he or she was defined as a citizen of an independent Homeland. If the pass was not in order, he or she could be arrested and subsequently fined, imprisoned or 'endorsed out' to his or her Homeland. Between 1948 and 1981 over 12.5 million people were arrested or prosecuted under pass law offences.

CONTROL THROUGH REPRESSIVE LAWS

One of the difficulties faced by opponents of apartheid in South Africa was the willingness of the government to introduce legal restrictions on their activities. The legal restrictions on individual and collective action were so open to interpretation and all-embracing that the authorities were able to silence many opponents and most organised, peaceful resistance over the years.

These legal restrictions were known collectively as the 'Security' Laws and under them the authorities had the power to detain people without trial, to ban people, organisations and meetings, to break up meetings, and to imprison people. The Government had developed these repressive laws since 1950, reacting to any new threat to apartheid with a new repressive law which allowed the legal system to deal with it. The main elements of the 'Security' Laws are outlined below.

1 The Suppression of Communism Act 1950

This Act made it illegal to be a member of the Communist Party or to promote communist ideas. It contained a very broad definition of communism. It was defined as "... any doctrine or scheme ... which aims at bringing about any political, industrial, social or economic change within the Union by unlawful acts or omissions ..." or which "aims at the encouragement of hostility between European and non-European races of the Republic." Having made such a sweeping definition of 'communism' the Act went on to declare any organisation "unlawful" if it was engaged in activities which were calculated to further the achievement of any of the objects of 'communism'.

The Act also gave the Minister of Justice the power to take restrictive action against anyone he considered to be a 'communist' or to be encouraging the achievement of the objects of 'communism'. He could impose any of the following restrictions on the individual:

a) Ban him or her from being in a specified area.
b) Place him or her under 'house arrest' which severely limited the person's freedom of movement.
c) Ban any visitors to his or her home.
d) Ban him or her from attending a concert, lecture or the wedding or funeral of a relative.
e) Remove him or her from his or her job if it wasin teaching or in a trade union.

In 1976, the Act was renamed the *Internal Security Act.*

2 The Unlawful Organisations Act 1960

This Act outlawed the African National Congress and the Pan Africanist Congress. However, other organisations were set up which the government viewed as 'fronts' for the ANC and the PAC and so they passed the *General Law Amendment Acts* (1962 and 1963) which gave them the power to declare such organisations illegal. These Acts were also used to ban many organisations after the Soweto riots of 1976, eg. the South African Students' Organisation, the Black People's Convention and the Union of Black Journalists.

3 The Terrorism Act 1967

This Act adopted a broad definition of what constituted terrorism in South Africa and then made all such actions illegal with the death penalty as punishment. A terrorist was anyone who used violent acts to try to "overthrow or endanger the State authority". Anyone arrested under this Act could be held until the police were convinced that they had answered all questions satisfactorily. Their relatives were not informed and they had no right of access to a lawyer. Peter Magubane was held for 586 days and Desmond Francis for 421 days under this Act - neither was charged with terrorist activities.

4 The Internal Security Act 1982

This Act removed all the above legislation but contained similar provisions plus additional measures. It introduced new offences such as: *subversion* and *incitement*. Subversion

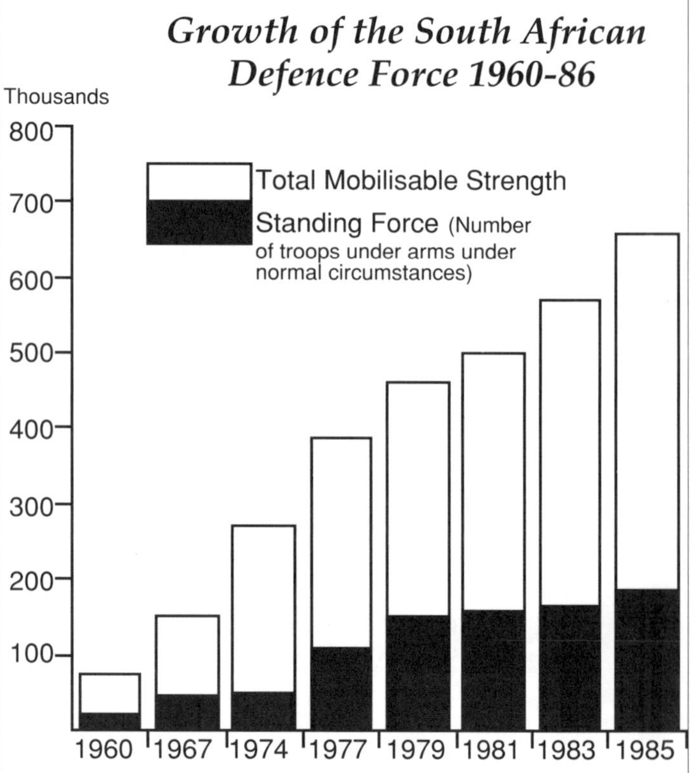

Figure 2.2 Source: *Apartheid The Facts*

was defined as any action aimed at "causing or promoting general dislocation or disorder" and affecting the normal business life of the community. Incitement was defined as any act which encouraged protest against any law or in support of any campaign for the repeal or modification of any law. The intention was to make illegal any form of protest, violent or peaceful.

REPRESSION - THE SECURITY FORCES

Protest in South Africa varied in its forms, but in this century developed from the nonviolent methods adopted by the African National Congress after its formation in 1912 to the more violent methods adopted after it was banned in 1960. Even after this development, most protest remained nonviolent. It was only after 1976 that violence and destruction of property by Africans became a more common response to the system of apartheid. White authorities, however, met most protest with a determination to destroy its leaders, organisation and grass roots support. They used all means at their disposal, often including violence, to combat any protests.

In most countries the police and armed forces are quite distinct, with the latter defending the country from external threats and the former protecting the people and their property by upholding the laws passed by Parliament. In South Africa the dividing line was not quite so clearcut with the police and the armed forces being used to quell unrest and protest arising from the apartheid system. By the 1980s, joint action by the police and the military had become frequent and routine in and around black townships during periods of protest and demonstration.

In dealing with such protest both the police and the armed forces had various responses ranging from occupation of the disturbed area to the use of whips, water cannon, CS gas, rubber bullets and live ammunition to disperse protesters.

The growing reliance on the police and the armed forces is illustrated by the increasing number of personnel recruited since the early sixties (see Figure 2.2). The increases in manpower were achieved by the introduction of conscription in 1967 and in subsequent years by the extension of both the time and age group it covers. Originally conscripts served only 9 months but this was increased to 2 years for all white males from the age of 16. After conscription white males become members of the reserve and they are liable for call-up until the age of 55.

3 APPLICATION OF APARTHEID

Establishing the Homelands did not cater for all the non-Europeans in South Africa for two main reasons. Firstly, the economy required a permanent supply of black labour, many of whom could not travel daily from their Homeland. Secondly, the coloured population was not included in the Homeland policy. Both these groups would be permanent in 'white' South Africa and so alternative arrangements were made for their settlement and control within the white areas.

COLOUREDS IN WHITE AREAS

The principle of land segregation was applied to Whites and non-Whites in 'white' South Africa through the *Group Areas Acts* (1950, 1957, 1966). It applied principally in urban areas and set out to establish group areas for the exclusive occupation of each racial group. This can be seen from the map of Johannesburg.

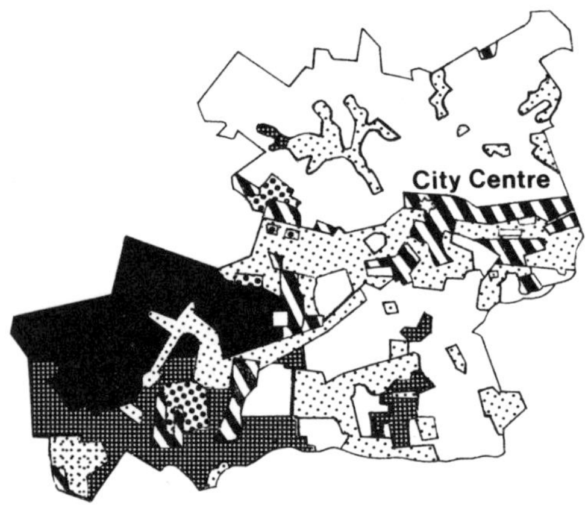

Establishing these urban divisions required the forced removal of families who had, before the Acts, been settled in areas which were now designated by the authorities for occupation by another racial group. By 1980 over 116,000 families, mainly Coloured and Indian, had been removed under this policy. The Acts resulted in non-Whites being forced into the outskirts of the towns and cities, and in 'white' areas dominating the land surrounding the city centres. Also, many Coloureds and Indians, forced to move to a new area, found that there was an inadequate supply of housing, with the result that many of them had to find accommodation illegally, in areas designated for Whites only. This was demonstrated in Pageview, an Asian area in the centre of Johannesburg. In 1981 the government flattened it for use by Whites and moved the Asian families to Lenasia, an Indian suburb well outside Johannesburg. Lenasia became very overcrowded and so many Asians from Pageview had to rent rooms illegally in 'white' areas. These Acts also prevented Blacks from buying land, trading or owning businesses within a so-called 'white' Group Area. As the business districts of most towns and cities were invariably in 'white' areas, this greatly limited the opportunity for Blacks to develop successful businesses.

The government sought a number of objectives with the Group Areas Acts. Firstly they satisfied the need for 'racial purity' in that social contact between Whites and Coloureds was reduced to a minimum. Indeed, one aim when organising the Group Areas in towns and cities was that different groups could travel to work without going through an area allocated to a different group. Secondly, the government believed that this would reduce inter-racial tension which it felt was increased by contact between the different racial groups. Thirdly, there is evidence to demonstrate that the government saw the Group Areas as a method of increasing social control of an urban population in which, it felt, the non-Whites were becoming a frighteningly large proportion. This aspect of the policy was referred to by Mr Kruger, the Justice Minister, in 1977 when he was reported to have said that "he did not think an organised 'guerrilla warfare' campaign would get off the ground. One of the big advantages of South Africa was that the residential areas were segregated". Finally, the government argued that its Group Areas policy allowed it to erase health hazards or slum conditions under which the poorer, mainly non-white, citizens lived. However, as a longtime opponent of the regime, Helen Suzman alleged in Parliament in 1961, "You do not need a Group Areas Act to clear slums; there is a Slum Clearance Act under which one can quite readily clear slums; and ... to put up great housing schemes in which those removed have been resettled, also has nothing to do with the Group Areas Act."

BLACKS IN 'WHITE' SOUTH AFRICA

> "Blacks are permitted in the white Homeland to do work that is there for them to do and not because they have equal claim to that of Whites for presence there. The converse applies to Whites in black Homelands."

This is the *Stallard Principle*, stated in 1922, which defined the status of Africans living and working in 'white' South Africa. According to the 1980 census, 9.5 million Africans were in this position, with 6 million of them living in urban areas. They live in the 'separate communities' which Stallard outlined - the townships, single-sex hostels and shanty towns.

For Blacks living in the 'white' areas the most important legislation was the *Black (Urban Areas) Consolidation Act*. Along with the regulations controlling the Homelands, this Act formed the basis of the government's 'influx control' - a phrase used to describe the measures which regulated the movement of Blacks in and out of the 'white' areas. Under this Act a Black was only allowed to live in an urban area if he or she:

1 had lived in an urban area continuously since birth;
2 had held the same job in the area for at least ten years;

3 was the wife or dependent child of someone qualifying under one of the first two rules;
4 was employed on contract in the urban area, their permanent residence then being in a Homeland.

These regulations were known as *Section 10 qualifications* and anyone found in an urban area illegally was likely to be "endorsed out", ie. deported to his or her 'Homeland'.

The combination of these regulations and the homeland developments led to an increase in migrant labour. Due to the lack of industry in the Homelands, the Africans had to seek work in the 'white' urban areas and on 'white' farms. They were put under contract, normally for eleven months, and usually lived in single-sex hostels separated from their families in the Homeland. Wives of such workers were allowed to visit them, but first had to gain permission from the authorities who might grant a 72-hour pass. To stay longer than this was to invite prosecution.

THE TOWNSHIPS - A STUDY OF SOWETO

Most Africans who qualified to stay in the Republic under Section 10 regulations were housed in one of the many townships. These are housing areas for the African labour force required by local industry and they are usually situated on the outskirts of an urban area. Soweto, situated 12 miles south-west of Johannesburg and housing well over one million Africans, is an example of one such township.

Soweto has 26 locations inside its boundaries; there are over 108,000 houses and, although some are modern and even relatively luxurious, the majority have no bathroom or indoor toilet. They were built to accommodate the labour required by Johannesburg's industry and commerce, but the number built has always been inadequate with an average of six to seven people living in each house. Most homes use candles, paraffin or gas lamps for lighting and coal stoves for cooking. Water is supplied to most houses by an outside tap from which residents carry supplies; only 3% have running hot water; 7% have a bath or shower and electricity is uncommon in houses - although the authorities agreed to introduce electricity after the 1976 riots.

Pupils are enrolled in Soweto schools according to ethnic groups and due to the shortage of teachers and school buildings, a 'shift system' is operated. This means that pupils attend school in one of the two sessions which are taken by the same teacher. (See page 49)

In the whole of Johannesburg there is only one hospital for Africans. Soweto has a number of clinics which deal with minor ailments and refer more serious cases to Baragwanath Hospital, which is situated on the outskirts of Soweto. It is a relatively well-developed hospital covering most areas of medicine. It takes Africans from all over South Africa in cases which require complex procedures or investigations. However, it is seriously under-staffed, especially by consultants. Although it has 2,500 beds, this number is inadequate as demonstrated by the need to occasionally put patients on the floor. According to Joyce Sikakane, standards are high at Baragwanath "but it remains inadequate in terms of the population it is supposed to serve." (See page 51)

Soweto mothers are not encouraged to stay at home. The system has created townships to house workers; normal family life was not part of the plan for Africans in the 'white' areas. Also, the low level of wages forces women to try to supplement their husbands' incomes. Child care is both difficult to find and hazardous for working mothers. There are few nursery facilities and young children are catered for in a number of ways. A granny or unemployed neighbour may be used. Joyce Sikakane recounts that when no 'grannies' were available more extreme measure were taken. "Our mothers were forced" by circumstances ... "to leave us locked alone in a room. They removed anything dangerous, leaving us with a plate of mealie pap, a mug of water and a chamber pot. Peeping through the drawn curtains and closed windows with window bars was the only enjoyable game. We did it in turns. Otherwise we had fights, cried or slept ... By the age of six our parents regarded us as responsible. We could be left with a house key so as to unlock the house to go to the toilet or to go out and play. When left alone like this, days used to drag on and on. You would cry for your mother until you fell asleep."

Political Control in the Townships

In 1977 the government passed the Community Councils Act which enabled Community Councils to be elected in townships to represent the Africans in matters of local concern. Most Africans saw the Councils as a fraud since they were not allowed to question the apartheid system and their response was to boycott the elections. In Soweto, for example, out of 30 wards, 29 candidates were proposed and 16 of these were disqualified by the white authorities for unspecified reasons. Only 2 wards were contested and 9 were filled without a contest - the other 19 were filled by appointees or in by-elections.

In the more middle-class area of Soweto, Dobsonville, 42% of the electorate voted. This respectable turnout could be explained by the fact that the people in this area had electricity and some security. Also rural wives were allowed to stay and so they had a lifestyle for which it was perhaps worth participating in local government.

This point was not lost on the government and they set out to give more power to the Councils in the hope that they could persuade more Africans that, by participating, they could influence their local community for the better. Consequently, the *Black Local Authorities Act* of 1982 and the *Black Community Development Act* of 1984 were passed as the basis for local government and the future development of the African urban areas.

In 1983 the old Community Councils were replaced in elections for 'Town' and 'Village' Councils in the townships. These had more powers than the Community Councils. However, instead of persuading the majority of Africans to participate in them, the extended powers maintained, or even increased, the feelings of alienation towards these Councils. This was demonstrated by the turnout for the elections when even fewer people voted than in the previous Community Council elections. The hostility was stoked by the new powers given to the Councils. They were made responsible for allocating and regulating accommodation within the townships which meant that they were participating in the administration of the influx controls which were at the heart of the apartheid system. Thus the national government removed itself from direct attack from urban Africans. Hostility towards the African Councillors was also fanned by the fact that the Councils were eventually to be financially self-sufficient. To achieve this, they would have to increase rents and rates for housing already considered to be inadequate. The result of the Councils' increased responsibilities was an increased financial burden which the Africans had to bear to support the areas laid aside by Whites for them in the urban areas. With such developments, it is not surprising that the African Councillors became a target for African frustrations in the riots and disturbances from 1984.

HOSTEL DWELLERS

The migrant workers on fixed-term contracts were not allowed to rent a house in a township. Their accommodation was provided by employers in the form of single-sex hostels, an example of which is at Alexandria, just outside Johannesburg. Alexandria was originally an African township, but that was removed to make way for 24 single-sex blocks to house 60,000 migrant workers.

Living conditions are very basic. The rooms accommodate from four to eight beds; windows are above eye level; and all facilities are communal, with 14 workers to a lavatory, 35 to a shower and 11 to a washbasin. Consequently life consists of endless queues to wash, to cook, to iron clothes and to catch buses. Every inmate must bear the number of his or her bed and mattress and each is allocated 14 cubic metres of space. The international minimum standard is 27 cubic metres. There are no possibilities for privacy and no outlets for frustration, depression and homesickness. Such tensions and inhuman social conditions inevitably affect behaviour, leading to alcoholism, drug addiction and other forms of anti-social behaviour.

THE SHANTY TOWNS

The main response to both the housing shortage and the attack on African family life by migrant labour policies was for Africans to live illegally in squatter camps, or shanty towns, in the urban areas. Probably the best example of this is Crossroads, a vast squatter camp of about 4,000 'illegal' families, a few miles outside Cape Town. In such camps Africans were willing to flout apartheid's regulations in order to retain family life. The camp flourished, with each household contributing to the cost of water, refuse disposal and education services. It evolved its own laws and elected a 30-member committee to run the area. Crossroads reflected an African demand to live a normal life and a rejection of the single-sex hostels for workers while their families were banished to the Homelands to face starvation.

THE HOMELANDS

Comprising no more than 13% of the total land in South Africa, the Homelands were expected to support, in theory, almost 73% of the population or 21 of the 28 million people living in the country. On the most fertile soil and with the most modern farming techniques, this would be an awesome task but the Homelands did not have optimum farming conditions and consequently the majority of Africans relied on work in the 'white' areas to sustain their families. This is demonstrated by the number of Africans living in the urban areas as shown in Table 3.1.

YEAR	AFRICANS LIVING IN URBAN AREAS (%)
1960	31.8
1970	33.1
1980	38.3
2000	60.0 (est.)

Table 3.1 Source: *IDAF Briefing Paper No. 13*

These figures also reflect the lack of job opportunities in the Homelands due to the lack of industrial development on the scale required to employ such a large proportion of the population. The need for a massive scheme of industrial development to make the Homelands viable was recognised by the Tomlinson Commission in 1954 when it said, "The choice is clear. Either the challenge must be accepted, or the inevitable consequences of the integration of the European and Bantu population groups into a common society must be endured." This challenge was never taken up by the white South African government and consequently large numbers of Africans 'commute' from the townships to work in 'white' areas.

Land Erosion and Overpopulation

The quality of even the best land in the Homelands was diminished by the demands placed upon it as more and more Africans were forcibly resettled in 'their Homelands'. Most Africans in the Homelands are subsistence farmers and as more people were forced into the Homelands, the demand for land increased. This has eroded the land. The scale of this problem was shown by the Tomlinson Commission in 1954 which found that 30% of all the Homelands was already "badly eroded".

Further, the Commission estimated that the Ngutu District in Natal, if fully developed agriculturally, could support only 13,000 people, although 30,000 lived there in 1951. However, with no significant agricultural improvements, the population of Ngutu had increased to about 80,000 by 1974 and to 200,000 by 1979 according to estimates by local doctors. Industrial development could have supplied the means of survival for such an increase in population, but this never occurred to any great extent.

Quality of the Land

The quality of the land allocated to the Homelands varies. The largest, Bophuthatswana, has a very large amount of desert and semi-desert, with only 6-7% of the land considered suitable for arable farming; the rest is too dry for anything other than livestock grazing. A similar picture can be drawn for the small, northern Homelands in the Transvaal - Venda, Gazankulu, Lebowa and Swazi - which have limited rainfall and periodic droughts and are mostly unsuitable for arable farming. However, the Homelands on the east coast contain some of the best-watered land in South Africa and in Transkei and Kwazulu pastoral farming is carried out. Indeed, it has been estimated that Transkei could produce enough maize for the entire population of South Africa if it was farmed by fewer people using modern farming methods.

Fragmentation of the Land

Even after their consolidation, which began in 1975, the Homelands remained fragmented, with pockets of land cut off from each other by 'white' areas. This created a number of difficulties for the development of the Homelands.

1 It was more expensive to develop essential infrastructure such as road and rail transport, housing, power lines etc.
2 People living in one part of the Homeland had much further to travel if industry was situated in another part.
3 Access to the Homeland authorities was more difficult.
4 The borders, arbitrarily drawn to satisfy white requirements, ensured that most major towns, industrial and mining developments were kept out.

In 1979 when Bophuthatswana was made 'independent', the *Johannesburg Sunday Times* was prompted to comment: "There is no possible basis in morality or history to justify the arbitrary borders assigned to Bophuthatswana. They are merely the minimum white greed could relinquish."

Search for Work

Due to the shortage of land and employment many Africans had to seek work outside the Homeland. The following patterns of employment practices operated:

1 Jobs could be sought in industrial areas which had been developed inside the Homelands. However, the number of jobs created in these areas wasinadequate to cater for the needs of the homeland population.

2 Africans could commute to industries in the 'white' areas close to the borders of the Homelands. The policy of industrial decentralisation which the South African government followed for a number of years, allowed industry to take advantage of cheap African labour from the Homelands. At the same time the South African government had no responsibility for the African workers or their families.

3 A large number of jobs were to be found in the urban areas too far from the Homelands to commute daily. Africans were allowed to enter and live in the 'white' area to do these jobs on fixed term contracts. This was the migrant labour force upon which much of the South African economy depended.

It has been estimated that at any one time 35 per cent of all employable males were absent from the Homelands and over 70% of the economically active population was involved in the migrant labour system. Thus the Homelands were left with a disproportionately large number of children, women, elderly and sick, ie. those who were of no productive use to the 'white' economy. The most disturbing consequence of this wasthe effect it had on African families in the Homelands. With wives only able to visit their husbands on a 72-hour pass, the links which bind families together were often broken and children in the Homelands were left fatherless. Also, an increasing number of illegitimate children wereborn in the 'white' areas. This wasthe price Africans in the Homelands had to pay for survival, however, as without the income from migrant workers the families in the Homelands would have starved.

Homeland Standard of Living

Some people in the Homelands had a very good standard of living, eg. those who were elected 'representatives' in the Homeland Legislature and government officials. For the vast majority of the population, however, living standards were very low by any criterion.

Living standards depend greatly on income levels and in the Homelands these were very low. A study of incomes in the Transkei in 1978 found that 95% of all households had an income of under R50 per month, which was well below the subsistence level; 50% had under R12 per month. The low level of income is also demonstrated by the fact that the Homelands accounted for only 3% of the Gross Domestic Product of South Africa.

Health standards were very poor by all accounts, although the government did not issue statistics on this, unlike other areas of homeland life. In 1972, one survey of Ciskei and Transkei found severe malnutrition. As a direct result of this, 50% of surviving children in the Ciskei were stunted in growth. In Kwazulu, a study of malnutrition found that it was changing the people's physique; people were becoming small, stunted and mentally enfeebled. Common childhood diseases such as measles and whooping cough became killers under such conditions and the infant mortality rate was very high.

REMOVALS AND RESETTLEMENT

The removal of 'surplus' Africans became a vigorously pursued objective after the 1967 instruction to officials of the Department of Bantu Administration that all "unproductive Africans should be sent to 'resettlement' areas in the Bantustan."

These removals can be defined according to the reason given for their implementation. There were generally four main reasons for removals occurring.

1 To get rid of 'black spots'. These were rural black communities, usually established for many years, which were situated in the middle of 'white' areas. Many Blacks living in such communities were forced into the Homelands.

2 Many rural Africans worked land in 'white' areas in return for which they paid rent or provided labour to the white owner. Such labour-tenant systems were removed and the Africans moved out of the 'white' areas to the Homelands.

3 Urban Africans also suffered this fate as some townships adjoining 'white' areas were razed to the ground, having been redefined 'white' or for the use of some other racial group. The families in this situation were often split as the 'breadwinner' was allowed to stay in a single-sex hostel and the family was dispersed to the Homeland. Squatter camps were also bulldozed for this purpose.

4 Even within the Homelands Africans were not safe from such upheaval. The implementation of the consolidation proposals of 1975 meant that the homeland boundaries were redrawn slightly. Any Africans living in the wrong place had to move out if their land was redefined as 'white'. Also each Homeland contained Africans who were 'citizens' of another Homeland and they had

Number of Africans Resettled between 1960 and 1980	
Type of Removal	*Numbers*
Eviction from 'white' farmland	1,129,000
Clearance of 'black spots'	500,000
Urban relocation	782,000

Table 3.2

to be removed from one to the other. The extent of these removals between 1960 and 1980 is shown in Table 3.2.

POLITICAL CONTROL OF THE HOMELANDS

Traditionally, political power was vested in the Chiefs of the African tribes and the organisation of decision making in the Homelands was based on a mixture of that tradition and elected representation. Each Homeland which became 'independent' had a legislature which was partly elected and partly appointed and the government Ministers were drawn from this legislature. All the Homelands depended upon Pretoria for considerable financial support, with about 80% of their budgets supplied directly from there. Government Ministers and members of the Assemblies received very high salaries and so had a vested interest in sustaining the system.

Many of the higher administrative jobs in the Homelands were filled by Whites who were paid by the South African government. These jobs were described by the pro-government press as "political parking places" for retired Nationalist politicians.

The democratic process was questioned in most of the Homelands as being not only inadequate but also corrupt. It was claimed that electoral malpractice was common and that obstacles were placed in the way of opposition parties which made them less effective. For example, in Bophuthatswana during the 1977 election, the newspaper, *The World*, reported that people were forced to register and to vote. Also, the registration of voters was in the hands of the ruling party; most opposition meetings were banned; and the opposition was not present at the count.

Repressive legislation, similar to that used by Pretoria, became a feature of some Homelands so that freedoms usually associated with a democracy were undermined. In the Transkei, for example, indefinite detention without trial and banning people and organisations were permissible acts by the authorities. In November 1979, the Transkei government banned the ANC, the PAC, Inkatha, the South African Council of Churches and Black Consciousness Organisations. As the *Guardian* put it in 1976, "If there is one bad habit the Transkei seems to have learned diligently from South Africa, it is contemptuous scorn for civil liberties."

4 MODERNISING APARTHEID 1979-1988

"We need them because they (the Blacks) work for us ... but the fact that they work for us can never - if one accepts this as one's own criterion one will be signing one's own death sentence now - entitle them to claim political rights." *(John Vorster, 1968)*

"Time is running out - time has run out - I don't think we have five years to play with."
(Rear Admiral Edwards, SADF, February 1978)

VORSTER'S LEGACY (1966-78)

John Vorster became Prime Minister in 1966 after the assassination of Prime Minister Hendrik Verwoerd. He will be remembered as the very symbol of unbending white supremacy in South Africa. The Soweto massacres of 1976 and the murder in police detention of Steve Biko in 1977 were justified thus: "When our survival is at stake, no rules apply." He was responsible for the passing of the *Idle Bantu Act* and the *Bantu Citizenship Amendment Act*, the latter of which deprived many black South Africans of their citizenship.

Yet he was also the architect of the reforms associated with his successor, PW Botha. It was Vorster who relaxed petty apartheid, proposed the extension of the franchise to the Coloureds and Asians and who initiated the process of reformulating apartheid. (Petty apartheid refers to the simple segregation of facilities such as trains, restaurants and toilets.) The highlight of his political career was his landslide victory in the December 1977 elections, when the Nationalists won 134 of the 165 seats. The white electorate endorsed his firm action against the black people and their tiresome leaders. Within a year he had resigned and in October 1978 he took up the ceremonial post of State President. However, the *Muldergate Scandal*, which erupted in June 1979, implicated Vorster and he resigned from public office, disgraced.

The scandal strengthened Botha's position within the National Party and there was strong hope that he would go beyond Vorster's tentative blueprint for reform and create a new South Africa that would satisfy the aspirations of its non-Whites.

'FACELIFT APARTHEID'

"To begin reform, is to begin Revolution."
(19th century British Prime Minister)

"There are higher things in life than to stare at the colour of a man's skin. We are prepared to allow black people into our kitchens to prepare food, but the moment a Black appears next to us in the post office, we say 'go away'. What kind of nonsense is that? ... I say one man, one vote in this country is out. I now want to say something further: don't try to do something unconstitutional or you will be sorry for yourself."
(PW Botha, 1979)

The above statement, made by Prime Minister Botha shortly after coming to power, defined the limits of his reformist policies. His purpose was to preserve the existing structure, not to destroy it; in short to introduce apartheid with a human face. Yet such a course of action carried the risk of alienating the more conservative elements of the white community without winning the support or gratitude of the black majority. The 'Verkramptes' (right-wingers) believed that to begin reform was to begin revolution and they actively opposed Botha, indirectly restraining the government's reformist zeal. Botha was called a "Kaffirbotie" (nigger brother) and a realignment within the Afrikaner 'Volk' occurred. The non-Whites were not impressed either. Bishop Tutu summed up this viewpoint when he declared, "We do not want apartheid liberalised, we wish it abolished."

Under Botha's rule changes did occur: petty apartheid continued to be dismantled - urban Blacks could eat and drink in International Hotels, attend mixed sports meetings, visit mixed beaches; Blacks could join trade unions, buy their own homes, set up their own businesses, travel without a hated passbook and be allowed greater freedom in running their own affairs. The Coloureds and Indians were given the vote and a say in decision making. Yet the fruits of these reforms were not peace and prosperity but the outbreak of massive black unrest which culminated in the first State of Emergency being declared in July 1985. A national State of Emergency, declared in June 1986, was to remain in force until 1990.

Reasons for Botha's Reforms

1 "We must adapt or die." Botha's words implied that the unrest of 1976-77, when over 500 Blacks died, would be

PW Botha

repeated unless meaningful reform was implemented.

2 A black middle class was created that would split African solidarity by setting the more secure township elite against the unskilled and unemployed majority.

3 The business community favoured the creation of a skilled, well-paid black work force committed to the free enterprise system. The apartheid system curtailed South Africa's internal market by lowering the standard of living of much of the population. Mr Harry Oppenheimer, a leading South African industrialist, stated in 1978, "The only way to bring about peaceful change is to allow a modern economy to build up which cannot exist without the participation of vast numbers of black people holding down skilled and highly paid jobs."

4 Reform would promote a new international image of a reformist South Africa that would end her status as an international pariah. The unrest of the late seventies had led to an arms and oil boycott against South Africa and the danger of economic sanctions being implemented by the United Nations was not lost on South Africa. Reform would also end her international isolation and restore her special relationship with the United States. (see page 31)

5 Extension of the franchise to the Coloureds and Asians would create a larger non-black minority and prevent an alliance between the non-white peoples of South Africa.

SOCIAL REFORMS

Botha continued Vorster's policy of eliminating petty apartheid, which improved the quality of life for the black elite. Hotels, restaurants and Sport Clubs could apply for international status which allowed them to serve alcohol to African guests. A permit also existed by which persons of different races could attend live performances in certain threatres. In short, wealthy Blacks could emulate the lifestyle of the Whites.

The coloured community especially benefited from the relaxation of barriers between the races, although it was still illegal for Coloureds and Whites to live in the same district. In Hillbrow, 'Jo'burg', one apartment block had both white and coloured residents; when a housing official tried to get all the Coloureds evicted the white residents signed a petition to let them stay. Generally if the white residents did not object to sharing an apartment building or beach with Coloureds then no notice was taken of the breach of policy.

Significantly, the government finally grasped the nettle of scrapping the 'heartbreak laws'. In April 1985, after years of deliberation, Botha agreed to rescind the laws prohibiting mixed marriages and inter-racial sexual relations. This recommendation was made by a parliamentary commission of the new tricameral chambers (see page 17) which included Coloureds and Indians - indicating perhaps their influence on government policies. In 1986 Botha abolished the hated Pass Laws.

Elimination of petty apartheid did not impress the black majority, nor improve the quality of life for the average African. Major surgery, not cosmetic change, was their prescription for apartheid. As one black leader stated, "The highpoint of my ambition is not to swim in a white pool or marry a white woman."

ECONOMIC REFORM

Two government-appointed Commissions set out the blueprint for economic change in the Wiehahn and Riekert Reports.

The report of the Wiehahn Commission into labour legislation made the following major recommendations:

- recognition of black trade unions with the prohibition on racially mixed unions being dropped;
- desegregation of facilities, eg. lavatories and canteens in factories and offices;
- the setting up of a manpower commission to oversee all labour-related issues;
- the scrapping of statutory job reservation - all 28 categories of 'trade reservation' should be eliminated;
- the opening of apprenticeship training to people of all races.

The government was slow in implementing the Report. It accepted that apprenticeships should be opened to all races in principle and that desegregation of facilities should take place. It created a national manpower commission and restructured the industrial tribunal as an industrial court empowered to adjudicate disputes.

In the field of job reservation the government was forced to tread softly. The white miners went on strike in March 1979 and the authorities immediately compromised by stating that job discrimination laws would be "phased out" in consultation with the unions. In fact, it was not until 1988 that job reservation was completely ended.

The government accepted black trade unions as it hoped to control them through legislation. Once unions are registered they are under the discipline of the Industrial Conciliation Act. The authorities agreed to mixed unions but refused to give the right of union membership to migrant workers. Only permanent residents in fixed (not contract) employment would be allowed union membership. The outcome was not the creation of pliant trade unions, but the growth in militancy of an articulate group prepared to challenge the apartheid regime. (see page 24)

The Reikert Commission's main recommendations were concerned with residence and citizenship rights.

- Its most controversial proposal was to question the myth of Grand Apartheid, namely that all Blacks are citizens of a Bantustan and not of South Africa. A settled and permanent African urban population now existed and any person who conformed to Section 10 should be given permanent status and specific privileges.
- These specific privileges would include security of tenure, the right to buy their own home, to set up their own business and to be given preference over rural migrants for jobs. Their children would qualify for Section 10 status, giving them a birthright of urban permanence.
- In return for 'rights' of citizenship, the burden of responsibilities would be imposed. The Report stated, "There is some merit in the argument that urban Blacks should themselves bear a greater share of the total financial burden in respect of housing service and transport."

The government only implemented the sections of the Report that strengthened the structure of control, ensuring greater misery for all Africans. The authorities quickly passed legislation that fined employers who failed to register their workers and also implemented the proposal of placing the financial burden onto the shoulders of urban Blacks. In return, Blacks would be eligible to purchase their own homes under a 99-year lease, and electricity and other amenities would be installed in the townships. Improvements also took place in retail business facilities. Africans can now own more than one type of business; own a business in an area in which they themselves are not resident; form partnerships with white businessmen in African areas as long as the black share is over 51% of the business.

POLITICAL REFORM

The Republic of South Africa reached a significant phase in its political history in September 1984 with the inauguration of its first executive State President (PW Botha), the opening of the country's first multiracial Parliament, and the swearing in of the first South African coloured and Indian Cabinet Ministers.

New Constitution

The new constitution was approved by Parliament in September 1983. A referendum was held in November of the same year and the white electorate endorsed this decision by a 2 to 1 majority. This ended the Westminster system of government practised since the establishment of the Union of South Africa in 1910. South Africa now has a presidential system of government. Moreover, the white-only Parliament was replaced by a tricameral Parliament composed of three separate chambers, one each for Whites, Coloureds and Indians. (see figure 4.1)

The executive State President is the head of State, chosen by an electoral college for the same period of time as Parliament. (see figure 4.2) The President has very wide powers: his office unifies and controls the cumbersome tricameral system. He appoints the Cabinet from members of all three population groups. The Cabinet has executive power in matters of general interest, such as defence, finance and foreign affairs, and is white dominated.

The State President also appoints the three Ministers' Councils, each of which consists of five members of the majority party of the respective Houses of Parliament. The Ministers' Councils have executive powers over such affairs as education, welfare and culture. Their respective chairmen are members of the Cabinet.

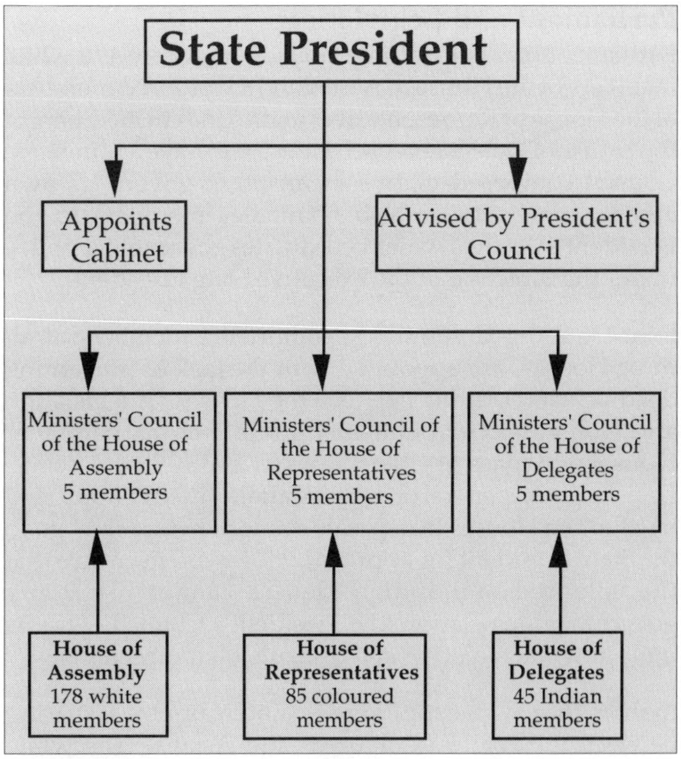

Figure 4.1

The President is advised by a President's Council in matters of general interest and in the ruling of disputes between the different Houses. The Council comprises 60 members chosen as follows:

- 20 are nominated by the House of Assembly (Whites);
- 10 by the House of Representatives (Coloureds);
- 5 by the House of Delegates (Indians).

The President appoints an additional 25 members, 10 of whom are members proposed by the opposition in the three houses.

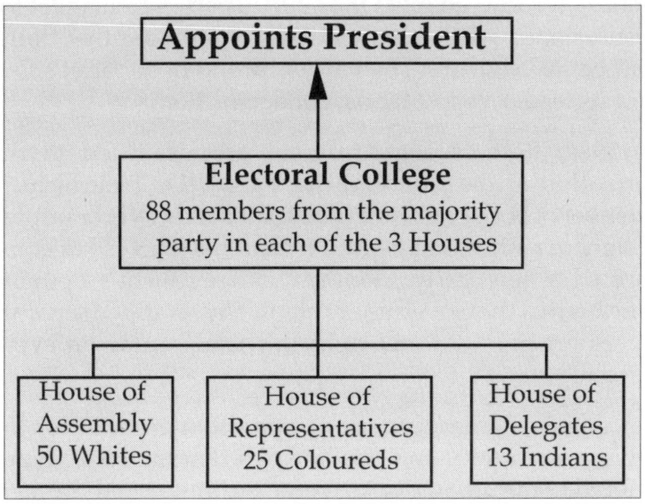

Figure 4.2

Parliament and Legislation

Parliament consists of three Houses: there are 178 white members of the House of Assembly, 85 coloured members of the House of Representatives and 45 Indian members of the House of Delegates. Each House will have a Ministers' Council composed of five members to govern its own affairs. Each House also nominates members to the President's Council which coordinates government policy under the direction of the executive State President.

Joint Standing Committees, comprising members of all three Houses, are appointed with the task of preventing deadlock and conflict between the Houses. If legislation affects only a specific population group, then that particular House will pass its own laws without interference. Legislation on general or national affairs must be approved by all three Houses in separate sessions before they go to the State President for approval. However, to ensure that the coloured and Indian Houses cannot block any government legislation, the President's Council, with its built-in white majority, can overrule their objections.

In short, the new constitution does not create power sharing between the Whites, Coloureds and Asians. The white Assembly has an overwhelming majority (50 to 38) in the electoral college and so its choice of State President is predictable - the white Leader of the National Party.

OPPOSITION TO THE NEW CONSTITUTION

The new constitution was vigorously opposed by the Blacks and led to the formation of the United Democratic Front. Grass roots opinion among the coloured and Asian communities was hostility and opposition to the proposals. However, unlike the Whites, they were not given the opportunity to voice their opinion - no referendum was offered.

White Opposition

Botha's constitutional reforms also infuriated the right wing of the National Party (the Verkrampte) and the backlash that followed bestowed respectability upon the extreme right-wing party, the Herstigte Nasionale Party (HNP). The reforms were also opposed by the Progressive Federal Party which objected to the exclusion of the Blacks.

The HNP broke away from the National Party in 1969 and for a decade it remained on the political fringe. However, Botha's reforms enabled the HNP to become a magnet for disillusioned Afrikaners who were convinced that Botha had betrayed them. The Party is proud of its racist stand and its leader, Jaap Marais, condemns Botha.

In 1982, Botha's constitutional proposals led to the formation of the Conservative Party. Dr Treurnicht, a member of Botha's Cabinet and leader of the 'Verkrampte', resigned and, along with 14 National Party defectors, formed a new party. Reform, in Treurnicht's opinion, "means that the Government has finally scrapped separate development. We will fight this fatal course on every terrain."

Once again, Botha faced strong opposition from within the white community and this ensured that the concessions offered to the urban Blacks would be limited and counter-productive.

Non-White Opposition

The proposed reforms were condemned by the black majority and created a split within the coloured and Indian communities. Even black moderates, such as Chief Buthelezi, accused those who participated in the new Assembly of betrayal and treachery. The (coloured) Labour Party agreed at its January 1983 conference to participate in the proposed new constitution and other minority parties followed this lead. As the Coloureds and Asians were not offered a referendum to test their opinion, a boycott of the August 1984 elections was the only effective weapon with which to register their disapproval. The turnout, even using government figures, was very poor: 30.1% of the coloured electorate and 20.2% of the Indian electorate voted.

Mr Dinkie Pillay, an Indian candidate for the Solidarity Party, whose house was petrol-bombed by opponents of the constitution, argued that involvement could act as a "catalyst" for change. "The future of South Africa depends on those who participate in shaping it, the new constitution creates an atmosphere in which negotiations could begin among all groups in South Africa. Let us not despise small starts."

The new constitution expressly excluded the black majority. Its preamble states "God gave South Africa to the Whites." Africans may enjoy their "separate freedom in the land allotted to them." However, the Soweto Riots of 1976 and the subsequent unrest convinced the government that some concessions had to be implemented.

Reform for Urban Africans

1 The townships were given greater control over local affairs through elected Community Councils and were referred to as "municipal homelands". However, these Community Councils have been a dismal failure. Organised boycotts of elections held in November 1983 ensured that the elected Councillors lacked a mandate from the people - only about 8% of the electorate voted. Nevertheless, the government proceeded with its plan to establish and use

(Yuri Cherepanov in *Pravda*)

these Councils as a basis for a political structure to accommodate Africans permanently living outside the Bantustan. The leaders of these Community Councils were regarded as traitors and the unrest in the townships in 1984-85 led to acts of revenge ranging from assassination to arson.

2 The government expected the townships to be self-financing and to this end central grants were greatly reduced. This forced the Community Councils to increase rents, bus fares and water rates by as much as 300%.

The outcome was predictable; the wrath of the urban Africans was directed against the Councillors. The unrest and black mobilisation engendered by the introduction of the franchise for Coloureds and Indians led to a spontaneous outburst of violence against the black servants of apartheid.

"... TO BEGIN REVOLUTION"

The Road to Uitenhage

The implementation of Botha's constitutional reforms at national and local level unleashed black fury and hatred against the apartheid system.

Fittingly, it was events in Sharpeville that marked the turning point in black opposition to apartheid. (In 1960, 69 black demonstrators were shot dead by the police in Sharpeville.) In September 1984, trouble began in Sharpeville and in five neighbouring townships following the announcement by the local council of a forthcoming massive increase in rents. The savagery that followed set the pattern that was to unfold throughout black townships in the months ahead. The crowd turned on the Lekaa Town Council (elected by a 14.7% poll). The councillors' homes were set ablaze and the deputy chairman, Sam Dalamini, was hacked to death and his body set alight. The government sent in the riot police to restore order and thus the vicious circle of repression and retaliation had begun. The riots quickly spread throughout South Africa and any hope of containing the unrest was ended by the police action at Uitenhage.

On the 25th anniversary of the massacre at Sharpeville, the police killed 19 Blacks and wounded 36 at Uitenhage. The victims were marching to a neighbouring black township for a memorial service that was being held to honour 13 Blacks who had been killed in recent riots. (Uitenhage is a small white town in the Cape province, and the 4,000 Blacks had to pass through it to reach the funeral at Kwanabuhle on the other side of Uitenhage.)

Conflicting versions of the tragic events were given. However, an investigation by the Progressive Federal Party refuted the police's accusation that petrol bombs had been in evidence and that "the police officer in charge had no alternative but to order fire in self-defence".

The Uitenhage massacre accelerated the downward slide to anarchy with the breakdown of law and order in the black townships. Moderate figures, such as Bishop Tutu, called on Botha to negotiate with the authentic spokespersons of the black community. Botha's response was to announce a State of Emergency in 36 districts (later 38 districts).

First State of Emergency

In July 1985 Botha declared a State of Emergency in 36 districts which included Johannesburg, the VAL triangle and most of the Transvaal and Eastern Cape Province. Botha justified this act by stating that "conditions of violence and lawlessness have become more severe and cruel, especially in black townships. This state of affairs can no longer be tolerated."

This State of Emergency gave the government powers to:

- impose curfews;
- tighten censorship of the news media;
- arrest and detain suspects without warrants for up to 14 days;
- interrogate prisoners without the presence of lawyers;
- license Security Forces to seal off curfew areas, close down businesses and take over all essential services.

Abolition of Discriminatory Laws 1982-1987

- Complete integration in sport and sporting facilities, subject to certain exceptions in the case of primary and secondary public school education. (*Group Areas Amendment Act No. 62* , 1982)
- Admission of non-Whites to tertiary educational institutions on a quota basis. (*Universities and Technikon Amendment Act*, 1984)
- Mixed business districts in previous exclusively White areas. (*Group Areas Amendment Act No. 101*, 1984)
- The repeal of the prohibition of mixed marriages and of inter-racial sexual relations. (*Immorality and Prohibition of Mixed Marriages Amendment Act*, 1985)
- The repeal of the prohibition of mixed political parties. (*Constitutional Affairs Amendment Act*, 1985).
- Abolition of all race restrictions on the sale of liquor. (*Liquor Amendment Act*, 1986)
- Abolition of influx control system, the so-called 'Pass Laws'. (Abolition of *Influx Control Act*, 1986)
- Restoration of a uniform South African citizenship, on application, to all citizens, including citizens of the Homelands. (*Restoration of South African Citizenship Act No. 73*, 1986)
- Conversion of 99-year leasehold rights into absolute ownership. (*Black Communities Development Act*, 1986)
- Creation of multiracial and integrated provincial administrative bodies. (*Regional Services Council Acts*, 1985 and 1986)
- End of job reservations (for Whites) in the mines. (1986 and 1987).
- Relaxation of the restriction on rights of residence in areas reserved for another population group (1986).
- Accessibility of Blacks to most publicly controlled recreational facilities, including beaches (1986).
- The proposal of an Integrated National Council comprising elected Black representatives for the black population for purposes of deliberating further constitutional reform. (*National Council Bill No. 109*, 1986)
- The establishment of Joint Executive Authorities ('JEA') for 'White' provinces and neighbouring Self-Governing Territories, as in the case of Natal and Kwazulu (1987).

Many of the powers listed above were already available to the government and in many ways the 'State of Emergency' was a symbolic gesture to the white electorate that the government had everything under control. Bishop Tutu condemned Botha. "This reaction is typical of the South African government. They have never known how to deal with dissent. The only response they know is the mailed fist."

The State of Emergency marked the failure of 'facelift apartheid'. Botha's reform package had been rejected by the non-Whites. It also marked the failure of Reagan's policy of "constructive engagement" and strengthened the demand for economic action to be taken against South Africa by the world (see page 32).

THE RESTORATION OF ORDER 1986-88

"As long as I live, reform will continue only on the basis of protection for the white man." *PW Botha*

This period marked the effective end of the reform programme. The limited State of Emergency in 38 districts had failed to crush black resistance and although this emergency rule was lifted for three brief months in early 1986 to coincide with the visit to South Africa of the Commonwealth Eminent Persons' Group (see page 33), it was clear that Botha was not prepared to remove the cornerstone of the apartheid system, the *Group Areas Act*. At a meeting of a special Congress of his Party in August 1986, he told delegates to ignore the review of the Group Areas Act. "Let us by all means make the Act more flexible, but let us cling fast to this cornerstone of the social system ... As long as I am leader of this country there will be no change in the principle of this law."

Botha's strategy was in many ways self-contradictory. His objective was to restore "order in the townships" and to create a political climate that would encourage 'moderate' black leaders to enter negotiations with the government to enable Blacks to participate in the political process. Botha was able to achieve his first objective: military might and repressive legislation did end the ungovernability of the townships but his search for dialogue with Black leaders ended in frustration. When Botha suffered a mild stroke on January 18 1989, six days after his 73rd birthday, it offered an opportunity to the reformist wing of the National Party to seize the initiative and reactivate the reform programme.

STATE OF EMERGENCY JUNE 1986

On 16 June, Botha declared a national State of Emergency which was to remain in force until 1990. In his 'go it alone' speech to the nation, Botha made it clear to the international community that he cared little for their threats of sanctions. He stated, "South Africans will not allow themselves to be humiliated in order to prevent sanctions. If we have to be dependent on our Creator and our own ability alone, then I say let it be."

Reasons for the State of Emergency

1 The immediate reason was to prevent widespread black demonstrations to commemorate the 10th anniversary of the 1976 Soweto uprising. Reports in the Afrikaans press had described "communist plans" to burn down the government's headquarters and other administrative nerve centres, set fire to white schools and to bomb shopping centres. Terrorist attacks such as the one in Durban on 14 June which killed three white women and injured 69 other people gave substance to these exaggerated reports.

2 An increase in support for the right-wing parties (see page 42), especially the extremist Afrikaner Weerstandsbeweging (Afrikaner Resistance Movement) had alarmed Botha. A joint rally organised by the Conservative Party, Herstigte Nasionale Party and the Afrikaner Resistance Movement on 31 May had attracted 15,000 supporters. They accused Botha of being too soft in dealing with the unrest in the black townships for fear of upsetting foreign opinion. The visit of the Eminent Persons Group (EPG) and its interference in South African affairs had infuriated Botha. The EPG, consisting of seven Commonwealth elder statesmen, had proposed to the government that the ANC should be legalised, its leader Nelson Mandela released, that the ANC in turn should renounce violence and that the two sides should begin negotiations about the country's future. Botha retaliated by displaying the Afrikaner tradition of Kragdadigheid (forcefulness); he refused to meet the EPG and on 19 May launched raids on Botswana, Zambia and Zimbabwe.

3 Botha had created an 'Imperial Presidency', heavily dominated by the military through the National Security Management System (see page 21). His advisers advocated a military solution.

RESTORING CONTROL

In the period 1985 (first State of Emergency) to 1988, over 40,000 people were detained without trial, at least 2,000 of them for over 2 years. Significantly, children formed a high proportion of those arrested - over 12,000 children were detained without trial. In the same period, 31 anti-apartheid organisations were silenced and 700 individuals were subjected to restrictions on their activities. Every form of opposition to Apartheid, the churches, trade unions, the media and political organisations, had their activities severely limited. Despite the draconian powers bestowed on the government by the State of Emergency, new restrictions were introduced every year in a vain attempt to restore 'order' similar to that achieved after the Soweto Riots of 1976.

Below is a brief outline of the action taken by the government to restore law and order.

Media Control

The government, aware of the tremendous damage inflicted on its image abroad by the international coverage of township unrest, was determined to restrict publicity by introducing savage censorship. The following limitations were placed on the media:

- Journalists were banned from reporting in any black residential area, or any other area in which unrest was occurring without prior permission.
- All live satellite transmissions out of South Africa by foreign television networks were prohibited.
- Intimidation was used against journalists, eg. in the first month of the State of Emergency 22 journalists were

detained and 4 foreign correspondents deported.

- The press could not publish news or comment upon those arrested or tried by the authorities. This silenced evidence of assault or torture of detainees.
- When newspapers challenged the rigid regulations by displaying blank spaces to indicate the censorship imposed on their reporting, they were informed that this act was "subversive".
- A new system of censorship was introduced on 28 August 1987. Any periodical, including newspapers, could be closed down for up to three months (later extended to six months). The first newspaper to be banned under the regulation was the *New Nation*, which was accused of "subversive propaganda". This new regulation also applied to the importation of foreign publications.

Political Control

The government tried to destroy the peaceful and legally organised opposition which had emerged in the 1980s. In particular, the leaders and members of the UDF were arrested and imprisoned. The UDF was declared "an affected organisation" and was prevented from receiving money from abroad. Two of its leaders, Mrs Albertina Sisulu and Archie Gumede were charged with high treason.

Numerous groups had their organisers detained and meeting places closed. The concept of civil disobedience was widened to include attendance at funerals, refusing to pay rents and participating in boycott campaigns of firms, products or educational institutions.

Educational Control

Emergency regulations outlawed the organisation of school boycotts and the use of People's Education materials in schools. The National Education Crisis Committee (NECC), which coordinated the activities of Parents - Teachers - Students Associations at the national level and directed the movement for People's Education, was banned.

In December 1986, a State of Emergency regulation made it illegal to offer "in any school any syllabus or work programme which had not been approved in terms of the Education Act". This regulation banned People's Education material, and also gave the police and army powers to expel any pupil carrying People's Education material or wearing a People's Education T-shirt. All pupils were also to reregister at school and to be issued with identity cards. Schools were placed under the authority of the police and army and were fenced and patrolled by security guards. These measures enabled the authorities to prevent political activists from attending school and receiving an education.

Township Control

The ANC had called on its people to make the townships "ungovernable" and in the period 1984-86 the 'young comrades' created their own forms of control within the townships. Unfortunately, an orgy of mindless violence occurred, symbolised by the 'necklace killings' - a revolutionary symbol as horrific as the guillotine of the 18th century French Revolution. The victim's hands were tied; one rubber tyre was put around his neck and another around his legs; they were then soaked with petrol and set ablaze.

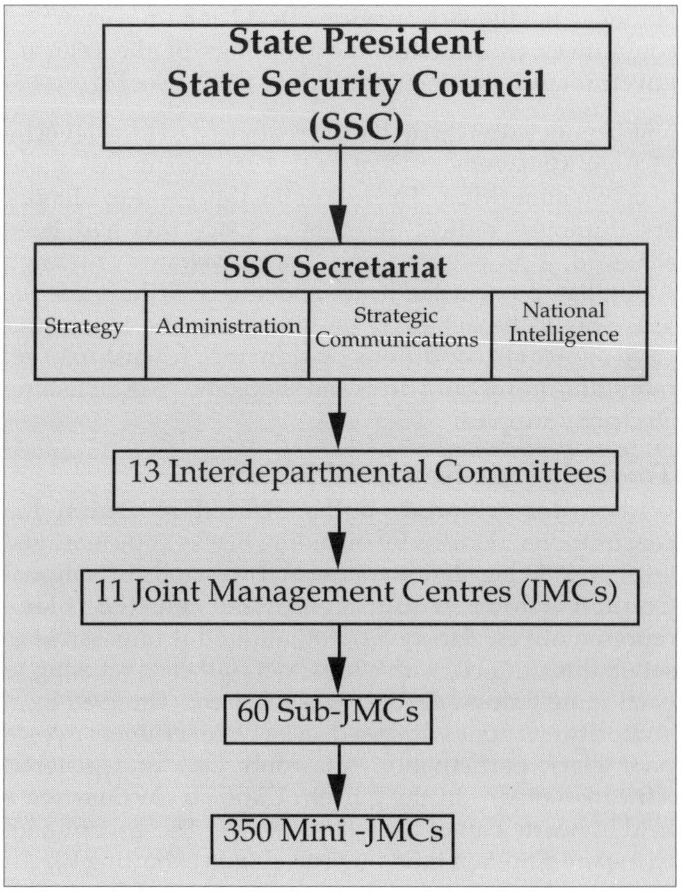

Figure 4.3

Many townships, especially in the Eastern Cape, had established alternative legal authorities to replace the hated local government structures. The 'Comrades' issued trading licences and fixed prices in black-owned shops; they policed the streets and set up 'people's courts' to try common criminals as well as suspected political informers; and they organised school and work boycotts.

The government's strategy was to isolate each township and to send in the police and army. A barbed wire fence was put round the township, with a single entry and exit to monitor movement. Systematically this 'army of occupation' searched each house, making mass arrests. In 1987, 400 people were killed by the police in the execution of their duties.

Central to this strategy of terror was the use of black vigilantes (older Blacks fed up with Comrade intimidation and street gangs) and the creation of extra black 'municipal local enforcement officers', nicknamed Kitskonstabels (instant constables). These groups carried out a reign of terror in the townships. The homes of known UDF supporters were set on fire and savage beatings inflicted while the police stood by.

National Security Management Scheme (NSMS)

The nerve centre of government action was the NSMS (National Security Management Scheme). It was set up in 1979 to coordinate national security in times of unrest and in 1984 it stepped out from the shadows. The top level of the NSMS centred round the State Security Council chaired by the President and in effect became Botha's 'inner cabinet'. Its membership consisted of senior Cabinet Ministers, military and police commanders and the head of the

National Intelligence Service. Its 13 interdepartmental committees coordinated the workings of the relevant government departments in various fields. (see Figure 4.3)

NSMS policy was carried out at regional and local level by 11 Joint Management Centres (JMCs), 60 sub-JMCs and over 350 mini-JMCs. The role of the JMCs was to identify and remove "radical activists". Once this had been achieved, a propaganda and "social welfare" campaign was initiated to win the "hearts and minds" of the residents. This was to be achieved by improving the living and environmental conditions within the Townships, eg. rebuilding burnt out offices and shops and re-establishing electricity supplies.

Towards Constitutional Reforms

With order restored, Botha offered to widen his constitutional reforms by including Blacks at the national level. In 1988, legislation was passed to establish a National Council which would comprise elected Black representatives. However, Botha found it impossible to set up this Council, with even Chief Buthelezi refusing to participate unless Mandela was released. The 1988 local authority elections witnessed, even in government eyes, a poor black participation rate (only 20% of registered Africans voted). In the Eastern Cape no elections were held in nearly half of the 50 townships. The government had spent 5 million rand on propaganda exhorting Blacks to vote and had clamped down on pro-boycott opposition groups, but to no avail.

The government had intended that the newly elected black councillors would form an electoral college to elect 9 of the 15 black representatives on the proposed National Council whose function was "to prepare a constitutional dispensation which provides for participation by all South Africans in the process of government". The low turnout reflected black opinion on the proposed National Council.

Restoration of Petty Apartheid

The 1988 local council elections also witnessed the further advancement of the Conservative Party. (In the 1987 General Election they had become the official opposition with 22 seats.) The Conservative Party won control of some 90 councils many of which tried to turn the clock back by restoring petty apartheid. Once again, 'White Only' signs appeared at swimming pools, parks and even at bus stops. However, a black consumer boycott was launched in two 'petty apartheid' councils, Boksburg and Carltonville, with devastating effect. The boycott in Carltonville, organised by the NUM (National Union of Miners), achieved its objective. A survey of 139 businesses in the town, conducted by the local Chamber of Commerce, found that 53% of shopkeepers estimated that sales had dropped by at least 40%. Although State of Emergency regulations made boycotts illegal, the government turned a blind eye and in fact enjoyed the spectacle of the Conservative Party being attacked by the local white business community. The boycott displayed black consumer power and was a further nail in the coffin of apartheid.

In November 1988, Botha released the ailing leader of the Pan Africanist Congress, Zephania Mothopeng and speculation arose over the possible release of Nelson Mandela. The ANC leader had repeatedly turned down Botha's offer of a conditional release if he renounced the ANC armed struggle. In August 1988 Mandela, receiving treatment for tuberculosis, had been removed from Capetown's Pollsmoor Prison and eventually placed in a house at Victor Verster Prison. The year ended with Mandela holding discussions with government leaders, including Botha himself, but they remained deadlocked.

5 INTERNAL OPPOSITION TO APARTHEID 1948-1988

Black opposition to apartheid was a recurring feature in the forty years of Afrikaner rule. The outlawing of mass organisations since 1960 and the repressive acts of the regime drove the liberation movement underground. The African National Congress (ANC), the Pan Africanist Congress of Azania (PAC), the Black Consciousness Movement (BCM) and the United Democratic Front (UDF) were all declared illegal. Political activity among black South Africans spanned a broad spectrum. It ranged from groups working within the system, such as the ethnic Zulu organisation and black trade unions, to support for the banned ANC.

EARLY YEARS OF RESISTANCE 1948-1970

It would be incorrect to imagine that African opposition to white dominance was a feature only of the post-1948 era. The ANC was formed in 1912 with the goal of forging national unity among Africans in their struggle for civil rights. The entrenchment of the apartheid system in the early 1950s turned the ANC into a mass movement. Despite the brutality of the regime, the ANC continued to preach and argue for nonviolent, nonrevolutionary change. Its leader from 1952 to 1960, Chief Albert Luthuli, was a dignified reformist in the mould of Martin Luther King.

Freedom Charter to Sharpeville

A significant factor in unifying and strengthening the nonwhite opposition was the adoption of the Freedom Charter by the African, coloured and Indian Congresses (The Congress Alliance). The Charter, which is still an integral part of ANC aims today, called for a nonracial, unitary, democratic state based on the socialist principles of nationalisation of key industries and services.

The Congress Alliance launched a nationwide campaign in which volunteers collected 'freedom' demands at meetings throughout the country. In addition, petitions were signed demanding civil rights for all. The authorities failed in their attempt to make support for the Freedom Charter a treasonable offence since the outcome of the Treason Trials (1956-61) was the acquittal of 156 Chartists.

The solidarity of black opposition suffered a blow in 1959 when a splinter group from the ANC formed the Pan Africanist Congress. Its supporters emphasised the need for Africans to act alone without the support of white liberals. Robert Sobukwe, the first President of the PAC, described its aims as follows: "Government of the Africans, by the Africans and for the Africans."

It was a PAC campaign against the pass laws that led to the Sharpeville massacre of March 1960, when police shot dead 69 demonstrators. The authorities declared a state of emergency and savagely crushed the peaceful black organisations. Over 20,000 people were detained, both the ANC and PAC were banned and their leaders tried and sentenced to long years of imprisonment.

The ANC went underground in 1960 and initiated an armed struggle. In 1964 Nelson Mandela, leader of the ANC, was sentenced to life imprisonment for attempting revolution by violence. For more than a decade, black opposition lay crushed and dispirited. However, in the 1970s, the struggle was taken up by a new generation and by 'the children'.

'THE CHILDREN AWAKE'

In 1976 and 1977, over 700 Africans died in what were referred to as the 'Soweto Riots'. The significance of these events was not the brutality of the regime but the resistance offered by the children of Soweto. This new generation had watched their parents retreat into sullen submission to the system: "You look at your parent and see a worn-out hopeless person."

The seeds for this reappearance of African pride and self-respect can be traced to the emergence in the seventies of a new layer of organised opposition that worked within the framework of apartheid. Its leader, Steve Biko, was a charismatic figure, who unified the people and revived the African spirit.

The riots started on 16 June when high school pupils began to march on Phefeni Junior Secondary school. This was the focal point of the protest against the introduction of Afrikaans as a medium of instruction in African schools. The protest march of up to 1,000 students began peacefully. They carried banners with slogans denouncing the use of Afrikaans - "We are not Boers" and "Viva Azania" - and sang the African national anthem 'Nkosi Sikel'i Afrika' (God Bless Africa).

The tragedy that followed was predictable. The police opened fire when the students started stoning them. Sophie Tema, a reporter from the black newspaper *The World*, witnessed the events: "I saw a young boy of about seven fall with a bullet wound. He had bloody froth on his lips and he seemed seriously hurt. I took him to Phefeni clinic but he was dead when we arrived."

The riots quickly spread throughout Soweto and to other townships. The Soweto Students Representative Council (SSRC) was set up to coordinate resistance. The school boycott was extended to a work boycott and this created resentment among the hostel workers who disliked being dictated to by the young. The outcome was a 'Zulu' backlash that turned Soweto into a city of terror and resulted in the death of 35 young Blacks.

The riots were a rejection not only of Bantu Education, but of the entire structure of apartheid. A leader of the SSRC stated, "We know that education is the tool of our liberation in the long run but not the second-class schooling we get under the Bantu Education Act. We must keep up the pressure to force the Whites to give us the same education they have."

The draconian actions of the government eventually brought disorder to an end. About 2,000 children were arrested and an equal number fled the country to join the ranks of the ANC in exile. One father remembers his daughter leaving home in April 1977; when he and his wife objected she asked them, "So you want your freedom to be won by other children, not your children?"

Although the school boycott ended in 1979, schools in Soweto never fully regained their previous enrolment level. By Christmas 1977, open resistance had been crushed. The government outlawed 18 movements and banned the newspaper, *The World*. Two months earlier, Steve Biko had died in police custody. Resistance had been crushed but the embers of black pride, dignity and aspirations could not be totally smothered. Steve Biko had not died in vain. As Peter Gabriel wrote, "You can blow out a candle but not a fire."

STEVE BIKO AND THE BCM

"When a newspaper delivery van turned into Pritchard Street in Johannesburg last night, every black man in the neighbourhood began to run after it. Posters stuck on the side of the van carried just two words, big and stark: BIKO DEAD. A crowd of incredulous Blacks gathered around a stack of newspapers. 'I didn't know what was happening,' Harry Alpern, a white South African who runs a second-hand clothing shop, said later, 'I asked one of the Blacks what had happened, and he said: "Steve Biko is dead." I said, "Who is Biko?" He looked at me as if I was mad, so I thought maybe this Biko was a famous jazz musician or a footballer. Then someone told me he was some Black who had died in prison.' " (From *Newsweek*, 26 Sept, 1977.)

Steve Biko died at the age of 30 and, like Harry Alpern, most white South Africans had never heard of him. In the early seventies the authorities had tried to 'silence' B iko. In 1973, he was forbidden to leave King William's Town, to publish anything, to be referred to in the press, or to be visited by more than one person at a time. He had to report once a week to the Police Station and was under constant watch by the Security Police.

To many Blacks, especially the young, Biko was South Africa's Martin Luther King. He was born in King William's Town on 18 December 1946 and for a brief period studied medicine at the University of Natal. His involvement in the struggle for black civil rights led to his expulsion from university and in 1968 he founded the (Black) South African Students Organisation (SASO). Biko travelled around the country to spread the gospel of Black Consciousness, instilling self-confidence, pride and dignity in the young.

The policy manifesto adopted by SASO in July 1971 outlined the philosophy of Black Consciousness. SASO believed that Whites must be excluded from the struggle for black freedom because of their privileges and involvement in an oppressive state. The Black Consciousness Movement (BCM) rejected tribalism and emphasised black unity at a time when separate (tribal) development was being implemented. Biko, as president of the Black People's Convention, stressed this point, "We are oppressed not as individuals, not as Zulus, Xhosas, Vendas or Indians. We are oppressed because we are black. We must use that very concept to unite ourselves, and to respond as a cohesive group."

The authorities arrested him for the fourth and last time on 13 August 1977. Their purpose was to discredit Biko by forcing him to confess to acts of terrorism. On 12 September, Biko died. His death shocked the world and an international outcry forced the Republic of South Africa to conduct a judicial inquiry. The Inquest Inquiry gave a disturbing insight into the workings of the Security Police. Biko was the 46th detainee to die in police custody. He was kept naked, chained to a grille and tortured. Finally, on September 11, he was put into the back of a Land Rover and driven 750 miles to a military hospital in Pretoria, where he died almost on arrival. The Inquest Inquiry lasted three weeks, with no charges being brought against any of the interrogation team.

In 1978, the rebirth of Black Consciousness occurred in the formation of AZAPO. Its leaders were arrested immediately, but its loose federation of various interested groups ensured its survival. However, it has lost much of its appeal and support, many of its former supporters returning to the fold of the ANC. Despite its emphasis on black integrity it agreed to work with the multiracial UDF. In May 1985, leaders of both AZAPO and the UDF declared at a prayer meeting in Soweto that their only enemy was apartheid.

TRADE UNION ORGANISATION

In 1979 Botha, partly in response to US pressure, legalised black trade unions. (See Riekert Report, page 17) It was also an attempt to bring black trade unionism within the limits of white industrial discipline; it failed miserably. The 1980s witnessed a rapid expansion in trade union membership and an increased militancy among black workers reflected in the rash of strikes that became an everyday feature of the industrial scene. Ironically the government helped to create what it always dreaded - a black South African version of Poland's 'Solidarity'.

Black trade unions are not new in South Africa. As far back as the 1920s a commercial union existed and several attempts were made in the 1940s and 1950s to form unions, although these were short-lived. It was not until 1973 that a concerted attempt was made to revive unionism. The government first tried to prevent this by 'banning' 30 trade union officials. However, grass-roots support was so strong, reinforced by foreign companies determined to implement the Sullivan principles, (see page 31) that the government was forced to accept trade unionism.

Growth of Unions

The period 1979-84 marked a rapid expansion in black trade unions, especially in distribution, motor assembly and the textile industries. The new Unions FOSATU, SAAWU and GAWU (see Table 5.1) were based on a principle of nonracism and initially concentrated on building up support at factory level. The period 1979-82 was also characterised by an outbreak of strikes. More Africans were now doing skilled jobs where they could not be readily replaced. In 1981 an estimated 171 strikes occurred and 1982 witnessed a strike in six coal mines which resulted in a substantial wage rise for black miners.

Multiracial (Black) Trade Unions

		Membership Figures 1985
FOSATU	Federation of South African Trade Unions	120,000
SAAWU	South African Allied Workers Union	100,000
GAWU	General and Allied Workers Union	80,000
CUSA	Council of Unions of South Africa	150,000
NUM	National Union of Mineworkers	150,000

Table 5.1

National Union of Mineworkers

In 1982 CUSA (Council of Unions of South Africa) sent a young Lawyer, Cyril Ramaphosa, to organise the half million miners, 90% of whom were migrant workers. Immediate recognition by two of the six Mining Houses was achieved. Anglo-American and Rand Mines enabled the fledgeling National Union of Mineworkers to consolidate its position; within a year the Chamber of Mines (which represents the owners) allowed the NUM to negotiate on behalf of the black miners.

Under Ramaphosa many longstanding grievances of black mineworkers were redressed; wage differentials between white and black miners dropped from 20:1 to 5:1, and job reservations were gradually eradicated. In 1983 the Chamber of Mines agreed that black workers could become samplers, surveyors and ventilation officers, but the right to gain a blast certificate in order to use explosives was blocked by the white union.

In 1984 and 1985 strikes broke out over the issues of pay and conditions. Significantly, the 1985 strike had political undertones. The unions demanded the lifting of the State of Emergency and the withdrawal of the threat to repatriate all foreign Blacks if economic sanctions were imposed on South Africa.

Government Repression

The government at first made some conciliatory gestures: in 1982 it accepted that black trade unions could register as nonracial and admit immigrant workers. It was also apparent that its attempt to control the black workers by legal statutes, 'parallel' unions and liaison committees at the factory floor level had failed. The regime now resorted to coercion. New legislation aimed at restricting the powers of the independent unions was introduced and numerous trade unionists were arrested. In February 1982 Dr Neil Aggett, a White working for black unionism, was found hanged in his prison cell.

The government's repressive acts towards the black community in general radicalised the black unions.
In October 1984, 7,000 troops and policemen sealed off four black townships south of Johannesburg and searched them. The unions reacted by calling a two-day strike which prompted the government to arrest Mr Pisoshaw and Mr Chris Diamini, the leaders of CUSA and FOSATU.

The proposed constitutional reforms also acted as a catalyst for politicising the unions. Several unions affiliated to the United Democratic Front and organised 'political' strikes. Even the moderate union, FOSATU, renounced its nonpolitical role and was prepared to act as the vanguard of black opposition. In May 1985, one of its shop stewards, Mr Andreas Raditsela, died of head injuries two days after being arrested. FOSATU turned his funeral into a one-day general strike. At the graveside Mr Diamini asserted that, "Everyone is becoming involved outside the work force."

A Black 'Solidarity' Union

In December 1985, the dream of a black 'Solidarity' trade union became a reality. Thirty six South African trade unions, with a total membership of 500,000, formed the Congress of South African Trade Unions (COSATU). Its leader, Elijah Barayi, former Vice President of the National Union of Mineworkers, immediately gave the government a six months time limit to dismantle apartheid. At a mass rally of union members he threatened a workers' boycott and greater union activity. He declared, "We are not going to be passive. We have been passive for quite a number of years. But now we feel we have to be seen to be taking an active part, politically, culturally and socially."

The trade unions played a crucial role in organising black opposition during the state of emergency. They organised strikes (such as the three-day stayaway of June 1988) and boycotts and they monitored the activities of the government. In turn, the authorities arrested 220 trade union officials and more than 2,000 rank-and-file members. Numerous acts of intimidation were carried out against trade union members. In April 1988 troops raided COSATU House and in the following month the union offices were bombed. Three members of the National Union of Mineworkers were sentenced to death.

INKATHA

The largest (and legal) political mass movement is Inkatha, "the national culture liberation organisation of the Zulus". Its leader and President is Chief Minister of Kwazulu, Buthelezi. He is hated by the ANC and feared by other black groups, but his power is built on a combination of Kwazulu patronage and refusal to accept homeland independence.

Inkatha, founded in 1974, is predominantly a Zulu movement, although it claims to be a national organisation. It straddles rural and urban areas with some 30,000 paid-up members and 700 registered branches. Inkatha rejects violence as the best means of bringing about racial change and favours nonviolent tactics such as consumer boycotts. Buthelezi denies that he is a puppet of Pretoria. In 1976 he stated that, "the Zulu people have rejected the policy of independence. I know I am vilified as a 'collaborator' for my cooperation with the government. But we have up to a point, not because we believe in apartheid but because since there was no alternative allowed, it was in the interest of a peaceful settlement of South Africa's problem."

Inkatha and the ANC were once fraternal organisations and initially Buthelezi was encouraged by the ANC to build up his movement. However, the ANC President, Oliver Tambo, accused Buthelezi of using Inkatha as a personal power base and of collaborating with the government. Inkatha's and the ANC's policies diverge on such major issues as sanctions and nationalisation. Inkatha

Mangosuthu Buthelezi, leader of the Inkatha Freedom Party

is against them and this infuriated the ANC.

The crisis of 1985-86 threatened to leave Buthelezi beached on a sandbank of moderation as a tidal wave of black fury and anger threatened to engulf the entire country. The revival of the ANC and the formation of the UDF weakened his power base. These groups accused Inkatha of preaching nonviolence against the government while using violence against black rivals. Tension between the UDF and Inkatha is especially prevalent in Durban (Eastern Cape Province). The murder, in August 1985, of Mrs Victoria Mxenge, a key member of the UDF, was blamed on Inkatha. At her memorial service, fighting broke out between Inkatha men and the mourners. This spread to the neighbouring townships and an orgy of looting occurred in the Indian township.

Buthelezi was unwilling to meet with Botha to discuss 'new black structures' - such an act would have been the kiss of death for Buthelezi's Inkatha movement and would have confirmed the suspicion that Buthelezi was a puppet of Pretoria. Buthelezi would only negotiate with the government if Nelson Mandela was freed.

Nevertheless, Inkatha witnessed a serious loss of support in its Natal stronghold. Trade union organisations such as COSATU supported the UDF in their struggle with Inkatha. (See page 55) In response, Inkatha resorted to coercion and forced recruitment and in June 1986 set up its own trade union, UWUSA (United Workers Union of South Africa), with secret government funds. Outwith Natal, Inkatha support has waned. An opinion poll in 1988 showed that support for Inkatha in the Johannesburg area shrank from 30 per cent in 1977 to less than 5 per cent in 1988.

UNITED DEMOCRATIC FRONT

At the January 1983 Conference of the coloured Labour Party, a decision was taken to participate in elections for the new coloured Assembly. This led directly to the formation of the UDF, a multi-racial umbrella group dedicated to opposing the new Constitution. (see page 18)

A central figure in the formation and activities of this body was Dr Allan Boesak, a coloured theologian, who was also President of the World Alliance of Churches. At the UDF's inaugural meeting on 22 January 1983, he denounced Allan Hendrickee, Leader of the coloured Labour Party, for his betrayal. Boesak declared, "We must reject the proposals aimed at drawing in so-called Coloureds and Indians and alienating Blacks from the new system. We ought not to play around with the evil. The situation calls for vigilance." The UDF quickly became the vehicle for national coordination and expression of popular resistance to the new constitution. Two of the most important groups that joined the UDF were the Eastern Cape Union, SAAWU (South African Allied Workers Union) and COSAS (Council of South African Students.

Despite the UDF's commitment to peaceful protest, the government tried unsuccessfully to crush it. However the UDF's loose structure was its strength. It was made up of 400 organisations drawn from every part of the country and every section of resistance. Although 36 of its leaders were arrested in 1984, the UDF simply regrouped with new leaders emerging. The government claimed that the UDF was a front for the banned African National Congress.

The State of Emergency intensified the pressure against the UDF and its affiliated groups. In August 1985 the government banned COSAS and arrested its leaders; at the same time 38 leading UDF members were charged with treason. The UDF was declared an "affected organisation" and effectively banned.

ARMED STRUGGLE - RE-EMERGENCE OF THE ANC

The Soweto Riots of 1976 and the demise of the Black Consciousness Movement rekindled the fires of the ANC. The 1980s witnessed a steady escalation of the acts of sabotage perpetrated by the military wing of the ANC (Umkhonto We Sizwe).

During this period, Nelson Mandela's role was that of a figurehead. Despite his long imprisonment and declining health, most black people referred to him as "Father of Azania" and used him as a mooring post for their political aspirations. The group's leader in exile was Oliver Tambo, who fled South Africa at the time of Mandela's arrest. Tambo's headquarters were in Lusaka, the capital of Zambia, and he had built up an estimated force of 6,000 men and women trained as saboteurs and urban terrorists.

Tambo insisted that armed struggle was the only way of ending apartheid. In 1983 he stated, "Never again are our people going to do all the bleeding. We have offered the other cheek so many times that there is no cheek left to turn."

The ANC received financial support and weapons from the countries of the Warsaw Pact. However, it denies that it was a communist organisation. Oliver Tambo established cordial links with the countries of the West and in October 1985 he received a standing ovation at the Labour Party Conference after calling on Britain to introduce sanctions against South Africa. Even South African industrialists, to the fury of Botha, held meetings with the ANC.

Botha's state of emergency curtailed the activities of the ANC. However, acts of sabotage against military and industrial targets were a common feature of the period 1986-88. Despite the ANC's decision not to engage in a terror campaign against civilian targets, bombs were set off in town and city centres, causing civilian casualties or injuries. However these were isolated incidents deplored by the National Executive Committee of the ANC.

Significantly the ANC's status as a legitimate organisation gained worldwide acceptance. Leaders of the ANC met with government officials in London and Washington. From a terrorist group in exile the ANC had been elevated to a government-in-waiting.

The Updated Freedom Charter

In 1988 the ANC released the document *Constitutional Guidelines for a Democratic South Africa*, which updated the Freedom Charter. The document provides for a centralised unitary state: "The state shall determine and guide, direct and control the economy to end economic and social inequalities produced by racial discrimination ..." and will encourage "... social well-being". The state should also introduce a policy of creating "a national identity and loyalty amongst all citizens. All other social, cultural and economic elements in society are under obligation to actively support these two objectives."

It also provides for universal franchise and freedom of association, subject to the obligation that "The state and all social institutions shall be under constitutional duty to eradicate racial discrimination in all its forms." Other forms of free association are protected in a Bill of Rights as well as in a Workers' Charter. The rights of women and the family are specifically protected.

6 EXTERNAL REACTION TO APARTHEID

SOUTH AFRICA - REGIONAL SUPERPOWER

The mid-1980s seemingly witnessed the realisation of Botha's dream of a constellation of neighbouring states dominated by South Africa. 1984 marked the high point of this vision when the pro-Soviet regimes of Angola and Mozambique signed non-aggression pacts with South Africa.

Yet a decade earlier the 'winds of change' had finally reached Southern Africa with the collapse of the Portuguese Empire in Mozambique and Angola. It was confidently predicted that this hurricane of black liberation would sweep away the white minority governments of Rhodesia and South Africa. In 1980 Robert Mugabe's electoral victory in Zimbabwe ended white control of that country. Ironically it was Mugabe's victory that forged the new aggressive foreign policy of South Africa towards the 'front line states'. Her 'mailed fist' policy was to use her economic and military might to destabilise her African neighbours. This action would prevent the 'front line states' from playing an effective part in the struggle for black rule within both South Africa and Namibia.

Economic Dominance

South Africa is the richest country in Southern Africa. It is responsible for nearly 80% of the region's total products and provides 75% of the region's output of coal, iron, wheat, maize, electrical power and rail transport. Since 1910 the countries of Botswana, Lesotho and Swaziland have been members of a customs union with South Africa. Their infrastructures are interlocked with that of South Africa; for example the South African company De Beers owns half of Botswana's diamond mines. In response to this dependence, these three countries joined with the five other front line states to form the Southern African Development Coordination Conference (SADCC). Its function is to coordinate efforts for economic development and to reduce economic dependence on South Africa. (see Table 6.1)

Countries of SADCC

	Population million	Area 000 sq km	GDP/Capita US$	GDP US$bn	Life Expectancy Years
Angola	9.2	1.247	470	4.32	44
Botswana	1.3	562	2,216	4.88	59
Lesotho	1.8	30	87	0.14	56
Malawi	8.4	118	160	1.31	46
Mozambique	14.3	802	136	1.89	44
Namibia	1.6	823	1,290	1.66	49
Swaziland	0.7	17	936	1.66	55
Tanzania	28.3	945	105	2.97	50
Zambia	7.2	753	250	1.80	53
Zimbabwe	10.0	391	580	5.80	58
SADCC	82.7	5,508	3,233	23.30	49.5
South Africa (1988)	35.9	1,100	2,437	87.50	Whites 72 Coloureds 61 Asians 67 Africans 62

Table 6.1 Source: *SADCC Annual Progress Report, 1989-1990*
SAIRR Race Relations Survey, 1988-9.

Angola

Despite not sharing a common border with South Africa, Angola has suffered greatly at the hands of South Africa because of her involvement in the Namibian struggle (see page 29). During the civil war of 1975-76, South Africa invaded Angola in an unsuccessful attempt to prevent the MPLA (Popular Front for the Liberation of Angola) from forming the country's first independent Marxist government.

South Africa actively supported the rebel forces of Sam Savimbi's UNITA (Total Independence for Angola). The rebels were able to occupy a considerable area of the country and their acts of sabotage and attacks on MPLA garrisons wrecked Angola's fragile economy. South Africa herself continually violated the sovereignty of Angolan territory and for long periods occupied the Kunene province of Southern Angola.

The Namibian settlement of 1988, which included the withdrawal of Cuban troops from Angola, opened the way for peace in this war-weary country. Both the superpowers agreed to cooperate and forced their respective clients to sit round the negotiating table. The war had been a costly quagmire for both superpowers, especially for the USSR. She had poured in 11,000 Russian advisers, 50,000 Cuban troops and $750 million in military aid to prop up the MPLA. Washington reacted by giving Savimbi's UNITA $60 million in annual covert assistance.

In June 1991 President José Eduardo dos Santos, head of the Angolan government, and Jonas Savimbi, rebel leader of UNITA, signed a peace treaty in Lisbon in the presence of James Baker, the US Secretary of State, and Soviet Foreign Minister Alexandr Bessmertnykh. A Soviet diplomat summed up the reason for this historic agreement: "Inside Angola exhaustion, outside Angola the end of the Cold War." The civil war had, in fact, destroyed Angola's infrastructure: roads, railways and water supplies stand ruined. Dos Santos asked the West for $2 billion in aid and agreed to the introduction of a mixed economy and to the holding of free elections. UNITA and the MPLA will form an interim government and a United Nations Peacekeeping Force will supervise elections in 1992. Troops of the MPLA and UNITA will be merged into a 40,000 strong national army.

STRUGGLE FOR NAMIBIA

Namibia, formerly known as South West Africa, is larger than France but with a population of only one million. In vast stretches of arid desert only snakes and lizards prosper and most of its inhabitants are native tribesmen living at subsistence level. However, it is one of the richest corners of Africa, possessing vast treasures of diamonds, uranium and other minerals.

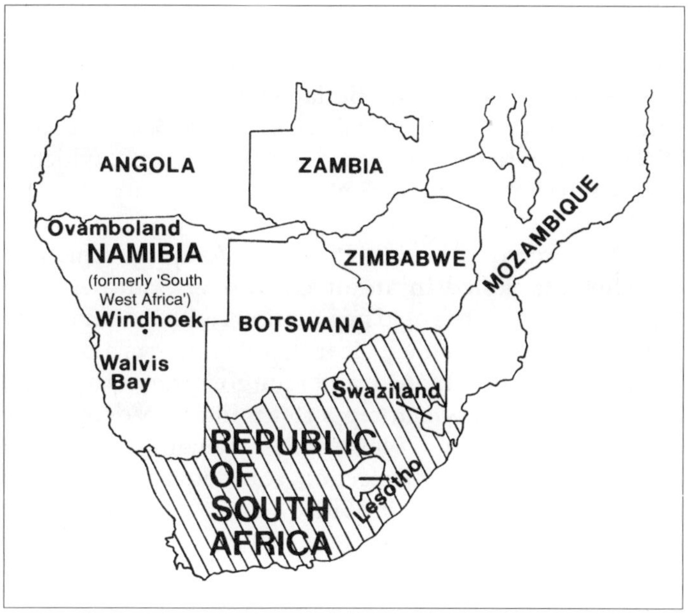

For 23 years South Africa waged war on the South West African Peoples Organisation (SWAPO), transforming the north of Namibia into a vast military camp and displacing the native population.

SWAPO, led by Sam Nujoma, is a Marxist-oriented movement whose political base is the 430,000-member Ovambo Tribe, Namibia's largest ethnic group. (Second largest is the Whites with 90,000 followed by the Hereros, the traditional enemy of the Ovambo, with about 60,000.) SWAPO had an estimated 4,000 guerrillas, most of whom were based in Southern Angola, and had been carrying out her struggle for independence since 1966. SWAPO had the support of the United Nations and in 1973 the General Assembly declared SWAPO "the authentic representative of the Namibian people".

Namibia was the last white colony left in Africa. It had been a German colony but after the First World War the League of Nations gave South Africa a mandate to administer South West Africa. In 1966 the United Nations ended this mandate and in 1969 the Security Council declared South Africa's occupation of the territory illegal and called for her withdrawal.

Democratic Turnhalle Alliance

South Africa, under international pressure, agreed "to prepare Namibia for independence". In 1977 it placed its support behind a white-led coalition of mixed racial parties with the aim of creating an anti-SWAPO alliance that would win an open election. The coalition adopted the name of the Democratic Turnhalle Alliance (DTA) and its leader was Dirk Mudge, a rich white 'verligte' farmer. The DTA won the 1978 election but did not gain international recognition as SWAPO had boycotted the election.

In January 1983 South Africa ended all pretence of a DTA-governed Namibia. Pretoria resumed direct control and the Council of Ministers and National Assembly were dissolved. Pretoria's policy was now to link Namibian independence to Cuban withdrawal from Angola and to this end she received the tacit support of the USA, to the dismay of black Africa. In June 1985, President Botha installed a new interim administration, formed by a coalition of six parties referred to as the Multi-Party Conference (MPC). The new multiracial government was, in theory, an experiment in power sharing.

The Steps to Independence

1988 marked the breakthrough in negotiations over Namibian independence. Negotiations between South Africa, Angola and Cuba, with United States mediation, commenced in May 1988. Subsequent meetings in Cairo and in New York led to the trilateral agreement signed on 22 December 1988 by the Republic of South Africa, the People's Republic of Angola and the Republic of Cuba. The agreement provided for the implementation of United Nations Security Council Resolution 435 (see below) and the withdrawal of Cuban troops from Angola.

The agreement reflected the changing political climate in South Africa, tempered by the 'winds of change' blowing out of the USSR. South Africa's claim that it was fighting a "total onslaught" orchestrated by international communism had become a hollow cry of self-delusion. Gorbachev's new foreign policy of disengagement from costly foreign adventures and the USSR's statement that it no longer supported the use of force as the method to achieve majority rule in South Africa ensured a new era of realism between South Africa and Angola. The peace plan marked a shift in South Africa's strategy from aggressive forward defence to a less assertive protection of the South African borders.

The November 1989 Election

The election which took place between 7 and 11 November was pronounced free and fair by the United Nations. Ten parties contested the election, the two leading parties being SWAPO and DTA. Throughout the election campaign, SWAPO emphasised the importance of national unity and reconciliation and this message of pragmatism was reflected in its election manifesto. SWAPO's programme was to eradicate racism from Namibia, to redirect economic activities in the interest of the Namibian people and to give priority to education, health and social facilities. However, learning from the bitter lesson of Mozambique, SWAPO aimed to do this without large-scale nationalisation and affirmed its support for a mixed economy.

The election was a triumph for the democratic process; 96% of the registered electorate voted in the five days set aside. As expected, SWAPO emerged victorious, but failed to achieve the crucial two-thirds majority which would have enabled SWAPO to write the constitution.

> ***SECURITY COUNCIL RESOLUTION 435***
>
> ***The 1978 resolution called for a ceasefire, the withdrawal of troops to camp, the release of political prisoners and holding a United Nations supervised election.***

On 20 March 1990 at the ceremony marking Namibia's formal independence, the new President, Sam Nujoma, and the South African President, de Klerk, watched as the South African flag was lowered and the flag of the new Namibia raised. President de Klerk had brought to an end a war that had been costing South Africa $2 million a day. More importantly, he had demonstrated to his white electorate that Whites could hand over power to the black majority in a peaceful manner. The message for South Africa was clear - negotiation, not warfare, would be the way forward for South Africa.

Walvis Bay

One issue that has still to be resolved is the future of Walvis Bay. This has not been restored to Namibia, despite United Nations Security Council Resolution 432 which stated that "the territorial integrity and unity of Namibia must be assured throughout the reintegration of Walvis Bay within the territories". South Africa claims that since Walvis Bay was not part of the German colony of South West Africa it is not, therefore, part of Namibia. Walvis Bay was annexed by Britain in 1878 and later was administered by the Union of South Africa.

Walvis Bay is of great economic and strategic importance. Namibia's only deep water port, it is the centre of her fishing industry and handles 90% of her overall export trade. South Africa has built up extensive military facilities in the area, including a naval and air base.

Namibian Nationhood

Nevertheless, Namibia's early experience of nationhood is encouraging. A national identity is being created, based on reconciliation and a democratic constitution. The government has reached new agreements with the multinational companies and is determined to reduce dependence on South Africa through participation in the Southern African Development Coordination Conference (SADCC).

Mozambique

Mozambique's proximity to South Africa and her direct support for the African National Congress's struggle against Pretoria exposed her to the constant threat of direct South African action. In January 1981, South African forces raided the outskirts of the capital, Maputo, and killed 13 members of the ANC. However, it was South Africa's support of the rebel Renamo movement that transformed Mozambique's security problem into a fully-fledged crisis; the famine of 1984 also accelerated this process.

Renamo guerrillas caused severe economic dislocation in the countryside - destroying roads, bridges, railway lines and even damaging the Beria - Mutane pipeline (the main fuel supply line for Zimbabwe). Mozambique's President, Samora Machel, finally capitulated to South African demands. He agreed that all ANC military elements would be ousted from his country. The Pact stipulated that neither side would allow its territory to be used to prepare acts of violence against the other. South Africa would end its support of Renamo and provide economic and financial assistance, such as the joint operation of the crucial Cabora-Bassa hydroelectric project.

However, South Africa failed to honour this agreement and continued to supply and train Renamo guerrillas for their campaign of terror. The devastation was immense; by 1990 it was estimated there had been 1 million war-related deaths and 1 million Mozambicans had become refugees in neighbouring countries. The United Nations Children's Fund (UNICEF) announced in 1989 that Mozambique had the highest child mortality rate in the world.

Zimbabwe has been forced to intervene to protect the railway systems and the Beria pipeline which delivers ninety per cent of Zimbabwe's fuel. Six thousand Zimbabwean troops are based in Mozambique, which is an obvious strain on the Zimbabwean economy.

The Mozambique leader, President Joaquim Chissano (Machel was killed in an air crash over South African territory in 1986), has held negotiations with Renamo. The Soviet Union has made it clear that it supports a political settlement. In 1990 the Mozambique government adopted a new constitution which supports a multiparty democracy and a mixed economy. Nevertheless, Renamo, aware that it would lose in an open election, was demanding to form a coalition government in 1991.

USSR

Until a switch in foreign policy priorities by Gorbachev in the late 1980s, Southern Africa was seen as a fertile ground for Soviet expansionism. The struggle for independent, black majority rule by the African liberation groups presented opportunities for the Soviet Union.

The government of South Africa continually reminded Western nations of the late Leonid Brezhnev's words to President Barre of Somalia in the early 1970s: "Our aim is to gain control of the two great treasure houses on which the West depends - the energy treasure house of the Persian Gulf and the mineral treasure house of Central and Southern Africa." Soviet policy towards Southern Africa in this period was shaped by the following goals:

- to create and maintain pro-Soviet or leftish states within Southern Africa;
- to reinforce its superpower status by playing a role in the resolution of problems in Southern Africa;
- to obtain air and naval access in order to counter US strategic forces and to monitor US military activity in the region.

Angola was Moscow's most important asset in Southern Africa. The Soviet Union had access to valuable air and naval facilities and was able to provide aid to SWAPO in Namibia. Moscow's surrogate forces, the Cubans, enabled the Angolan government to withstand attacks from UNITA. In September 1983, shipments of Soviet arms to Angola were stepped up. These included Soviet SA8 surface-to-air missiles, new T72 tanks, helicopters and assorted small arms.

Both Angola and Mozambique had signed Treaties of Friendship and Cooperation with the Soviet Union and their economic development was assisted by numerous Soviet and East European technicians. However, economic assistance has been limited. For example, Mozambique was refused admission to COMECON (the Soviet equivalent of the EC). The actions of the South African-backed Renamo movement increased Mozambique's reliance on Moscow. The Soviet Union also furnished assistance to Mozambique-based members of the ANC. Moscow provided economic, military and humanitarian support to the ANC, which has strong links with the South African Communist Party.

Gorbachev's Foreign Policy

Under Gorbachev the USSR moved away from revolutionary activities and expansion. Brezhnev's policy of Soviet expansion was a recipe for prolonged and increasingly costly entanglement in regional conflicts which were damaging to both Moscow's relations with the West and also often to Soviet prestige. Furthermore they were a massive drain on the Soviet economy. In the context of South Africa, the USSR wished to negotiate rather than export revolution. The Soviet leadership had changed its analysis of the South African situation. The unrest in the townships in 1984-86 was not the forerunner of violent revolution and the complete destruction of the capitalist system. For this reason, the USSR in the late 1980s advised the ANC to move away from its armed struggle to negotiation.

The Soviet position in Southern Africa has evolved from actively opposing American efforts to resolve conflict in the region to collaboration in diplomatic undertakings towards that end. The peace treaty and elections in Namibia, the withdrawal of Cuban troops from Angola, the end of the civil war in Angola and the possibility of peace in Mozambique are all by-products of this 'new realism' in foreign affairs. In November 1990 the first official Soviet trade delegation visited South Africa. The Soviet mission coincided with a visit from a Bulgarian delegation and was preceded by similar visits to South Africa by delegations from Hungary and Poland.

SOUTH AFRICA AND THE USA

South Africa is of strategic and economic importance to the countries of the West, and Pretoria continually stressed her role as a bulwark against communism in Southern Africa. Nevertheless, the existence of a political system that denied civil rights on the basis of colour naturally provoked the United States' condemnation. This dilemma of moral indignation versus national self-interest faces all Presidents of the United States.

President Reagan's Constructive Engagement

The architect of the 'constructive engagement' policy was Chester Croker, the Assistant Secretary of State for African Affairs. In an article written in 1980 he questioned the merits of President Carter's policy of open criticism and hostility towards South Africa. In his view, reform and progress in South Africa (and Namibia) could only be achieved by open dialogue with Pretoria. "The way you get the South African government to move forward on ending apartheid," he stated, "is by breaking down the siege mentality that has influenced them for years."

Initially this strategy seemed productive. US firms in South Africa followed the Sullivan code of conduct and achieved economic and social improvements for their African work forces. American foreign policy objectives also benefited from making Botha's regime the linchpin of its own regional policy. The spread of Soviet influence in Southern Africa was not only curtailed but seemingly rolled back.

In 1976 a black preacher and director of General Motors, the Reverend Leon Sullivan, drafted a voluntary code of six principles for US firms operating in South Africa (see below). These principles would eliminate the effects of apartheid from the work environment. Over 125 US companies became signatories to the code. Significant progress was made during the Sullivan era. Federal and private agencies sponsored everything from scholarships for non-Whites at American universities to subsidies for legal aid centres in black townships. Salaries, as well as conditions of employment, improved under the enlightened management of US firms.

Free South Africa Movement

Within the United States a powerful backlash against 'constructive engagement' emerged. This resurgence of grass-roots anti-apartheid feeling within American society was, in part, a by-product of Reagan's sweeping electoral victory over Mondale in the November 1984 Presidential Election. The issue of civil rights in South Africa united the Liberal Coalition as well as recreating the euphoric atmosphere of America's own Civil Rights campaign of the 1950s and early 1960s.

The Free South Africa movement began in November 1984 when three black leaders went to the South African embassy in Washington to urge the release of 20 South African trade unionists imprisoned after a work stoppage. A spontaneous sit-in occurred, the embassy called in the police and had the demonstrators arrested. Suddenly, South Africa's race problems became a major domestic issue.

Botha's State of Emergency and the crushing of democratic groups within South Africa fuelled the campaign for economic action being taken against South Africa. Even

The Sullivan Principles

A statement of principles of American-based firms operating through affiliates in the Republic of South Africa.

1 Non-segregation of the races in all eating, comfort and work facilities.
2 Equal and fair employment practices for all employees.
3 Equal pay for all employees doing equal or comparable work for the same period of time.
4 Initiation and development of training programmes that will prepare, in substantial numbers, Blacks and other non-Whites for supervisory, administrative, clerical and technical jobs.
5 An increase in the number of Blacks and other non-Whites in management and supervisory positions.
6 An improvement in the quality of employees' life outside the work environment in such areas as housing, transportation, schooling, recreation and health facilities.

the Reverend Leon Sullivan reassessed the merits of constructive engagement and in 1987 he urged US companies to pull out of South Africa. This appeal fell on fertile soil because South Africa had become a liability for most US companies. Anxious to placate the general public at home, numerous US firms pulled out of South Africa. Household names such as IBM, Kodak and Ford Motors led the stampede. The number of US companies with direct investment in South Africa declined from 330 in 1983 to under 130 by the end of 1989. Banks such as Chase Manhattan and Barclay's also withdrew from South Africa.

Significantly, Botha's crackdown ensured that the disinvestment campaign was not simply the clarion call of the Democrats. In June 1986, for example, the University of California, with the support of the Republican Governor George Deukmejian, voted to sell off 3 million dollars in stocks and bonds in companies which had South African dealings.

US Sanctions

In America, throughout 1984-85, both Houses of Congress initiated legislation relating to 'sanctions' against South Africa. In August 1985 both Houses agreed on a compromise Bill that united both the Republican and Democratic Parties and isolated Reagan. The resultant measure would commit the United States to a policy of gradualist sanctions. This action forced President Reagan to pre-empt the Congress Bill by issuing an executive order that imposed the following mild range of sanctions:

- Ban on the export of computers to South African military establishments.
- No export of nuclear technology.
- Ban on loans to the South African government except on those promoting the welfare of *all* South Africans.
- Prohibition of US sales of South African Krugerrands.

However, this pre-emptive bid did not satisfy Congress and in October 1986 , overriding a presidential veto, the *Comprehensive Anti-Apartheid Act* was passed. This Act banned all US imports of South African iron, steel, coal, uranium, textiles and agricultural products; it also forbade new US loans and investments in South Africa. The United Democratic Front hailed this Act as being of historic importance. Congress had derailed Reagan's constructive engagement policy and had set America's sights on campaigning for a multiracial South Africa.

Significantly, the Act allowed the President to suspend it if South Africa achieved the following five objectives:

- The release of all people persecuted for their political beliefs and detained unduly without trial and the release of Nelson Mandela.
- The repeal of the State of Emergency and the release of all prisoners held under it.
- The unbanning of all democratic political parties and permitting all South African free political expression.
- The repeal of the *Group Areas Act* and the *Population Registration Act*.
- Agreement to enter into negotiations in good faith and without preconditions with truly representative black delegates.

The reform programme introduced by President de Klerk in 1990-91 had obvious implications for the rescinding of the Comprehensive Anti-Apartheid Act. Both Nelson Mandela and FW de Klerk visited America in 1990, each with the objective of winning the support of the American public and the administration. In June 1990, as part of his world tour, Mandela made an eight-city tour. He had three main objectives: to thank supporters, to ensure that the West continued sanctions and to raise money. In his speech to the joint meeting of the House and Senate he urged the US to stand firm and to support the black majority in South Africa. "Our people continue to die to this day, victims of armed agents of the state who are still determined to turn their guns against the very idea of a racial democracy," he declared. However, the ANC's economic policies and Mandela's praise of the PLO and Colonel Gadaffi of Libya reinforced the American right's perception of the ANC as a terrorist left-wing organisation.

In September 1990 President FW de Klerk became the first South African head of government to come to America since Jan Smuts in 1945. President Bush praised President de Klerk for his courage and declared that the process of dismantling apartheid was now "irreversible". The Bush administration was eager to end sanctions, despite the misgivings of many Congressmen. Bill Gray, a Democratic Congressman and majority whip in the House of Representatives, stated, "Although we welcome the reforms of Mr de Klerk, the fact is that South Africa is still not free. There are 23 million black South Africans who don't have the right to vote."

Lifting of Sanctions

In July 1991, President Bush announced that he was rescinding the 1986 Comprehensive Anti-Apartheid Act, as the South African government had fulfilled all the conditions laid down in this Act. During the same week South Africa was readmitted to the Olympic Games and to the International Cricket Council. (South Africa had last competed in the 1960 Rome Olympics and in 1970 had been expelled from the Olympic Movement.)

The ending of sanctions and a return to the Olympic Movement strengthened President de Klerk's position within the white community and also his negotiating position with the ANC. Despite white euphoria, the lifting of sanctions will not dramatically transform the economy. Black urban unemployment is nearly 40 per cent and the economy needs to grow at 5.6 per cent each year simply to prevent unemployment getting worse. It is doubtful that the approximately 200 American companies that disinvested will rush back.

BRITISH COMMONWEALTH

Ever since South Africa's withdrawal from the Commonwealth in May 1961, Commonwealth pressure on South Africa has steadily intensified. The consensus of the 49 member states was that Britain, with her close historic and economic ties with South Africa, had a moral duty to actively bring about the abolition of apartheid.

However, the Conservative Government of Margaret Thatcher supported Reagan's policy of 'constructive engagement' and was also influenced by the fact that

Britain's investments in South Africa total £11 billion. In contrast, the opposition parties, both Labour and the SLD, supported a more active stance against apartheid with the introduction of some form of sanctions. Apartheid became an issue of concern to many people in Britain. Oliver Tambo, President of the ANC, spoke to the House of Commons Foreign Affairs Select Committee. Several leading retail firms decided to boycott South African goods, and churches, universities and local authorities took action ranging from ending financial ties with South Africa to symbolic gestures. In 1985, Glasgow District Council renamed St George's place - Nelson Mandela Place, (the South African Consulate has its offices in this square) and granted the freedom of the city to the imprisoned Nelson Mandela.

The Nassau Agreement, 1985

The question of the most effective way of influencing the South African government came to a head at the October 1985 summit meeting at Nassau in the Bahamas. At the conference, Britain faced strong criticism from her fellow members over her reluctance to introduce sanctions. However, the pressure was so intense that the British Prime Minister was forced to compromise.

Eminent Persons Group (EPG)

This group of seven prominent Commonwealth spokespersons visited South Africa in 1986. Its two joint Chairmen were Malcolm Fraser, the former Australian Prime Minister, and General Olusegun Obasanjo of Nigeria. The Group proposed that Pretoria should release Nelson Mandela, unban the ANC and pull the troops out of the townships, while the ANC should agree to suspend violence and begin negotiations. The Group met with Nelson Mandela and were impressed with his positive comments and lack of bitterness. Progress seemed to be achieved and therefore on their return visit in May, the EPG were stunned by the aggressive reaction of Pretoria. Hours before a meeting with the President's Constitutional Committee they were informed that South Africa had raided three neighbouring countries, namely Zimbabwe, Zambia and Botswana. The EPG returned home; Botha had turned his back on dialogue with his policy of Kragdadigheid.

The Nassau Agreement

1 Britain was to extend her boycott of the Krugerrand gold coin trade.

2 Britain was to end trade promotions with South Africa.

3 A request was to be made by all the Commonwealth countries to the South African government to end the state of emergency; to release Nelson Mandela and all others imprisoned; and to end the ban on the African National Congress.

4 A review was to be held in six months time of the steps taken by the South African government to implement meaningful reforms.
The Accord stated - "If in their opinion adequate progress has not been made within this period of six months, we agree to consider the adoption of further measures. Some of us would, in that event, consider the following steps among others. A ban on air links with South Africa and new investment or reinvestment of profits earned in South Africa; a ban on the import of agricultural products and the termination of double taxation agreements with South Africa; all government assistance to investment and trade with South Africa to be ended along with government procurement in South Africa. Furthermore there would be a complete ban on government contracts with majority-owned South African companies and the promotion of tourism to South Africa."

5 A Commonwealth Review Body made up of "eminent Commonwealth persons" was to be set up to monitor progress within South Africa.

The Group's report was published in June and heavily criticised the South African government: "Pretoria was not yet prepared to negotiate fundamental change, nor to countenance the creation of genuine democratic structures, nor to face the prospect of the end of white domination and white power in the foreseeable future." The Group was convinced that "there can be no negotiated settlement in South Africa without the ANC; the breadth of its support is incontestable; and this support is growing." The Report concluded that strong measures were essential: "We are convinced that the South African Government is concerned about the adoption of effective economic measures against it."

The Commonwealth's Response

The Special Commonwealth Summit meeting of August 1986 set the pattern for subsequent meetings of Commonwealth heads that followed in the late 1980s. Margaret Thatcher, despite Botha's crackdown, refused to support the introduction of the wide-ranging measures or sanctions agreed to in the Nassau Accord of 1985. She agreed initially only to voluntary bans on promotion of tourism in South Africa and on new investments there. She stated: "I do not believe that further sanctions will bring about internal change in South Africa. On the contrary, I very much fear that they will be counterproductive." The rest of the Commonwealth Heads of Government were not impressed. Kenneth Kaunda of Zambia summed up the collective viewpoint when he said: "Mrs Thatcher is committed to British vested interests in South Africa at the expense of human beings." Six of the Commonwealth states, Zambia, Zimbabwe, Australia, The Bahamas, Canada and India, agreed to a package of thirteen measures. Among other things, they banned airline links, agricultural imports, new investments, government contracts with South African firms and the import of coal, uranium, iron and steel. Thatcher, put under severe pressure, conceded further measures including a ban on the import of coal, iron, steel and gold coins from South Africa.

At the Commonwealth Summit of October 1989 at Kuala Lumpur, Margaret Thatcher stood isolated in her support for President de Klerk and in her opposition to an escalation of sanctions. Mr Lee Kwan Yew, Prime Minister of Singapore, stated that it had been a case of 48-1 against Mrs Thatcher.

Predictably, Britain reacted swiftly to President FW de Klerk's reform package and announced the end of British sanctions against South Africa. The October 1991 Commonwealth Summit held in Harare, saw no major disagreements among the leaders. The question facing them was *when* and not *if* sanctions should be ended. Britain, while making her own position clear, accepted the final communique which stated that sanctions should be lifted only once a new constitution had been completely written.

EC AND SOUTH AFRICA

The EC is South Africa's largest trading partner, and it has attempted to implement a uniform policy towards apartheid. In 1977, for example, the Community adopted a code of conduct for subsidiaries of EC corporations operating in South Africa.

The 1985 crisis within South Africa and the imposition of US sanctions forced the EC to implement its own mild sanctions against South Africa. In fact it was Britain who delayed EC action by refusing at first to take such mild measures as withdrawing the EC countries' military attachés from their embassies in Pretoria. It was France who took the hardest line against South Africa. She recalled her Ambassador from Pretoria, suspended new foreign investment and, to the dismay of Britain and the USA, introduced a resolution in the UN Security Council denouncing apartheid.

The 1986 State of Emergency placed pressure on the European Community to take action against South Africa. In September 1986, the EC followed the example of the United States and introduced its own range of sanctions. With German support, Britain was able to soften the measures and remove coal from the list of sanctions. An EC ban on coal would have hurt South Africa as two-thirds of her coal exports go to the Community. However, an EC ban was placed on new investments in South Africa and on the import of Krugerrand gold coins and iron and steel products. France and Denmark placed an embargo on South African coal.

In February 1990 Britain lifted its voluntary ban on new investments and restored academic, cultural and scientific contacts with South Africa. In December 1990 the EC followed Britain's lead and agreed to drop sanctions against new investment. In 1991 the EC lifted all the sanctions imposed in 1986.

South Africa attaches major importance to its relationship with the EC. South Africa is Europe's seventh biggest trading partner and despite sanctions, South Africa's exports to the EC rose by more than 90 per cent between 1985 and 1988, reaching $7 billion or 26 per cent of total South African exports, while the EC supplied over 40 per cent of South African imports. (Less than one per cent of the Community's imports from South Africa were covered by the 1986 sanctions package.)

Lomé Convention

The Lomé Convention of the EC offers South Africa future possibilities for greater access to European markets and technology. (The Lomé Convention covers groups of developing countries, all of whom are former colonies of one of the European states, including all of South Africa's neighbours.) South Africa can argue its eligibility for Lomé membership on the grounds of its status as a former UK colony and its 'Third World' as well as 'First World' economy. Membership of the Lomé Convention would allow most South African exports to enter the EC duty-free and would provide funds to stabilise export prices of mineral and agricultural products in the event of fluctuations in the world market.

Impact of Sanctions

Despite Botha's proud boasts that South Africa could go it alone, sanctions have hurt the South African economy. In the week that Bush ended the sanctions imposed by the US Congress, a leading Afrikaans newspaper stated, "The nasty truth is that our economy has been knocked to pulp by the punitive international measures of the last six years."

While the disinvestment of US and EC companies made headline news, its impact on the South African economy was minimal. Many of these companies sold their businesses to local shareholders, often establishing licensing agreements with the new owners. Rod Compton, a Durban based union leader, declared: "Disinvestment as it has been practised is almost without exception an exercise in corporate camouflage, designed mainly to confuse an audience back home (in the USA)." Again most of the trade sanctions were not particularly severe and others could be evaded at a price.

However, the sanctions that have hurt fall into three main categories: trade bans, bans on direct investment and restrictions on government lending. Since 1985 South Africa has been starved of foreign capital. Economists at the South African Trust Bank estimate that South Africa missed out on $16 billion in loans and direct investment over the past five years. They also estimate that South Africa lost $4 billion worth of exports because of trade sanctions (most notably on coal, iron, steel and fruit). This missing trade and investment created an economic recession in South Africa which weakened the Rand, increased inflation, forced interest rates up, created high unemployment and depressed consumer spending. According to the Trust Bank's economists, the economy's 2 per cent annual growth in 1985-89 might have been nearly 4 per cent had it not been for sanctions.

However, sanctions have also brought some benefits. John Patrick, in a special advertising section in *Time* magazine placed by the South African government, wrote: "In some respects the sanctions imposed upon South Africa during the past two decades have worked to the country's advantage. They have forced the Government to impose strict monetary and financial disciplines. By 1990, South Africa's import growth rate had fallen to zero, and with exports at $22.4 billion, the country's Balance of Payments surplus stands at a healthy $2 billion. The total 1990 GDP (over $89 billion) although 1% down on the 1989 figure, still reflects a healthy productive capacity, and a 4% reduction in the rate of inflation in the same period (from 18.4% to 14.7%) demonstrates a willingness and ability to tackle the most insidious of economic ills."

South African exporters have found new customers in

South-East Asia and elsewhere. Helped by a weak Rand, South Africa's non-gold exports have risen 136 per cent in Rand terms since 1985. The government has cut the public sector and introduced a policy of privatisation. (In November 1989 it sold off Iscor, the state steel company.) Nevertheless, the future economic prosperity of South Africa and its ability to tackle the massive economic and social inequalities, for example in housing, education and health, depend on the return of foreign capital. Ironically the ending of sanctions does not guarantee the flight of international capital back into South Africa.

THE UN AND SOUTH AFRICA

The United Nations plays an important part in orchestrating world opposition to the racist regime of South Africa. South Africa is in violation of the 1948 International Declaration of Human Rights and is also a threat to international peace and security. In 1963 the Security Council instituted a voluntary arms embargo against South Africa and called on all states to participate in this boycott. On 4 November 1977, this voluntary arms embargo was made mandatory in a unanimous decision by the Council's 15 members. The Soweto Riots and the death of the black leader Steve Biko ensured that the countries of the West would not use their veto.

Although South Africa formally remains a member of the UN General Assembly, in effect she has been expelled. In 1974 the General Assembly voted to reject the credentials of the South African delegation on the grounds that the government was not representative of the people of the country. The United Nations General Assembly has, in successive years, reaffirmed its recognition of the African National Congress (ANC) as the authentic representative of the people of South Africa. The Assembly declared South Africa's occupation of Namibia illegal (see page 29) and refused to recognise the independence granted to the four Bantustans of South Africa.

On 22 June 1990, Nelson Mandela made an emotional and historic speech at a meeting of the United Nations Special Committee Against Apartheid in New York. He thanked the Special Committee Against Apartheid, the Secretary General and all the member states of the organisation for making it possible for him to be there. He also urged the United Nations and its individual member states not to relax sanctions.

7 DISMANTLING APARTHEID

BOTHA'S REMOVAL

The "mild stroke" President PW Botha suffered on 18 January 1989, six days after his 73rd birthday, marked the beginning of the end of his political career. Chris Heunis, Minister for Constitutional Development, became Acting President. Botha's decision to stand down as Leader of the National Party on 2 February resulted in the Party appointing FW de Klerk as its new Leader. Thus Heunis' role was reduced to that of a figurehead, with effective power in the hands of de Klerk.

FW de Klerk's appointment revived the National Party's enthusiasm for 'renewal' and a clear switch of allegiance took place. However, Botha refused to resign gracefully from office and to the consternation of Party members he announced on 2 March that he planned to resume his duties after Easter, with the firm intention of leading the Party into the next election. Party members reacted swiftly; on 13 March all 130 Nationalist MPs voted in favour of a resolution that in effect asked Botha to resign as President. Finally in August 1989 Botha appeared on television to announce his resignation. In a bitter and emotional speech he attacked FW de Klerk for having met with Kenneth Kaunda, President of Zambia. Botha felt betrayed. He had introduced wide-ranging reforms which had transformed the lives of millions of South Africans, yet his achievements had not been recognised. The final insult was the implementation of sanctions by the international community.

Frederik Willem de Klerk

FW de Klerk was born in 1936 in the Northern Transvaal, which is the cradle of Afrikaner nationalism. His family had a history of political involvement and, after graduating as a lawyer, he became an MP in 1972. In 1978 he became Post Office Minister and when Treurnicht left the National Party to form the Conservative Party, de Klerk replaced him as provincial Party Leader of the Transvaal. Botha appointed him Minister of Education and his record in this post gave no hint of his reformist zeal. In fact he had tried unsuccessfully to reduce the number of Blacks enrolling in white universities.

De Klerk is the first Nationalist Leader not to have been involved in the creation of the apartheid system. This perhaps explains his pragmatic approach and his willingness to dismantle the system.

SEPTEMBER 1989 ELECTIONS

On 6 September 1989, the non-Black peoples of South Africa voted together for the first time. The National Party faced strong opposition, both from the right (the Conservative Party) and from the left (the newly formed Democratic Party). Indeed there was speculation that the outcome might be a hung parliament with the National Party losing its overall majority.

The election was once again targeted by the Black majority who were excluded from the electoral process. The Mass Democratic Movement (MDM), a loose coalition of banned anti-apartheid organisations, launched a 'defiance campaign'. It did not constitute itself formally as an organisation and thus avoided being banned. The MDM challenged the use of segregated facilities and also organised a strike to protest against Blacks being excluded from the election. On 2 August, over 270 black patients, in the company of supporters, entered 'white only' hospitals throughout the country. In Durban some 10,000 people swam and picnicked on a 'white only' beach before police broke up the protest and arrested 58 of them. In Cape Town police whipped and baton-charged black people at an exclusively white beach. In the mines, members of the National Union of Mineworkers (NUM) used changing rooms, kitchens and canteens reserved for white workers. The high point of the defiance campaign was the two-day strike of 6 and 7 September, with an estimated 3 million workers taking part.

The elections for the House of Representatives (coloured) and the House of Delegates (Indian) were once again marked by a low percentage poll (with about 28% of

How they voted

Seats in South Africa's white House of Assembly

Total seats: 178

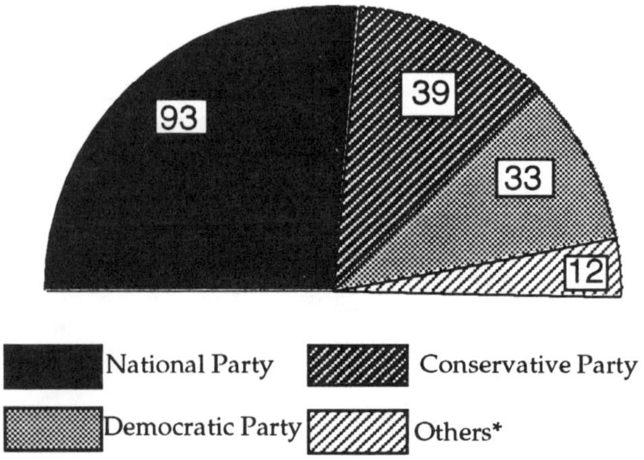

*Eight elected by Members of Parliament, four nominated by the President
NB: one constituency was tied

Figure 7.1 Source: *Economist* 9 September 1989

Coloureds and 32% of Indians voting). The boycott called by the Mass Democratic Movement (MDM) had been successful.

Despite the opposition and the defiance campaign, de Klerk was able to retain a comfortable majority in the white House of Assembly, although the number of Nationalist MPs fell from 123 to 93. He even declared that the result gave him a mandate for reform. (see Figure 7.1) The Democratic Party won 33 seats, displaying strong support among sections of the white community for the abolition of apartheid. The Conservative Party, while strong in the Transvaal (31 seats) was only able to gain 37 seats. A political analyst summed up the election thus: "The NP no longer has purely Afrikaans-speaking support and the more 'verligte' DP no longer purely English support."

ELECTIONS FOR THE TRICAMERAL PARLIAMENT - 6 September 1989

Extracts from the Manifestos of the main white Parties

NATIONAL PARTY

OVERALL OBJECTIVE

The National Party intends to create a *new South Africa* in which every South African can live in safety, prosperity and dignity, as an individual and within a group.

Such a South Africa must be a *democracy* in which:

- no group *dominates or is dominated,*
- the *independence of the judiciary* is upheld and honoured,
- *civilised norms* apply,
- a dynamic economy thrives, based on *free enterprise,*
- everybody lives in *safety* and *harmony*, and
- in *good neighbourly relationships* with the international community.

1. A DEMOCRACY: PARTICIPATION FOR ALL

South Africa is one undivided state with one citizenship for all. Every South African has the right to participate in political decision making on all levels of government which affect his interests, subject to the principle of no domination.

KEY OBJECTIVES

The National Party commits itself to pursue the following objectives during the next five years:

- to promote a set of common values, as a basis for a peaceful political system, without inhibiting the identity of groups;
- to engage recognised leaders of all groups committed to the pursuit of peaceful solutions in talks and negotiations about the political, social and economic systems for a new South Africa;
- to make a definite start, based on these discussions and negotiations, with the setting up of institutions in which the leaders of all groups can participate in the creation of a new system.
- to reassess the functions and powers of the head of state in a new system, his role or otherwise as head of government, and the manner in which he should be elected.

THE NATIONAL PARTY'S PLAN FOR NEGOTIATED PARTICIPATION FOR EVERYONE IS THE ONLY PLAN THAT CAN CREATE A JUST SOUTH AFRICA OF WHICH ALL SOUTH AFRICANS CAN BE PROUD

2. NO DOMINATION: GROUP PROTECTION

The South African population consists of a variety of groups that evolved as a result of cultural and historical factors. This can easily lead to a power struggle and to domination, dictatorship and tyranny - as has often happened elsewhere. To avoid this, the diversity of groups must be fully taken into account in a new South Africa of the future.

The National Party therefore believes that every group should participate as a component in the process, and that, in principle, all groups should agree before an important decision can be taken.

Because full agreement is not always feasible and the administration of the country must continue, it is necessary to create institutions geared to promote consensus, settle disputes and deal with obstruction of government. ...

7. THE INTERNATIONAL COMMUNITY

The Republic of South Africa must regain its rightful place in the international community, while maintaining the honour and dignity of our country.

This includes the restoration of sound economic and cultural relations worldwide, international competition in world sport, membership of international institutions and organisations in all walks of life, and the expansion of diplomatic relations.

THE DEMOCRATIC PARTY

A GOVERNMENT IN THE MAKING

We are going for power

South Africa is moving into a new era of political equality. Every day this movement gains momentum and, despite apartheid laws, has become unstoppable.

The reason is simple. Most South Africans have outgrown the National Party. Their policies have made us poorer, unsafe, and have isolated us from the rest of the world. We have had enough! We want to be proud of our government again.

Constitutional Vision

There are two reasons why South Africa's present constitution is unworkable; it is based on race and it excludes the majority of South Africans.

Real Negotiation is the Key

The Democratic Party will change the constitution. Our new constitution must be the result of negotiation between the true leaders of all South Africa's groups and communities.

However, *real* negotiation cannot take place while many of these leaders and their organisations are banned, the state of emergency is still in force,and apartheid laws are on the statute book. The Democratic Party is already speeding up the negotiation process by defusing conflict and creating a climate of mutual trust and respect.

The type of constitution we would negotiate would be based on:

Bringing government closer to the people

Our opponents often claim that the Democratic Party stands for one man, one vote in a unitary system. This is not true. We stand for a universal adult franchise in a federal system. South Africa should consist of federal states or provinces that will conduct their affairs in whichever way they choose, provided this does not conflict with the constitution or Bill of Rights. The central government should deal only with matters of national concern, eg. foreign affairs, national finance.

Making everyone's vote count

Each party would be represented at all levels of government in proportion to their support. This means, for example, that if a party gets 10% of the vote it gets 10% of the MPs.

Protecting everyone's rights

In many democratic countries the rights of individuals and communities are successfully protected by a Bill of Rights.

The Democratic Party will introduce a Bill of Rights along the lines suggested by the South African Law Commission. It will include the right of every South African to vote in free elections, the right of every South African to own property, and will protect the language, culture and religion of communities.

THE CONSERVATIVE PARTY OF SOUTH AFRICA

The CP is the Solution

A MANDATE FOR FREEDOM WITH JUSTICE

In this election the Conservative Party is asking for a mandate from the White voters to:

- ensure that the most basic right of every people, namely the right to rule over themselves, is guaranteed as an inalienable right for the White community and every other individual community;
- take appropriate steps to protect the lives and property of the community through the improved enforcement of Law and Order and the prevention of crime;
- ensure that the White's exclusive and separate community life not be overwhelmed and disrupted by other communities;
- launch a national culture building programme through which:
  - patriotism and love of the fatherland can be promoted;
  - moral values and the observance of Sunday as a holy day will be restored. Negative moral influences will also be removed from our community life.

POLICY PROGRAMME

1. POLITICAL DEVELOPMENT

THE MULTICULTURAL REALITY OF SOUTH AFRICA

The Conservative Party acknowledges as a reality the existence of a wide variety of people and groups in South Africa who are all entitled to self-determination within the boundaries of their own states. At the same time the Conservative Party rejects the vision that South Africa is merely a community made up of individuals all entitled to equal political rights in a unitary state.

THE CHALLENGE FACING SOUTH AFRICA

The challenge facing South Africa today is to establish a constitutional framework wherein the self-determination rights of every community are maintained without domination by one people of another.

PARTITION IS THE SOLUTION

The Conservative Party believes that the only way in which a people can effectively be protected against domination and can unhindered exercise their right to self-determination is in their own states under their own governments. This can be realised by PARTITION. Partition brings an end to the domination of one people by another.

PARTITION WAS BUSY SUCCEEDING IN SOUTH AFRICA

The Conservative Party rejects the unfounded criticism that partition failed in South Africa and maintains that it was just beginning to succeed when the new National Party began to steadily replace it with an integrationist policy.

THE IMPLEMENTATION OF PARTITION

The Conservative Party will use all measures at its disposal to help develop the Black states so that the maximum number of Blacks can be accommodated in their own states and the minimum remain in White South Africa.

The Conservative Party will encourage and promote DECENTRALISATION and border industries in or near the Black states.

INFLUX CONTROL will be reintroduced.

LABOUR PREFERENCE AREAS will be introduced whereby for example Natal will be a labour preference area for Zulus, the Eastern Cape for Xhosas and the Western Cape for Coloureds.

NON-WHITE URBANISATION will be restricted to a minimum in White South Africa and be encouraged within the Black states.

THE SO-CALLED 'URBAN BLACK'

The Conservative Party is not prepared to share power with the so-called urban Black. The CP will point out to them the success of partition. In any negotiations over the exercising of non-White political rights the White community's right to self-determination will always be non-negotiable.

REMOVALS

The Conservative Party proposes negotiation, thorough planning, decentralisation, job creation and other similar measures whereby settlement patterns can be regulated and which will make removals unnecessary.

OWN COMMUNITY LIFE

The Conservative Party is committed to the creation and maintenance of an own community life for White people, which includes, amongst others, separate residential areas, schools, educational institutions, public facilities, transport and recreational facilities.

LAW AND ORDER

The Party will give immediate and intensive attention to the restoration of Law and Order.

Era of Conciliation

De Klerk quickly displayed that his administration would be less confrontational and more tolerant of dissent. He declared, "The State President in South Africa is ... the leader of all South Africans and not only of those represented in Parliament." In the first major test of his administration, he allowed a huge protest march organised by leading churchmen to take place in Cape Town. This massive peaceful protest was the first in a series of such events throughout the country.

A new era of negotiations and conciliation had begun. On 8 October , prominent political prisoners, including five of those jailed for life with Nelson Mandela, were released. The most prominent of the Rivonia trialists was Walter Sisulu. (see box page 41)

The release of the prisoners was seen as testing the waters for the possible release of Nelson Mandela. The Government was now moving towards a timetable for the release of Mandela. To this end President de Klerk met with Mandela in December to discuss the terms of his release. It was clear that the Government was now prepared to drop its demands for the ANC to renounce violence before beginning negotiations.

Beach Apartheid was abolished in November 1989 - a move well timed to defuse holiday season protests and confrontation. De Klerk also announced that the Government would repeal the laws that allowed local officials to segregate public facilities. It was hoped that this would make it impossible for town councils controlled by the Conservative Party to use the 1953 *Separate Amenities Act* to continue to bar Blacks from public places. The 1953 Act empowered, but did not oblige, local councils to reserve public facilities such as halls, toilets, swimming pools and parks for Whites. (The Act did not cover schools or hospitals.) Significantly, in December PW Botha's giant security web, the national security management system, was dismantled and in the same month national service was halved to a year.

De Klerk had created the conditions for a new era of negotiations with 'genuine' black leaders. Banned since 1960, the ANC had dramatically returned to the political stage. The Government had, in essence, granted the ANC provisional legal status. The question now was when, not if, Nelson Mandela would be released.

1990 THE YEAR OF CHANGE

Events in South Africa in many ways resembled the upheavals that took place in Eastern Europe in 1989. A state ideology - Communism in Eastern Europe and Apartheid in South Africa - was declared dead. In South Africa it was a giant step away from the past, with the government willing "to renounce its sole occupation of the heights of Government". De Klerk had crossed the Rubicon. (See De Klerk's Reforms page 40)

Reasons for de Klerk's Reforms

1 The 1989 election manifesto of the National Party (see page 37) had offered the electorate a programme for future reform. For this reason the election results gave de Klerk a clear mandate for reform. The combined strength of the National and Democratic Parties (126 MPs) completely overwhelmed the 33 Conservative MPs. Separate Development was now the policy of the Conservative Party and the far right. De Klerk's new style of leadership had rekindled the demand for reform within the National Party and had revived the hopes and expectations of those opposed to apartheid both within and outwith South Africa.

2 Even within the Afrikaner community the demand for reform was intensifying. Professor John Heyus, the leader of the Dutch Reformed Church to which most Afrikaners belonged, had called on the government to drop its insistence that the ANC renounce violence as a precondition for talks. Significantly, the Broederbond (see page 4) was at the forefront of the reform movement. In June 1988 it drafted a document setting out its proposals for a new South African constitution based on "freedom and equal rights and opportunities for all South Africans". The Broederbond concluded that neither a black President nor a government in which the majority of members were black would be detrimental to Afrikaner survival - provided that the presidency was stripped of its executive power and that the constitution contained safeguards against domination by any one racial group. Astonishingly, the Broederbond, once the high priests of apartheid, were now openly advocating its destruction. In fact such was the reformist zeal within the Broederbond that one of its members became joint leader of the Democratic Party.

3 South African isolation from the outside world was affecting her economy, especially in the area of investments. (see page 34) The demand for further sanctions was growing, with the possible nightmare scenario of the introduction of United Nations economic sanctions. De Klerk admitted that sanctions were harming South Africa: "The Government is aware of the important part the world at large has to play in the realisation of our country's national interest. Without contact and cooperation with the rest of the world we cannot promote the well-being and security of our citizens." The White business community had long supported reform. During the 1984-86 black uprising they had published anti-apartheid advertisements in their newspapers. Before his resignation as Governor of the Reserve Bank in 1989, Gerhard de Kock baldly stated that no economic solution would be found until there was a political solution that would redress black political grievances.

4 The State of Emergency provided both an opportunity and a warning to de Klerk. The township revolt had been crushed with even the ANC admitting that its ability to continue the "armed struggle" was at a low ebb. Paradoxically, therefore, the restoration of law and order by Botha offered de Klerk the opportunity to negotiate from a position of strength. Nevertheless, the State of Emergency had not crushed black opposition, with the churches and unions taking the lead. The turning point was the detainees' hunger strike in February 1989, when PW Botha was recovering after his stroke and so was unable to overrule the Cabinet's decision to release the detainees.

The dominance of the military was resented within the National Party. Botha, through the National Security Management System (see page 21) had, in many ways, created a military dictatorship. The 'military option' had reduced the influence of the Party and so the election of a new leader outwith reformist policy resulted in the reassertion of the NP's will to govern as a party.

5 Finally, the changes in the world balance of power and the resolution of conflicts in Southern Africa weakened the far right's claim that "communism would take over in South Africa". Perestroika in the USSR, global superpower cooperation, the collapse of communism in Eastern Europe, independence in Namibia and moves towards national reconciliation in Angola and Mozambique all combined to redefine South Africa's regional role. It was clear that the USSR wished to end apartheid through negotiations rather than by bloodshed. Therefore,1990 was to the be year of change in South Africa.

Opening of Parliament, February 1990

Expectations of de Klerk's speech to Parliament on 2 February were rivalled only by those of his predecessor in 1985, when Botha had gone to the Durban town hall and ended all further hopes of reform in his 'Rubicon' speech. De Klerk, however, did not disappoint his supporters. (See extract on page 40) He stunned MPs by announcing that the ANC and other black nationalist movements would be legalised immediately and that Nelson Mandela would be freed. He also announced a moratorium on executions - in 1987 South Africa hanged 164 people - a reduction in the number of capital crimes and the repeal of the law which made the death penalty mandatory for murder. The moratorium brought relief for 279 people on death row including the Upington 14 - condemned in a controversial 'necklace' trial - and Barend Strydom, the right-wing extremist sentenced to hang for shooting eight Blacks at random in Pretoria. (see page 42)

The reaction throughout the country was electric. Spontaneous celebrations broke out in the townships around the country. The sweep of de Klerk's address stunned Archbishop Desmond Tutu - "he has taken my breath away". The ANC announced an urgent review of the new situation which had emerged and predictably the Pan Africanist Congress (PAC) reacted with complete hostility. In a statement issued in Dar es Salaam it said, "The reforms announced by de Klerk today are irrelevant

Extract from the address by State President FW de Klerk at the opening of Parliament on 2 February 1991

The season of violence is over. The time for reconstruction and reconciliation has arrived ...

The steps that have been decided are the following:

- The prohibition of the African National Congress, the Pan Africanist Congress, the South African Communist Party and a number of subsidiary organisations is being rescinded.
- People serving prison sentences merely because they were members of one of these organisations or because they committed another offence which was merely an offence because prohibition on one of the organisations was in force, will be identified and released. Prisoners who have been sentenced for other offences such as murder, terrorism or arson are not affected by this.
- The media emergency regulations as well as the education emergency regulations are being abolished in their entirety.
- The security emergency regulations will be amended to still make provision for effective control over visual material pertaining to scenes of unrest.
- The restrictions in terms of the emergency regulations on 33 organisations are being rescinded. The organisations include the following:
  National Education Crisis Committee
  South African National Students' Congress
  United Democratic Front
  Cosatu
  Die Blanke Bevrydingsbeweging van Suid-Afrika.
- The conditions imposed in terms of the security emergency regulations on 374 people on their release are being

and meaningless because apartheid cannot be reformed. We cannot talk about ending apartheid. We can only eliminate it."

The reaction from the Conservative Party and the far right was one of fury and anger. The Conservative Party threatened a campaign of demonstrations and strikes to force de Klerk out of office. Treurnicht thundered, "If a Government does not protect the rights of its people what can be expected but that the volk will protect itself." The neofascist Afrikaner Resistance Movement (AWB) (see page 42) sent hundreds of khaki-clad heavily armed marchers into Pretoria shouting, "Hang de Klerk, hang Mandela." Treurnicht's accusations that de Klerk had acted without a mandate and that he had betrayed his people were seemingly confirmed in June 1990 at the Umlazi by-election in Natal. A 27% swing to the Conservatives turned a safe government seat into a marginal one. However, while the Conservatives more than doubled their share of the vote to 44%, the National Party's share of the votes slipped only marginally to 48%, from 51% in the general election of September 1989. Significantly, the Democratic Party's vote had collapsed, with many of its supporters switching to the National Party. Not only had the National Party stolen the policies of the Democratic Party, it was also stealing its supporters.

De Klerk's Reforms

"There is neither time nor room for turning back. There is only one road - ahead." *De Klerk*

1990

February 2: De Klerk lifts the ban outlawing the ANC, the South African Communist Party and other political groups.
February 11: After 27 years in jail, Nelson Mandela is freed.
May 2: The ANC and the government hold their first formal talks and agree to negotiate a new nonracial constitution.
June 7: De Klerk ends the national State of Emergency with the exception of Natal Province.
June 19: The *Separate Amenities Act* is repealed.
August 6: The ANC agrees to suspend its armed struggle.
August 31: The National Party opens its ranks to all races.
October: State of Emergency lifted in Natal.

1991

February 1: De Klerk announces repeal of the *Land Acts, Group Area Acts and Population Registration Act*, the remaining pillars of Apartheid.
June 17: The three racially defined houses of South Africa's Parliament vote to repeal the *Population Registration Act*.

Walk to Freedom

On Sunday 11 February 1990, at 4.15 pm local time, Nelson Mandela walked out of the Victor Verster Prison Farm near Cape Town. The event, televised live around the world, was described by an announcer of the South African Broadcasting Company as "the moment that a majority of South Africa and the world had been waiting for." Archbishop Desmond Tutu summed up the mood of euphoria and expectation that had swept through the black community. "We want to touch him and say 'Here he is', this man who has such a crucial role to play in the making of this new South Africa."

In a series of speeches, Mandela made it clear that he was "a loyal servant" of the ANC and that he stood by the Freedom Charter. Whites were alarmed by his call for the nationalisation of industries, his appeal for continued Western sanctions and his salute to the South African Communist Party. However, Mandela also stressed reconciliation and the need to restore peace. To a crowd in Soweto he declared, "I must make it clear that the level of crime in our townships is unhealthy and must be eliminated as a matter of urgency." Mandela also impressed the world with his lack of bitterness towards his jailers and the

Nelson Mandela

Black nationalist leader Nelson Mandela and his wife Winnie salute well-wishers as he leaves Victor Verster prison on 11 February 1990

Nelson Mandela was born in 1918, son of a chief of the Tembu, Transkei's largest tribe. He went to Fort Hare College and was suspended in 1940 for leading a strike for students' rights. In 1944, at the request of the ANC, Mandela joined with Walter Sisulu, Oliver Tambo and others to establish the ANC Youth League. The League espoused 'direct action', including boycotts, strikes, civil disobedience and noncooperation.

In 1952 he graduated in law from the University of Witwatersrand and formed a legal practice with Oliver Tambo in Johannesburg. Both lawyers were active members of the ANC, with Mandela becoming President of the Transvaal African National Congress. Along with numerous other African activists, he was accused of treason but all were acquitted at the 'Treason Trials' (1956-61). During a break in this trial he met Winnie Madikizela who became his second wife in 1958.

In 1961, he went underground, organising the military wing of the ANC (Umkhonto We Sizwe). Mandela declared "the time comes in the life of any nation when there remains only two choices: submit or fight. That time has now come to South Africa. We shall not submit and we have no choice but to hit back by all means within our power in defence of our people, our future and our freedom."

Mandela was eventually arrested on a farm at Rivonia, near Johannesburg, and in 1964 he was sentenced to life imprisonment for attempting to overthrow the government by violent revolution. He was imprisoned on Robben Island until 1982, when he was transferred to Pollsmoor Prison, near Cape Town.

In prison, Nelson Mandela met with both government officials and Cabinet Ministers in a search to end the growing conflict and violence through genuine negotiations for a peaceful solution. Finally, on 11 February 1990, he was released from prison.

Walter Sisulu

Walter Sisulu was sentenced with Nelson Mandela at the 1964 Rivonia treason trial, accused of sabotage and conspiracy to overthrow white rule. Sisulu co-founded the ANC's Youth League with Mandela and Oliver Tambo and later became secretary general of the ANC. In 1962 Sisulu went underground to join Umkhonto we Sizwe (Spear of the Nation), the ANC's military wing.

His wife Abertina was Co-president of the United Democratic Front and restrictions on her activities imposed under South Africa's State of Emergency were only lifted in early October 1990. Their son Zwelakhe was editor of the Roman Catholic weekly, *New Nation*, until he was detained in December 1986. On his release two years later he was placed under a crippling restriction order banning him from journalism and rigidly controlling his movements and contacts.

The Democratic Party

The Democratic Party (DP) came into being on 8 April 1989 following the merger of the Progressive Federal Party (PFP), the Independent Party, the National Democratic Movement and the so-called 'Fourth Force' of dissident Afrikaners. For the first time in over three decades, the entire white parliamentary opposition to the left of the government was unified into a single party. It fought the 1989 election on a platform of a universal adult franchise in a federal system, with the first step being the scrapping of apartheid and negotiation with the ANC. The economic policy of the Party offered support for private ownership and free enterprise.

However, President FW de Klerk's policy of negotiating with the ANC and ending all apartheid laws left the DP in a state of disarray. The National Party had stolen its policies and at the Democratic Party Conference in September 1990, a clear division emerged on the future direction of the Party. The debate centred around whether the Party should link up with the National Party or the African National Congress. Proposing an ANC pact, the MP David Dalling argued that the DP's campaign against apartheid was "to identify with those who have suffered under apartheid rather than with those who had imposed it." The 'progressives' within the Party supported the pact on the grounds that "we are moving from the politics of five million to the politics of 35 million." It was essential, they argued, for the Party to be identified with the black majority or it would cease to have a relevant role.

However, the Party faithful were against such a pact. They wanted no alliance with a Party that had strong ties with the Communist Party and were also distrustful of the ANC's economic policy of nationalisation and redistribution of wealth. To avoid a split, the Party leaders agreed to explore the different options. Significantly, the new Party Leader, Zach de Beer, a retired senior executive of the giant Anglo American Corporation, favours links with the National Party. A compromise proposal to allow dual membership with other organisations (ie. the ANC) was rejected.

government. He stressed the need for compromise and the necessity to overcome the strife and misery caused by four decades of apartheid. He also emphasised the need for a national consensus to build a united nonracial and democratic state in the interests of all the people of South Africa. Half a century of oppression had not weakened his vision and he renewed the pledge he made at his trial in 1964: "I have cherished the ideal of a democratic and free society in which all persons live together in harmony and with equal opportunities. It is an ideal which I hope to live for and to achieve. But if needs be, it is an ideal for which I am prepared to die."

The release of Mandela had cleared the major obstacle to

The Right Wing in South African Politics

There are numerous right-wing organisations in South Africa. Below is a summary of the major groups.

Eugene Terre Blanche, leader of the extreme rightwing AWB

Herstigte Nasionale Party
Formed in 1969, it is the oldest of all right-wing groups. In 1985 it won a by-election at Sasolburg and gained its first seat in Parliament. However, it has been eclipsed by the Conservative Party and its electoral fortunes have declined. It lost its seat in the 1987 election when it contested 83 seats and only retained four deposits. It refused to form an electoral pact with the Conservative Party and remains a 'fringe' party. Nevertheless, it still retains a small core of support drawn from the white working class. HNP supports the original apartheid blueprint whereby independent black Homelands would be set up in the 13% of land allotted to the Blacks.

Conservative Party
The Conservative Party was established in March 1982 after 16 Nationalist MPs rejected Botha's reforms. (see page 18) The CP's support is concentrated mainly in rural and urban working-class and lower middle-class constituencies. The Party is supported by a range of different organisations with varying policies. These groups share the belief that partition is the only constitutional solution for South Africa. However, each organisation believes that its model of partition is the most viable and each group devotes much time and energy to proving that the other models are unworkable.

The Conservatives' model is the present status quo with all of the black Homelands becoming independent. New 'independent Homelands' would be created for the coloured and Indian people and large townships like Soweto would become independent city states.

They argue that Grand Apartheid can work if applied with sufficient resolve and vigour. The Homelands would have stronger agricultural and industrial sectors; influx control would be reintroduced, involving a mass forced removal campaign.

Right-wing organisations are divided on whether black workers should be employed within the 'white' economy. Officially, the Conservative Party sees no contradiction in a separate white nation dependent on black labour. It regards black workers as guest labourers, comparable to Turks working in Germany, but many of its members reject this. "If we are serious about having our own country, we must be prepared to clean the streets and work the factories, to wash our own dishes and care for our children. That may mean a drop in our living standards, but it is a small price to pay for survival."

The Conservative Party won 31% of the white vote in the 1989 election and is confident of victory in any forthcoming election. FW de Klerk, though, has no intention of holding a general election. The CP are refusing to take part in constitutional talks.

Die Afrikaner-Weerstandsbeweging (Afrikaner Resistance Movement - AWB)
The most notorious and infamous right-wing organisation is the Afrikaner Resistance Movement (AWB). Its leader, Eugene Terre Blanche, refuses to divulge the size of the organisation which mixes superstitious Christianity with nostalgia for the nineteenth century. It is estimated that the AWB, which was established in 1933, has about 6,000 signed-up members and 150,000 supporters who regularly attend its meetings. Many AWB followers, including Terre Blanche, are open admirers of Nazism and Fascism. Although the AWB is registered as a political party, it does not contest elections and works more as a pressure group. In the 1987 and 1989 elections it supported the Conservative Party.

The organisation has its own paramilitary force ready to crush any black uprisings. Many of its members carry arms and have formed death squads. In November 1988, a member of the AWB, Barend Strydom, shot dead eight passers-by and wounded a dozen more black people in the name of the White Wolves.

The AWB believes that Afrikaners have no legal or moral right to govern any land outwith the nineteenth century Boer Republic founded by Afrikaners who trekked north to escape British rule and settled in the Transvaal, the Orange Free State and northern Natal. However this model, while historically sound, ignores the demographic and economic realities of South Africa today and therefore is deeply flawed. This Boersvolkstaat would include Soweto and English-speaking Whites and would obviously exclude Afrikaners living in all other parts of South Africa.

Die Blanke Bevrydingsbeweging (The White Liberation Movement - BBB)
Established in 1985 by Professor PC Schabort, this group openly preaches racial hatred and the superiority of the white race. The BBB's policy is based on "total partition" which means that every black person would be repatriated to a homeland — by violence if necessary. Ironically, the BBB (and all right-wing groups) accept that Whites will have to endure economic hardship to ensure racial purity. "We would rather be poor and free than rich in a common society" is the BBB's slogan.

negotiations. The Government hoped that it was turning a myth back into a man and the ANC from a movement of underground heroism into a political party. *The Citizen* newspaper, in its editorial, summed up the mood of its Afrikaner readership: "Whites are divided, uncertain, angry or bewildered. The Blacks are at each others' throats cock-a-hoop with thoughts of victory or just as uncertain and fearful as the Whites."

CONSTITUTIONAL TALKS

The unbanning of the ANC led to a series of meetings between the Government and the ANC to prepare the way for formal talks. The ANC's negotiating position centred round the Harare Declaration of 1989. Meaningful negotiations could not take place until certain obstacles had been removed. Once this had been achieved, an interim government should be set up to rule South Africa during

VIEWPOINTS OF FW DE KLERK AND NELSON MANDELA

FW de Klerk — **Nelson Mandela**

Economic Policies

FW de Klerk:

At the same time, my Government is not insensitive to the needs of the less privileged in our society. It has repeatedly expressed its desire to eliminate imbalances and rectify past injustices, particularly in education, health care, housing and job creation. This cannot be done without rapid economic growth to create the resources needed for socio-economic development.

Confidence is vital to economic growth. Investors from Europe and elsewhere will not invest in a country unless they are assured of its stability and economic potential.

The Government's basic point of departure is to reduce the role of the public sector in the economy and to give the private sector maximum opportunity for optimal performance ... The Government is endeavouring to reduce security-related expenditure in the national budget in favour of social welfare expenditure

Nelson Mandela:

The economy must be restructured so as meaningfully to raise the living standards of the entire South African population. Since the private sector is the prime wealth creator, those factors leading to income and wealth generation by that sector must be promoted.

Much debate has been sparked off by the ANC policies on the economy relating to nationalisation and the redistribution of wealth. We believe that apartheid has created a heinous system of exploitation in which a racist minority monopolises economic wealth while the vast majority of oppressed black people are condemned to poverty.

South Africa is a wealthy country. It is the labour of black workers that has built the cities, roads and factories we see. They cannot be excluded from sharing this wealth. The ANC is just as committed to economic growth and productivity as the present employers claim to be. Yet we are also committed to ensure that a democratic government has the resources to address the inequalities caused by apartheid.

Our people need proper housing, not ghettos like Soweto. Workers need a living wage - and the right to join unions of their own choice and to participate in determining policies that affect their lives.

The nationalisation of the mines, the financial institutions and monopoly industries is the fundamental policy of the ANC and it is inconceivable that we will ever change this policy ... The economy of this country is based partly on nationalisation. The railways, the post office, South African Airways, are all in the public sector. The steel industry was only privatised towards the end of last year (1989)

Sanctions

FW de Klerk:

South Africa is asking neither for aid nor charity. It merely wishes to compete openly and fairly on the world's markets for investment capital, trade and credit. If restrictions in this regard were to persist, the government of the new South Africa will inherit an economy which will be worthless, also to those in the Southern African region and the rest of Africa. After all, their fortunes are inextricably linked to ours.

Nelson Mandela:

Today's reality (June 1990) is that the Apartheid system is still in place. We are still ruled by a white minority government. We wish to emphasise that it is our firm belief that sanctions must be maintained ... As I have pointed out, when I went to jail, I could not vote. I have come back after 27 years: I still cannot vote.

A Future South Africa

FW de Klerk:

We believe majority rule is not suitable for a country like South Africa because it leads to domination and even to the oppression of minorities ... We are convinced that power based on full participation by everyone, as well as protection against domination, is the only workable answer ... a common voter's role applied in a constitutional system based on a winner-takes-all situation is not acceptable to the National Party ... I believe in universal franchise and a power-sharing formula not dissimilar to that of the United States.

Nelson Mandela:

We call on our white compatriots to join us in the shaping of a new South Africa. The freedom movement is a political home for you too ... Universal suffrage on a common voters' roll in a united democratic and nonracial South Africa is the only way to peace and racial harmony ... We are not thinking in terms of a one-party state. Nor is the ANC a Marxist organisation. We have got an alliance with the Communist Party and that alliance has been there since the 1920s.

Legacy of Apartheid

FW de Klerk:

Mistakes have been made on all sides in South Africa over many years.

Nelson Mandela:

The apartheid destruction on our sub-continent is incalculable. The fabric of family life of millions of our people has been shattered. Millions are homeless and unemployed, our economy lies in ruins and our people are embroiled in political strife.

the process of transition to a genuinely democratic constitution based on universal adult suffrage with a common non-racial electoral roll and with no built-in veto powers to protect racial or 'group' rights.

However, the Government made it clear that it was not prepared to abdicate power and commit political suicide. As de Klerk stated, "The idea that the present, lawfully constituted government should simply relinquish its powers, obligations and responsibilities and hand them over to some or other temporary regime cannot be considered in any internationally recognised sovereign and independent state."

The Groote Schuur Minute

A three-day meeting in May 1990 witnessed the first formal talks between the ANC and the Government at Groote Schuur in Cape Town. The Groote Schuur Minute of 4 May set up a joint working group to deal with the release of political prisoners and the return of exiles. Meanwhile, temporary immunity from prosecution would be granted to ANC officials and anyone else returning to the country to take part in talks.

Pretoria Minute

On 6 August, after 15 hours of talks, the Pretoria Minute was signed by the ANC and the Government. Paragraph Three of the Minute announced the ANC's suspension of "armed actions" and all related activities in the interests of moving as speedily as possible "towards a negotiated peaceful political settlement". The Minute also recorded the acceptance by both sides that certain crimes could be known as political offences. This would be used in the process of granting pardon and indemnity to political prisoners and exiles. Target dates for the release of prisoners and return of exiles were set: the process was due to be completed by 30 April 1991.

Nelson Mandela made it clear that the ANC regarded the mass mobilisation tactics of protest marches and boycotts as being legitimate actions of a people still deprived of political rights. The Government tried to link the release of political prisoners to the end of mass mobilisation campaigns and the ANC accused the Government of using prisoners and exiles as hostages. (It was not until August 1991 that President de Klerk announced a general political amnesty, thus ending this obstacle to serious negotiations on a new constitution.)

The events of 1990 clearly identified two issues that were major obstacles to the negotiation processes. These were: (i) the violence in Natal, and (ii) the issue of state violence. (see Chapter 8)

AFRICAN NATIONAL CONGRESS (ANC)

At present the ANC is transforming itself from a banned underground organisation with its leadership operating from outwith South Africa into a mass political party. In December 1990 the ANC held a national consultative conference in Johannesburg. The Conference agreed to support negotiations but attached two conditions: that they should not be secret and that the ANC's regional branches be consulted on the main issues.

National Conference - June 1991

This, the first national conference of the Party held on home soil for 31 years, witnessed the formal transformation of the ANC from a revolutionary liberation movement into a political party ready to form a government. The party accepted it had to become more democratic and accountable to its membership. In its journal *Mayibuye* the ANC declared that faced with a repressive government "its structures had gradually become smaller and more secretive ... decision-making powers were vested among smaller numbers of people. Our priorities now are to build a mass-based democratic ANC which can lead the process of transition to the transfer of power to the people".

The first stage in this process was the election of the new Executive Council. Nelson Mandela was elected unopposed as President (Oliver Tambo, who stood down as President, was given the honorific title of National Chairman). Mandela, in his opening speech to the Conference, made it clear that negotiations with the government would be lengthy and tough. Significantly, he no longer referred to President de Klerk as "a man of integrity"; instead he told the Conference, "We are dealing with a group of politicians who do not want to negotiate themselves out of power."

The elections held under secret ballot produced a new integrated leadership with some "old wood being cut out". Walter Sisulu, the 79 year old veteran of Robben Island, was persuaded to stand as Deputy President to avoid a divisive fight within the Party. A wounding contest had been expected between Chris Hani, Chief of Staff of the ANC's underground army and Thabo Mbeki, the secretary for international affairs. While both men are members of the Communist Party, Hani is regarded as a hardliner with Mbeki willing to compromise over future negotiations. Cyril Ramaphosa , General Secretary of the NUM (National Union of Miners) was elected to the post of General Secretary. Ramaphosa represents the new generation of ANC leaders who were actively involved within South Africa against the apartheid system. (The UDF - United Democratic Front - ended its separate identity in August 1991 and formally merged with the ANC.) Ramaphosa is revered by his black workers and respected by white business leaders. "He is without the shadow of a doubt the most competent negotiator I have come across anywhere," said Bobby Godsell of Anglo American Corporations; "This (NUM) is an organisation that does answer its telephones, that does respond to faxes and does turn up at meetings."

Links with the Communist Party

> "I salute the South African Communist Party for its sterling contribution to the struggle for democracy. You have survived 40 years unrelenting persecution ... I salute General Secretary Joe Slovo - one of our finest patriots. We are heartened by the fact that the alliance between ourselves and the Party remains as strong as it always was." *Nelson Mandela, February 1990*

There are no sinister reasons to explain the popularity of the South African Communist Party (SACP) among the black population. The black people remember with gratitude that communists were the first Whites to identify with their cause in the 1920s when the Party opened its doors to Blacks and helped them form trade unions. They also remember the apartheid government's long persecution of the Communist Party. For these reasons the bond between the ANC and the Communist Party is tight. Membership of the organisations overlaps. The new executive council of the ANC and organisations such as the Congress of South African Trade Unions (COSATU) have significant communist membership.

The government regards the SACP as a "parasitic organisation using the ANC as a pool in which to recruit the best and the brightest for membership". The SACP in its new programme rejects a one-party state as being incompatible with democracy and now calls for the abandonment of the principle of "the dictatorship of the proletariat". The Party's economic policy, with its demand for an equitable redistribution of the wealth of South Africa, obviously finds support among the black population.

NATIONAL PARTY CONSTITUTIONAL PROPOSALS

In September 1991 the National Party unveiled its proposed framework for the forthcoming constitutional negotiations. Under de Klerk's planned constitutional change, Blacks would receive the vote but would be denied outright power . Parliament would consist of a First House elected proportionally so that parties would be allocated seats according to their share of vote nationally. However, the Second House, based on an equal number of seats from each of nine regions, would be able to veto legislation proposed by the popularly elected Chamber and would have special powers to guard the constitution and protect minorities and regions.

In place of a president, there would be a rotating presidency made up of the leaders of at least the three biggest parties. It would appoint Ministers to a multi-party Cabinet. The proposed constitution would, therefore, institutionalise power sharing. De Klerk justified his position by stating that it would "put the leaders of the largest political groupings in a position to act as statesmen rather than politicians, to decide things together and to be called to account together, to build a new system together, a system in which distrust and conflict must be replaced with mutual understanding and cooperation." De Klerk made it clear that a form of power sharing was the only way forward for South Africa. He stated, "We are certainly not prepared to exchange one form of domination for another. Black domination is as unacceptable as white domination."

The proposals were described by the ANC as "a recipe for disaster, designed to deny a future South African government the power to truly liberate the country from the misery that apartheid has wrought." The ANC declared that the proposals "would produce a weak parliament and executive hamstrung by arrangements requiring broad consensus amongst small interest groups." They were "no less than an attempt to disguise an effective minority veto, designed to prevent effective government by a majority party." The ANC further criticised the proposals for their failure to address the issue of the four 'independent' Bantustans - Transkei, Ciskei, Venda and Bophuthatswana. It was not good enough for the National Party to contend that "their relationship with the new South Africa will have to be negotiated with each state individually."

THE ANC PROPOSALS

The ANC supports a united democratic and nonracial South African Republic with only limited powers devolved from central to regional and local structures and no special dispensation for minority groups.

Its key components and features, while open to future negotiations, revolve around:

- A unitary state that would include the four "independent states with a strong central government."
- A President who would be head of the executive and head of state.
- Two Houses of Parliament, the first being a National Assembly elected on the basis of proportional representation by universal suffrage. The major legislative power would be vested in this house. The second House, the Senate, would also be elected by universal suffrage but on a different electoral system allowing for regional representation. The Senate as the "Guardian of the Constitution" would refer Constitutional disputes to the appropriate courts and have the power to review. It would be able, where appropriate, to delay legislation from the National Assembly but not to veto it.
- A Constitutional Court, appointed by the President, would be responsible for the interpretation of the constitution and the application of the law of the land.
- Local and Regional government would be elected by universal franchise. These authorities would have wide discretion over local policies provided they were not in conflict with national policies. Regions would be based upon the distribution of population, availability of economic resources and urban/rural balances.
- A Bill of Rights would protect rights and freedoms, including economic rights. All legislation inconsistent with the Bill of Rights would be invalidated.

CODESA

In December 1991 the opening session of the Convention for a Democratic South Africa (CODESA) took place. Despite a public row between FW de Klerk and Nelson Mandela, the convention established a structure which it is hoped will create a new multiracial democracy in South Africa.

Mandela had reacted angrily to de Klerk's attack on the ANC for refusing to dismantle its underground army (Umkhonto we Sizwe). He stated that de Klerk was not fit to govern but he was "...prepared to work with him in spite of all his mistakes" ...and ..."to make allowances because he is a product of apartheid who has very little understanding of democracy."

This outburst on the opening day did not prevent progress. At the end of the Convention the delegates agreed to set up five specialist working groups to produce detailed proposals on a new constitution to be presented at the CODESA meeting in March 1992. Significantly, de Klerk implied that he was prepared to accept a multiracial, all-party, democratically elected government to rule until a new constitution had been negotiated and was in place. In short, constitutional changes would be implemented which would bring black politicians into the government and parliament.

8 LEGACY OF APARTHEID

While the final structures of apartheid were dismantled in 1991, the social and economic inequalities between the races still remain. Reviewing the legacy of apartheid, Maasdorp, a South African economist, identifies the following main features of South African society:

- Whites control most of the land, only some 13.4 per cent being reserved for African use, mostly on a communal basis of tenure.
- Whites fill most of the skilled, well-paid positions in the economy, enjoying per capita incomes on average 12.9 times that of Africans in 1980.
- Whites own and manage almost the entire spectrum of large businesses in the economy.
- Whites enjoy far higher standards of education and other services such as health, and receive a disproportionately high share of state expenditure on these items.

> "Pity South Africa's first black ruler. His followers expect the conquest of apartheid to bring more than just the vote. Activists want jobs in the new bureaucracy. Peasants want white farmland. Trade unions want a minimum wage. The country's 7 million squatters want legal homes, and many even of those whose homes are legal are still waiting for electricity and hot water.
>
> Besides these expectations, the new leaders will inherit the problems that plague politicians all over Africa. The population is growing at 2.5 per cent a year, which means that the need for new houses and schoolrooms will be mushrooming even as they struggle with the backlog. After a century in which Blacks were forcibly kept from moving to the towns, shanties are springing up around South Africa's gleaming cities; greater Durban is said to be the fastest growing metropolitan area in the world." (*The Economist*, 26.5.91)

Before examining the key areas of Education, Health and Land Distribution, an examination of a broad statistical summary of economic and social indicators will clearly highlight the need for economic and social restructuring to reduce the imbalance between the races. The outside world, while applauding the dismantling of apartheid laws, has failed to recognise the legacy that it has left behind. Apartheid has achieved its purpose. It has created such vast economic and social inequalities between the races that their lives do not touch, except in a master/servant relationship. (see page 47)

EDUCATION

Education has been used by the government to fit the apartheid mould. The Afrikaner view on the role of education was made quite clear by the future Prime Minister, Verwoerd, in 1954 when he said, "The native must be taught from childhood that equality with Europeans is not for them. There is no place for him in the European community above the level of certain forms of labour ... Until now he has been subject to a school system ... which misled him by showing him the green pastures of European society in which he is not allowed to graze." To the Africans it was simply a case of "the Boers wanting to indoctrinate African children into being perpetual slaves of the white man."

The values and attitudes expressed in these statements were enshrined in the 1953 *Bantu Education Act* which transferred all authority for education to the central government in the shape of the Department of Native Affairs. This enforced strict segregation in education and sought to limit the education of Africans to the confines of the state-controlled schools. For example, it was made illegal for an African minister to teach his congregation to read the Bible; no white person was allowed to teach his or her African servants to read. Similar legislation was passed for Coloureds and Indians.

The subject matter in the schools reflected white dominance. One of the main aims was to condition the different groups for the roles they were supposed to play in South African society. Joyce Sikakane, reflecting on her own education in Soweto, summed up how Blacks viewed their education:

> "Bantu Education meant being taught of a tribal identity. In their history books, it meant that the white man 'discovered' the 'savage' African and civilised him. The derogatory word 'Bantu' was used instead of African.
>
> It meant being taught that our national heroes like Tshaka and Hintsa were brutal murderers yet they were African patriots who fought against the white invasion of our country. It meant being taught that the white man is superior to the black man. Above all it meant the unquestionable acceptance of the philosophy of apartheid."
>
> (From *Window on Soweto* Joyce Sikakane)

In 1959, segregation was extended to university education, with separate universities being established for Whites, Coloureds, Indians and Blacks. Blacks were only allowed to attend white institutions if the government Minister had given his approval. Again the access to universities was unequal, as demonstrated by the 1980 student roll with 160,000 Whites, 16,000 Indians, 12,000 Coloureds and 10,500 Africans.

The segregated education was unequal in its provision as is shown by Figures 8.4 to 8.8 on page 48.

People's Education

Education has been an important battlefield between the government and black opposition groups. Despite draconian measures taken during the State of Emergency, (see page 21) the government failed to break the link between education and national liberation established by groups such as COSAS (Congress of South African Students) and the NECC (National Education Crisis Committee). The watchword of the 1980s was 'People's Education'. People's Education, according to the declaration of the Soweto parents crisis committee in December 1985, was education that "enables the oppressed to understand the evils of the system and prepares them for participation in a nonracial democratic system;

ECONOMIC AND SOCIAL INDICATORS OF DISADVANTAGE

Births in 1986 and Population Growth Rate 1987 by official race group

(Figures exclude independent bantustans)

	Total Births	Annual Growth %
African	769,000	2.8
Coloured	81,825	1.92
Indian	19,560	1.85
Whites	72,955	0.83
Total	943,340	(Average) 2.3

Table 8.1 Source: *Minister of Home Affairs and Department of National Health*

INCOME DISTRIBUTION IN 1987

	African	Indian	Coloured	White
Percentage of income	27.0%	3.5%	7.5%	62.5%
Percentage of population	74.0%	3.0%	9.0%	14.0%

Table 8.2 Source: Race Relations Survey 1988/9

Income per person (Rand), 1987

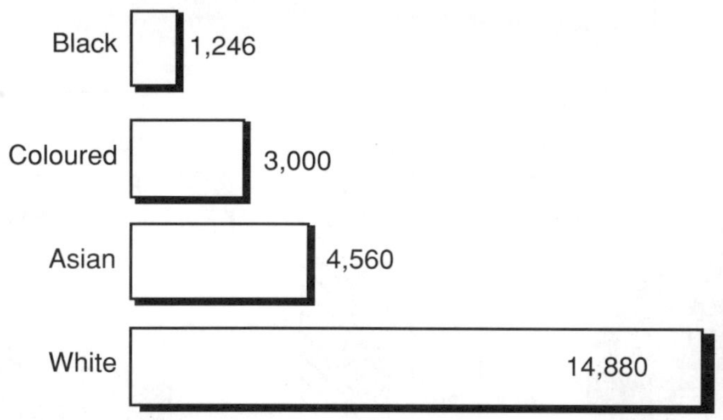

Figure 8.1 Source: *South African Institute of Race Relations*

Old Age Pensions, 1990 (Rands per month)

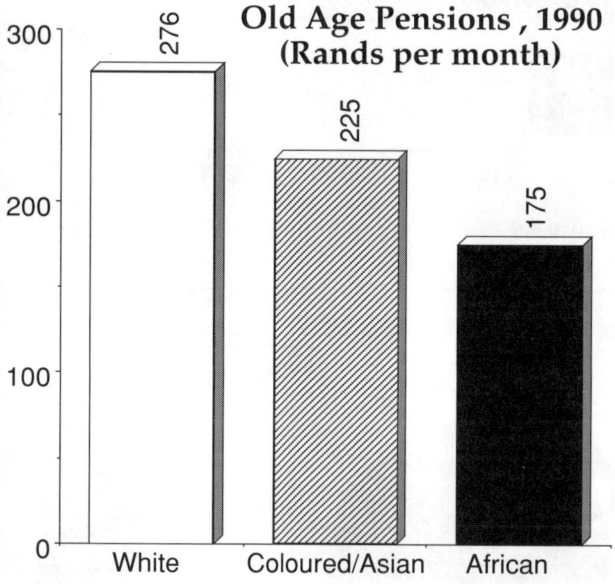

Figure 8.3 Source: *Star* 28.3.90 quoted by IDAF

Occupational Structure (selected occupations) 1985

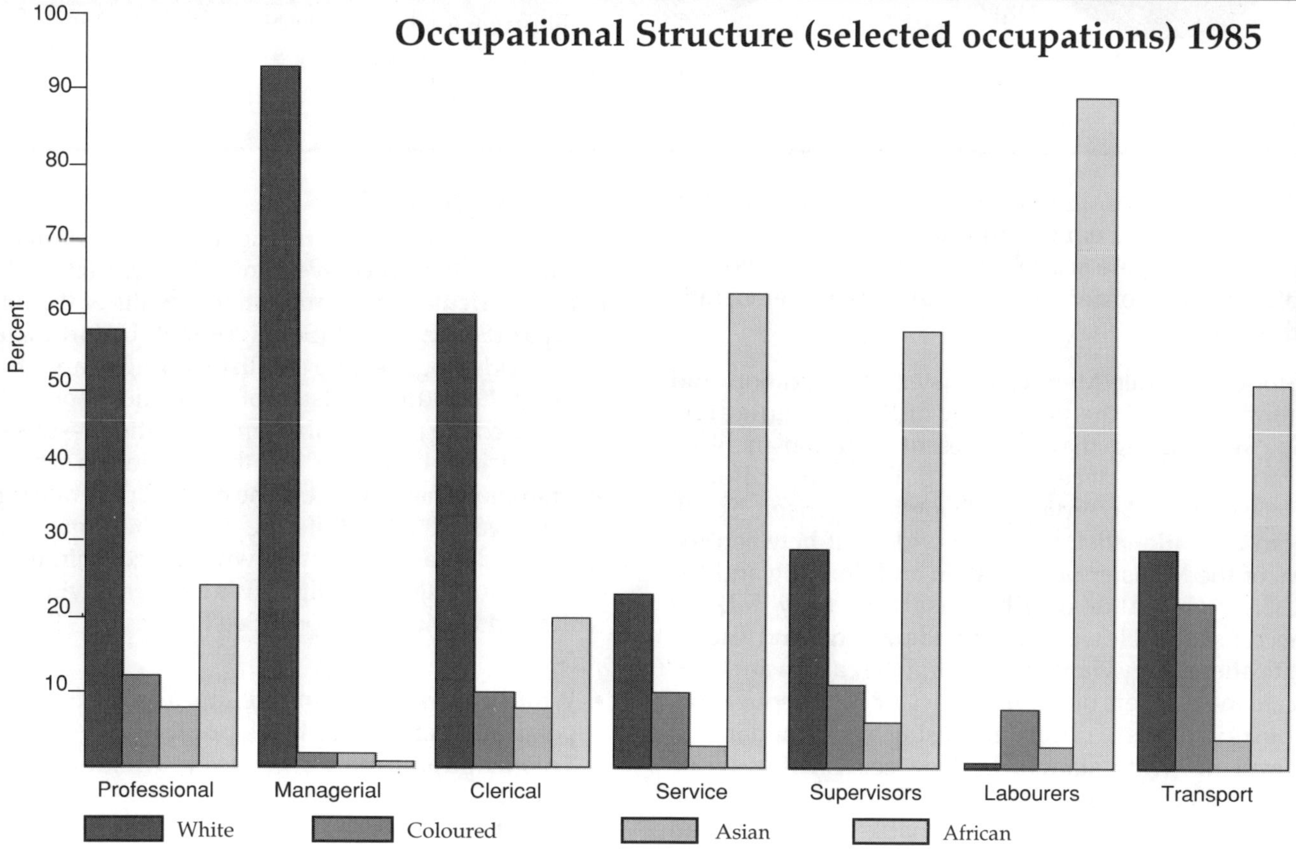

Figure 8.2 Source: *Levy & Mbali 1987* quoted by IDAF

INDICATORS OF EDUCATIONAL DISADVANTAGE

State Spending per Pupil 1987-88 (Rand)

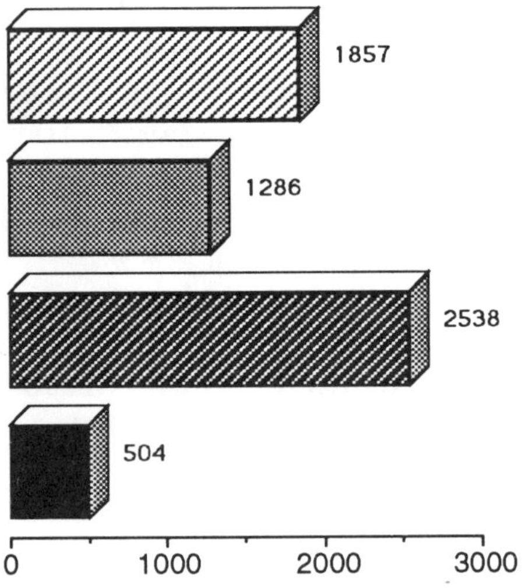

Figure 8.4

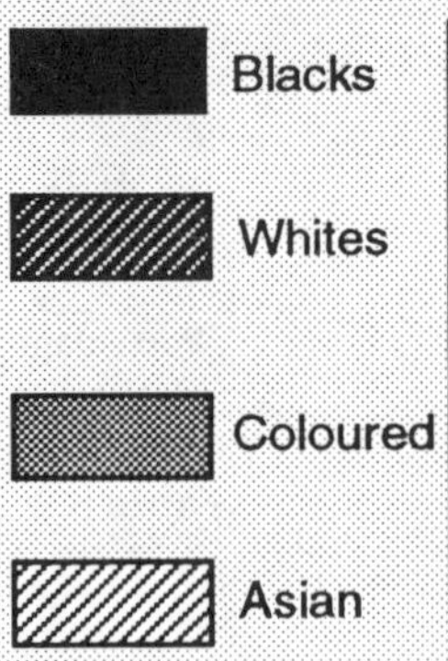

Literacy Rates, 1984
(% of Adult Population)

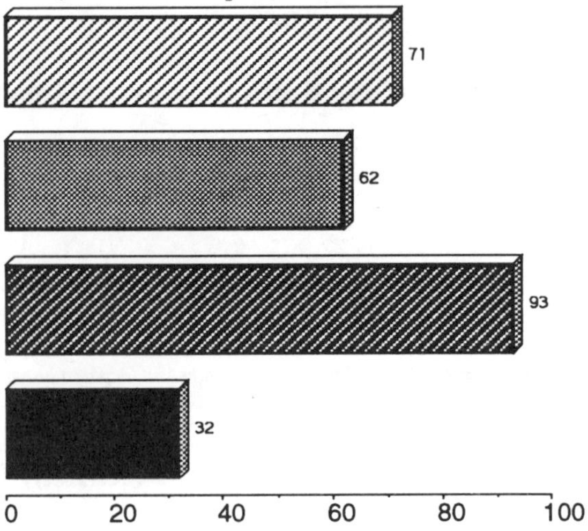

Figure 8.8

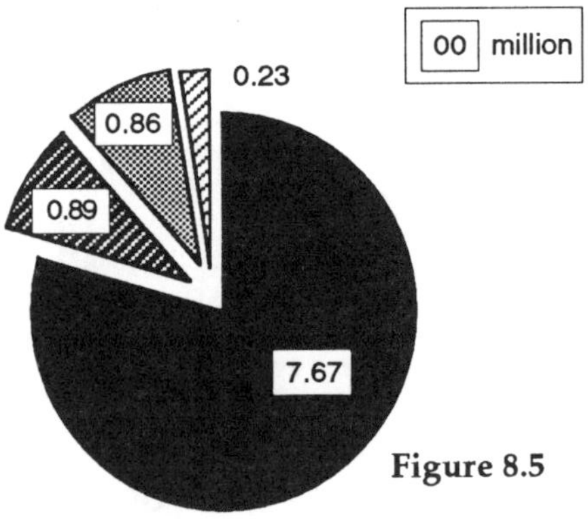

Figure 8.5

Total Number of Pupils: 9.65 million

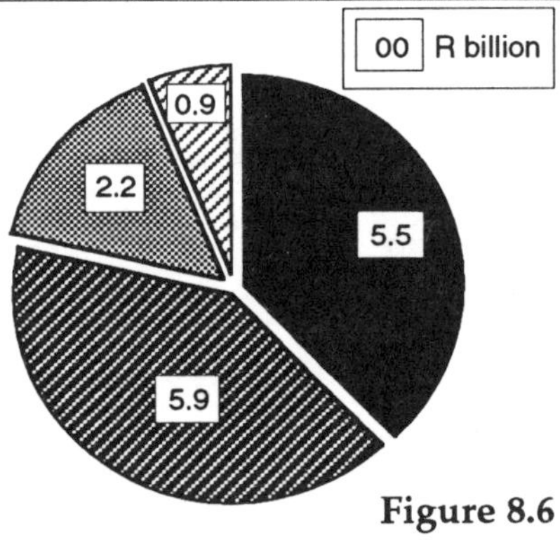

Figure 8.6

Total Expenditure: R14.5 billion

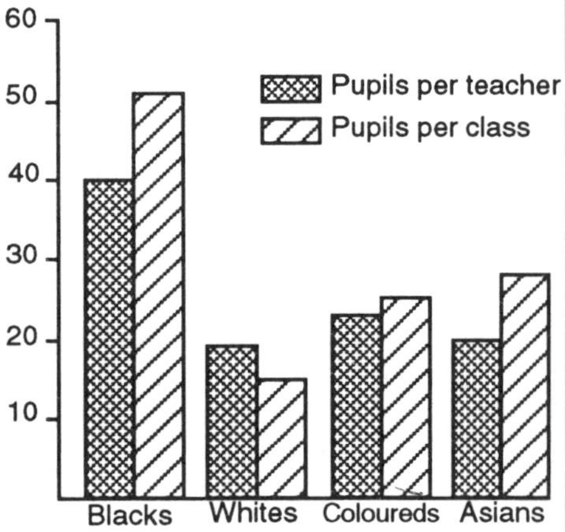

Figure 8.7

eliminates illiteracy, ignorance and exploitation of any person by another; equips and trains all sectors of our people to participate actively and creatively in obtaining people's power in order to establish a nonracial democratic South Africa."

Dr Stoffel van der Merwe, Minister of Education and Training, attacked the philosophy of People's Education while "recognising that the present situation in black education is not acceptable and there are colossal shortcomings." According to Douglas Morrison, South African educationalist, there is a wide gulf between the views of the Minister of Education and Training and the NECC: "He talks of liberalisation; they talk of democratisation. He wants to upgrade facilities and teacher qualifications; they want that too - but they also want to re-educate the teachers out of the legacy of Bantu education. He thinks in terms of ultimately raising black standards to the level of white standards; they see existing white standards themselves as a problem. The norms, according to this view, should be set at an attainable level lower than the present white standards but above the present ones set by the Department of Education and Training."

Crisis of Inequality

A clear indication of the impact Bantu education has had on the educational achievements of nonwhites can be seen in the matriculation (examination) results of the different groups in South Africa. (See Figure 8.9) Unfortunately the gulf is widening, despite the dismantling of apartheid. In January 1991 the Minister of Education and Training announced the poorest black matriculation results ever in South Africa. Under 40% of the candidates who sat the examinations had passed. (The highest pass rate figure in Soweto was 30%.) While the school boycotts, teachers' strikes and anarchy in the townships contributed to the dismal results, the real culprit was the great divide between white and black education. (See Figures 8.4 - 8.8)

- White pupils get about five times as much capital expenditure per head as black pupils.
- Teacher:pupil ratio for Whites is 1:16; for Blacks it is 1:40.
- In 1988 there was a shortage of 37,781 classrooms for black pupils.
- While 82% of Whites entering school reach the final

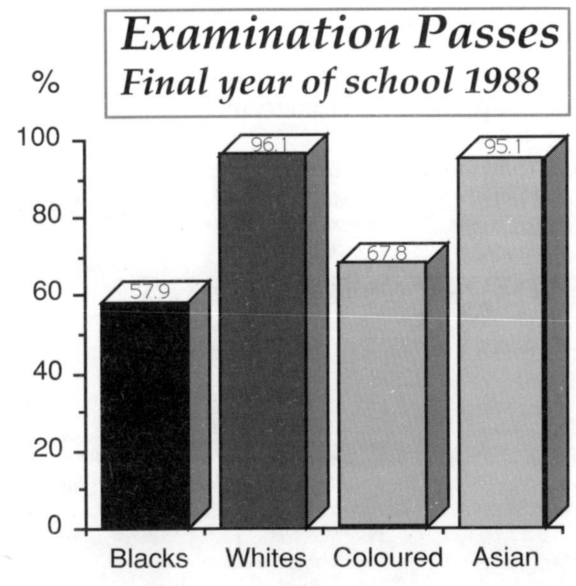

Figure 8.9 Source: Race Relations Survey 1988/89

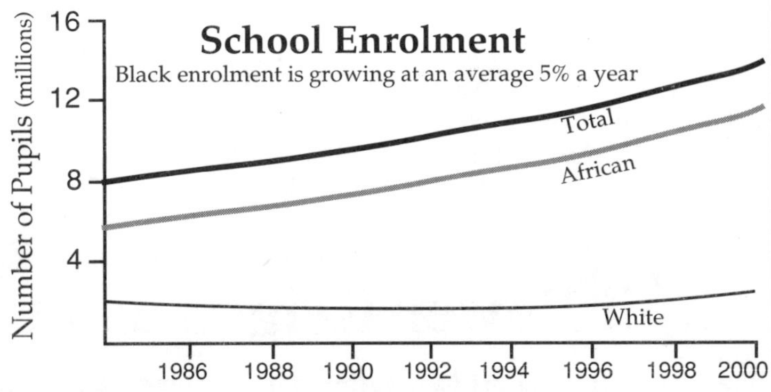

Figure 8.10

years of study, the figure for Coloureds is 20% and for Blacks, 16%.

- 170,000 black pupils left school in 1988 without having passed Sub A and were therefore illiterate.
- At more than 800 black schools, double sessions (where the same teacher takes 2 classes a day) and the platoon system (teachers for two classes but in the same room) were in operation.

Nevertheless, the culture of violence and the alienation of youth have contributed to the poor performance of black students. They are not easily swayed by authority, whoever it is. When Nelson Mandela told students to throw their pangas into the sea and go back to school, some of them showed their displeasure by cutting his face off their T-shirts. According to Dr Hartshore, consultant to the Centre for Continuing Education, schooling of black South Africans has reached crisis point. "It has produced people who do not know how to learn and who do not want to learn." Monde Tulwana, a teacher at ID Mkhize Secondary School, Guguletu township outside Cape Town, states: "Gangsterism is rife in the township and affects children who might want to come to school." According to figures released in January 1991 by the Education Department, 33 schoolchildren died and 204 were injured in unrest in 1990; 48 schoolgirls were raped and 18,000 township children who left school in 1989 were on the street.

The Demographic Timebomb

According to researchers at Witwatersrand University, more than 200 white schools have been closed in the last 10 years, while the shortage of black schools keeps an estimated 3.5 million children away from lessons - more than the total white school enrolment. At present there are 7.6 million black schoolchildren (see Figure 8.5) and this figure will rise to 12.3 million by the year 2000. (See Figure 8.10) Despite these white school closures there are still 200,000 places vacant in white schools. Pressure has obviously mounted on the government to allow Blacks to fill the empty places. The absurdity of the white education department closing precious educational resources while the black community is desperate for places has been seized upon by both the Democratic Party and the English-speaking press as conclusive evidence of the need to create a unified education system and of the wastefulness of the present segregated system. Although educational policy and apportionment of finance are controlled by the Minister of National Education, the administration of education continues under separate authorities. White education is controlled by the Department of National Education, while coloured and Indian education falls under the Department of Education and Culture, and African education is either under the Department of Education and Training or Bantustan authorities.

In March 1990, Piet Clase, Minister of Education and Culture, proposed two educational models which would cater for mixed schools. Provided that 72% of all parents agreed in an 80 per cent poll, a state school could either become a private school - and receive a 45% state subsidy - or remain in the state sector. Parents also have the right to vote on whether to admit non-whites, but at least 80 per cent of parents must vote, and at least 90 per cent of those voting must vote in favour of the change. However, the

Closure of Western High School

The gradual disintegration of residential segregation transformed Homestead Park from an all-white suburb into a mixed area which, by 1990, had a 60 per cent coloured and Asian population. The roll at the local white school, Western High, had fallen from 500 to 138 and it was to be closed at the end of 1991.

Homestead Park's non-white parents meanwhile had to send their children to overcrowded Indian and coloured schools five miles away. "It's crazy," declared Ismael Munshi, an Indian resident of Homestead Park. "I have to look at these empty classrooms across the road while my two children go to a school in Fordsburg that was built for 500 pupils but has 700. The conditions there are terrible; there is no space for a playground and part of the building has been condemned."

The white parents voted overwhelmingly for integration but the Minister of Education refused and as a result the school closed and Homestead Park lost its school.

school must retain its 'white' characteristics and the Minister can still refuse permission even if the white parents do vote for integration. (See Closure of Western High School.) As part of the solution to overcrowding, the government has purchased some of the closed white schools for black pupils and for the children of African National Congress exiles.

Unfortunately this has created a violent right-wing reaction. In July 1991 Hillview High School in Pretoria (a former white school closed in 1981) was blown up just days before the return of up to 700 children from Tanzania.

The NECC (National Education Coordinating Committee) announced in July 1991 that it intended to occupy 50 empty

Pupil Power Reigns as the Struggle Sharpens

Extracts from a report by George Walker, Head Teacher of the Cavendish School, Hemel Hempstead, on his visit to South Africa.

I am teaching a Standard 9 class in Luhlaza senior secondary school in Khayelitsha, a sprawling black township of boxes, shacks, huts and concrete houses dumped on the sandy dunes of the Cape Flats, some 10 miles from the centre of Cape Town. Estimates of its size vary from 30,000 to half a million but no one can ever know because another 7,000 or so flood into the Cape Peninsula every month now that the Pass Laws have been removed.

Luhlaza has about 1,350 pupils but only 37 teachers of whom eight, unusually, are white, including the school's acting principal. The vacancy for principal arose in February when a pupil activist came to the staff room at lunchtime to announce that the incumbent must go or there would be serious trouble; he had been judged to be a collaborator with the government's hated Department of Education and Training which is responsible for black education. His notice to quit had already been delivered in the form of a bold red cross painted over his reserved parking space and he had no option but to join the growing ranks of officials forced out by militant Student Representative Councils and Parent, Teacher and Student Associations.

Since the violent revolt in the schools in Soweto against the imposition in 1976 of Afrikaans as a medium of instruction, township schools throughout South Africa have been in the front line of black opposition to apartheid. Learning has taken a back seat to political activity and teachers and their students have been subjected to all kinds of political, moral and physical threats. As a result, a whole generation of black pupils has missed out on its education and more than 4 million black youths are uneducated and unemployed 'somewhere out there': a thought that terrifies the white population.

Back at school we pick up a bright 18-year-old about to sit his matriculation exams. He is hoping to get a place at Cape Town University to study science but his education, already hopelessly disadvantaged in terms of resources and teaching quality, has been further put at risk by the strikes and boycotts that have affected every year of his education. The comparison of black and white matriculation results tells the story with the black pass rate falling from 54 per cent in 1988 to 42 per cent in 1989 and widely predicted to fall by a similar amount in 1990.

This boy, like thousands of other pupils across South Africa, has been following the matriculation revision programmes on television each morning, sponsored by Caltex Oil and Argus Newspapers, and now we are taking him to an after-school maths revision class staffed by local teachers and by students from the black University of the Western Cape. Dozens of these semi-formal opportunities for help have been established, many of them under the auspices of the ANC-backed National Education Coordinating Committee, but despite this desperate injection of last minute learning, his chances of achieving the grades set by the University of Cape Town are slim.

Not so far away in terms of distance, another group of matriculation pupils has been watching the television revision programmes, prerecorded on video by a qualified librarian in the school's well-equipped resources centre. Fifteen miles down the coast from the Cape Flats and Khayelitsha, towards the Cape of Good Hope, lies the very English seaside town of Fish Hoek. Only the deep red of the bougainvillea, the deep blue of the Indian Ocean and the presence in the bay of a school of whales, betray Fish Hoek's location as South Africa and not South Devon.

Fish Hoek senior high school has about 530 white pupils aged 16 to 18 and 44 teachers. It has the kind of buildings that win architectural awards, a smart blazered uniform, a school song, a powerful group of prefects and, like all white schools, 'voluntary' school fees of around £50 a term.

Fish Hoek SHS provides quality education and is highly regarded among its community, but now it has a problem: how to persuade its parents to vote 'yes' in sufficient numbers to enable the School Management Council - its governing body - to change the admissions policy from next January to allow pupils of all races to attend the school. The Minister of White Education, Piet Clase, has at last responded to increasing pressure from white teachers and their professional associations, in particular the influential and well-respected South African Teachers' Association, to allow white state schools to open their doors to other racial groups. At the same time it would enable the schools to recruit non-white teachers, a point not lost at Fish Hoek where earlier in the year the school had lost a bitter battle with the Minister to recruit an outstanding black teacher of Xhosa.

But Clase has set the schools a tough target: a minimum of 80 per cent of parents must vote and at least 90 per cent must vote in favour of the change. Even then, the Minister has reserved the right to turn down the request. The Fish Hoek school community, drawn more closely together by this new experience of democracy, is quietly confident that it will join the dozen or more Cape schools (including one in deeply conservative Uitenhage) that have already declared resounding percentage votes in favour of going open. But nothing is being left to chance ...

The school now has about 175 spare places. In marked contrast to the black population which will double in the next 20 years, white numbers have been falling and this has given a powerful impetus to the admission of non-whites to white schools that will otherwise face closure ...

After such a professional campaign, there is little doubt that Fish Hoek will be in the vanguard of the open schools movement but to satisfy conservative parents the Management Council has set its own criteria for entry. In the first year only about 50 non-white places will be offered so that pupil:teacher ratios are not adversely affected; fluent English will be required; pupils must not be more than two years different in age from the average of their standard and they must be able to benefit from the school's strong academic tradition. In practice, therefore, the school will take the cream of the pupils from Ocean View High School that serves a large coloured community nearby, but despite this, the principal of Ocean View has lent his support to the campaign.

(George Walker on his second visit to Luhlaza)

This time I am better prepared, at least knowing what classes I am going to teach. But the school is not prepared for me. During my absence the simmering violence has erupted into serious rioting that left eight bodies in the hospital's mortuary and over fifty injured. Dozens of buildings have been burned out and from the comfortable white suburbs of Cape Town, we observed the cloud of black smoke over the township and watched the police helicopters flying overhead. It was something to do with the rent increases, we were told, and the conflict between the ANC and the puppet town council, but from where we lived no one seemed either sure or very bothered.

After the pictures and the reports in the Cape Town press, I am surprised even to get back to Khayelitsha - at one point all access roads were sealed off - but on the morning of my arrival all is quiet at Luhlaza as groups of pupils drift back. Quiet perhaps, but far from normal and for at least an hour something very close to pupil anarchy prevails. Nothing violent, nothing even unpleasant but it is nonetheless clear that the pupils and not the teachers are in charge. Indeed many of the teachers retreat discreetly to the staff room to sit it out.

Eventually, the efforts of a handful of dedicated teachers who hold the school together prevail and some sort of learning gets into low gear where it sticks for the rest of the day with pupils drifting aimlessly around the buildings. The standard 10s gather in the hall to write the first paper of their matriculation exams on which their future life chances will depend. Sixteen-year-old Ricky Dyaloyi, who will become one of South Africa's great artists, shows me a selection of his pastels and woodcuts. I help the Standard 9s with the chemistry of the halogens, whose relevance to the problems of Luhlaza, Khayelitsha and South Africa is not immediately obvious. But never mind, they are gaining knowledge and confidence, enjoying it and possibly beginning to move down the very, very long road to something better.

The day started with an outdoor assembly. At eight o'clock only two dozen pupils had emerged from the strife-torn township but by the end several hundred had arrived. I talked briefly to them about a school I knew in Hertfordshire - but was it on the same planet? Then they sang me the Lord's Prayer in Xhosa and it was hard not to cry.

(Times Educational Supplement, 23.11.90)

white schools in and around Johannesburg. Amon Msane of the NECC stated, "This is not a symbolic step. We need this accommodation."

Education Renewal Strategy

In June 1991 the government unveiled its new education strategy in an attempt to defuse the tension in black schools and to secure the cooperation of black leaders. The plan proposed the creation of a single central authority responsible for a core curriculum and policy and standards in electorally accountable regional bodies.

Under the plan, the first seven years of schooling would be free and compulsory for all children. However, while the state would bear the cost of compulsory primary education, parents would be expected to contribute towards secondary schooling, which would be more vocationally oriented. Dr Johan Garbens, Director-General of National Education, stated that the criteria for the new education system would be integrity of language, religion and culture and not race. However, he did acknowledge that this would enable the white community to retain segregated state schools. Nevertheless, progress has been made towards redressing inequalities. According to the Institute of Race Relations, the 1991 education budget witnessed a 53 per cent increase in spending on black education. It also found substantial improvements in black pupils' attendance. On integration, the Institute stated that some 10 per cent of white schools had opened their doors to all races.

HEALTH

In June 1990, the Minister of National Health and Population Development, Dr Rina Venter, announced that hospitals would be opened to all population groups. Once again the realities of population pressures - of empty white hospital wards and overcrowded and inadequate black wards - had forced the final collapse of yet another segregation stronghold. The inequalities in hospital provision led to the absurd situation of Johannesburg Hospital being underutilised, with whole wards closed down, while in Baragwanath Hospital in Soweto patients slept under as well as on top of the beds.

Dr Venter stated: "While a lot of our hospitals are overcrowded with bed occupancy rates of more than 100 per cent, there are hospitals which are totally underutilised ... if a norm of three beds per 1,000 of the population applies there is a surplus of 11,700 beds in white hospitals while there is a shortage of 7,000 beds in black hospitals."

Yet, while the government congratulated itself for ending segregation, the issue of redressing the vast inequalities in provision and health standards still remains. The depressing statistics (see Tables 8.3 - 8.7) illustrate the vast gulf between the 'First World' health care of the Whites and the 'Third World' health service administered to the Blacks. The statistics also highlight the contrast between urban and rural (Homelands) African health provision.

A major factor in this disparity of health provision between the races is their contrasting lifestyles and socio-economic position. Poverty - with its checklist of inadequate housing and sanitary conditions and poor diet - is the major culprit. Dr Venter accepts that "restructuring (of health care) must go hand in hand with the socio-economic upliftment of

RACIAL DIVISIONS IN HEALTH EXPERIENCES

Infant Mortality Rate by Race Group, 1986 **(per 1,000 births)**

African	80.0
Coloured	31.6
Indian	13.6
White	7.0

Table 8.3 **Source: Central Statistical Service 1988**

Projected Life Expectancy at Birth

	1985-90	1990-95	1995-2000
African	62.2	64.9	66.4
Coloured	60.9	62.6	64.4
Indian	67.2	68.5	69.9
White	71.4	72.3	73.2

Table 8.4
Source: Central Statistical Service as in *SA Barometer*, 16 March 1990

Maternal Mortality Rate 1986 **(per 100,000 Population)**

African	18
Coloured	16
Indian	15
White	3

Table 8.5 Source: *SA Barometer*, 14 July 1989

Rural/Urban Differentiation in Infant Mortality Rates 1981-85 **(Deaths per 1,000 births)**

	African	Coloured	Indian	White
National	94 - 124	52	18	12
10 major urban areas	39	26	17	12
Rural and semi-rural	100 - 135	66	20	12

Note: Figures exclude the 'independent' bantustans where mortality is often higher.
Table 8.6 Source: *SA Barometer*, 21 April 1989

Nutritional Status of Children (1 to 5 years) 1985

	% Stunted	% Underweight	% Wasting
African - Rural	41	43	3
African - Urban	12	28	7
Coloured - Urban	20	49	11
Indian - Urban	6	35	15
White - Urban	4	16	8

Note: Stunted children have less than 90 per cent of expected height for age. Underweight children are under 80 percent of expected weight for age. And wasting children measure less than 80 percent of expected weight for height.

Table 8.7 Source: *SA Barometer*, April 21 1989

communities so that disease stemming from poor living conditions can be limited and overcrowding of hospitals can be prevented ... The building of more hospitals will not solve the problem."

Nevertheless, the desegregation of Health Services was welcomed by anti-apartheid groups, who had made it a main demand of the defiance campaign of 1989. (see page 36) Fazel Randera of the anti-apartheid National Medical and Dental Association (NAMDA) declared, "We have been struggling and fighting for years for a nonracial health service. This is what South Africa is looking forward to in the future."

Significantly, private health care is a growth area in South Africa. At present it provides 20% of hospital beds and 90% of the white community relies on private rather than on state funded medical care. Private hospitals have been open to all races for some time, but their high fees ensure that very few Blacks can afford to be treated in the private sector. In short, a two-tier health system based on racial lines still exists in South Africa.

LAND DISTRIBUTION

> "Any reforms with regard to the usage of land will have to take into account the principles of free enterprise, security of tenure and vested property rights."
> President FW de Klerk

> "The intention of the proposed land reforms is to legitimise and entrench the legacy of apartheid while repealing the laws which create it."
> African National Congress

The above quotations highlight the debate over the emotive issue of land reform in South Africa. It is clear from the White Paper on Land Reform (see page 53) that the government has no intention of returning the land taken from the African and coloured population. According to the Surplus People's Project, 3.5 million people were forcefully moved, sometimes at gunpoint, from 'black spots' and herded into their allotted tribal homelands. (See Table 8.8)

A government Minister, Mr De Villiers, has stated openly: "White farmers have been repeatedly assured by the authorities that their title deeds are safe. The objective has never been and will never be a redistribution of land by means of nationalisation or expropriation." He continued, "Apart from the fact that a redistribution programme to restore historical land rights is almost impracticable, it also holds the potential for serious conflict. How far back in history must one go to determine who really has a right to a specific territory?" He further infuriated anti-apartheid groups by blandly stating, "I wish to emphasise that more land has been expropriated from Whites to be given to black people than vice versa and that people were indeed compensated for their land."

Estimated Number of People forced to Move, 1960-82

Type of Removal	Number Moved
Removals under Group Areas Act	834,400
Township relocation in bantustans	730,000
Eviction of squatters in informal urban settlements	112,000
Eviction of farm workers and labour tenants	1,129,000
Black spot and other evictions for bantustan consolidation	687,500
Removals within and between bantustans	30,000
Total	3,552,900

Table 8.8
Source: Surplus People's Project, cited in *Unterhalter* 1985 , p.142

The government's refusal to restore land, except by ending the restraints on Blacks to take part freely in the land market and by offering loans and aid on a nonracial basis, is symbolic of their inability to recognise the evils created by the apartheid system. De Klerk has never admitted that apartheid was wrong, thus avoiding the need to offer reparations. The repeal of the *Land Acts* of 1913 and 1936 by President de Klerk might end the enforcement of racially discriminatory laws, but it certainly does not redress the grievance of 13% of the country's land being given to 80% of its people.

The ANC has criticised the government for not consulting them before publishing the White Paper which is, according to the ANC, "a racist document that cannot break loose from the racist rut of the past". The ANC is committed to the restoration of land to the victims of forced removals (see article page 54) and argues that the White Paper "absolves the white population of all responsibility for the long, tragic history of black dispossession." The Pan Africanist Congress (PAC) is united with the ANC on this issue. Their argument is simple: the land was stolen from the original inhabitants by white settlers and it is illogical to expect African people, assuming they could afford it, to buy back land which was stolen from them. As far as Clarence Makwetu, President of the PAC, is concerned, repeal of the land laws without compensation for their victims is land apartheid "dressed up in new clothes".

Homelands

The White Paper on Land Reform did not affect the status of the four independent Homelands. The Acts, which

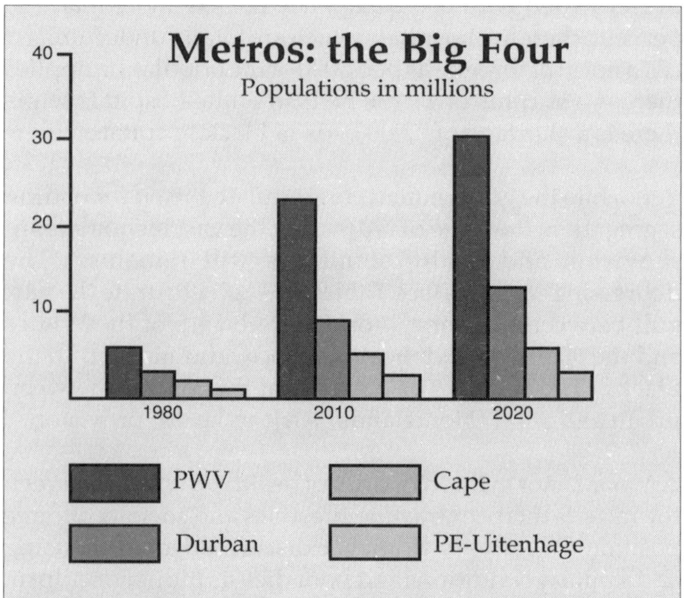

Figure 8.11

Extracts from White Paper on Land Reform

The White Paper is supported by five Bills, viz:

a) *Abolition of Racially based Land Measures Bill*
The principle aim of the Bill is the repeal of the *Black Land Act* 1913, the *Development Trust and Land Act* 1936, the *Group Areas Act* 1966 and the *Black Communities Development Act* 1984, as well as the deletion of racial restrictions on land tenure in all other laws, including laws relating to rural areas for the coloured group and laws of the self-governing territories.

Since the South African Development Trust (SADT) comprises a complex network of rights, structures and measures it cannot be abolished overnight. The Bill accordingly provides for the phasing out of the SADT through the systematic integration of its services, assets and staff. The phasing out will be administered by the establishment of the Advisory Committee on Non-racial Area Measures.

b) *Upgrading of Land Tenure Rights Bill*
The primary objective of this Bill is to rationalise land registration systems and the upgrading of lower-order land tenure rights to full ownership. To prevent exploitation of tribes, it is provided that no land belonging to a black tribe may be leased, sold or otherwise disposed of to any person other than a member of the tribe without the permission of a court.

c) *Residential Environment Bill*
Provision is made for the prevention, combating and restoration of physical decline in cities and towns.

d) *Less Formal Township Establishment Bill*
Provision is made for the urgent provision of suitable land for the settlement of homeless people in a less formal but orderly and upgradable manner, for shortened procedures for the establishment of less formal towns, and for measures in connection with land which tribal communities intend to use for communal forms of residential settlement.

e) *Rural Development Bill*
The Bill provides for the establishment of a rural development corporation with the object of contributing towards and coordinating the development of rural areas at a national level with reference to the development needs of such areas.

The unproductive use of high potential agricultural land must be discouraged. The purchase of land by tribes and tribal communities poses this very risk, namely that high-potential agricultural land may be lost as a result of communal use of such land in accordance with unproductive traditional systems of land tenure.

deprived a million Blacks of South African citizenship by making them citizens of the independent Homelands, also remain unchanged. In 1986 the *Restoration of South African Citizenship Act* offered Blacks the right to reclaim South African citizenship. However, because of red tape very few Blacks regained their South African birthright. Transkei, Venda and Ciskei wish to reverse their independence status while Bophuthatswana is watching developments in South Africa and will, if necessary, make a constitutional amendment. The government's view is that the status of the four independent Homelands will be considered at the constitutional talks. They assume that the leaders of the four independent Homelands (along with the other self-governing Homeland leaders) will participate in the talks.

Urbanisation

The scrapping of the Pass Laws and the Group Areas Act has accelerated the movement from the countryside to the towns. Pushed by population growth, poverty and opportunity, people are flocking into the major metropolitan areas. Figure 8.11 estimates the impact this will have on the major urban areas.

LEGACY OF VIOLENCE

Despite numerous denials by FW de Klerk, there was clear evidence - even before Inkathagate (see page 57) that elements of the military police force were hostile to his reforms and had used excessive force to deal with black protests. Criticism has even come from within the police force itself. A coloured policeman, Lt Gregory Rockman, publicly labelled the South African Police riot squads "mad dogs" following election night killings in the Western Cape on 5 September 1989. Rockman and 40 other nonwhite police officers met with the Minister of Law and Order to present their grievances. In November 1989 Rockman helped to set up the Police and Prisons Civil Rights Union to protect the basic human rights of its members. However, at its first meeting on 13 November, Rockman and 20 others were arrested and charged under the Internal Security Act. He was also suspended from the police force and charged under disciplinary procedures.

The Civil Cooperation Bureau

In 1990 the existence of 'death squads' was admitted by the government. The police discovered that inside the Defence Ministry a separate unit existed responsible for arson, bombing and murder. The Defence Minister, Magnus Malan, lamely stated that he had only discovered its existence in November 1989 and that he had immediately taken action to end its activities.

The scandal surfaced when Captain Dirk Coetzee, a former 'death squad' commander, defected to the ANC in 1989 after telling his story to the Afrikaans anti-apartheid newspaper *Vrye Weekblad*. Coetzee admitted, among other things, that he had helped to plan the murder of civil rights lawyer Griffiths Mxenge.

President de Klerk set up a judicial inquiry under Justice Louis Harms. The commission discovered that the Civil Cooperation Bureau had been set up in April 1986 and had carried out some 200 operations, ranging from plots to

Home thoughts in Botshabelo

"If you want to see a symbol of apartheid, then look no farther." In the grasslands of the Orange Free State, social engineering has herded half a million people into a township, second in size only to Soweto.
Report: Ian Mayes

If you drive about 35 miles towards the east from Bloemfontein, through the white farmlands and across the plains of the Orange Free State, you will come upon a place that does not appear on the map. It is revealed suddenly, just off the main road, a great straggle that has grown there in little over 10 years.

It used to be called Onverwacht, which in Afrikaans, means 'unexpected'. Today its new name is spelt out in stones on the low hills which rise to one side of it: Botshabelo. In the language of the south Sotho people it means 'place of refuge'. Social workers describe it more accurately as a dumping ground for Blacks who are surplus to the requirements of the local economy.

This is a township - a city - of some 500,000 rural people, second in size only to Soweto but with practically none of the things which usually support communities on this scale. Made-up roads are spasmodic and peripheral. Brick built homes are few and mainly for employees of the government. Water is from taps which may mean a walk of half a mile. Little more than three per cent of homes have electricity, about two per cent have flush toilets and at a recent count, in the entire place there were 33 telephones. Transport is confined to the subsidised buses that take nearly 15,000 manual workers and domestic servants to and from Bloemfontein every day. Beyond that it hardly matters. No one is going anywhere.

What Botshabelo does have is huge unemployment - one report a year ago put it at 80 per cent - and it has hunger and all the diseases of poverty. "If you want to see a symbol of apartheid," a French doctor said, "then look no farther."

She was right. Botshabelo is a product of the complicated mess of the government's hated homelands policy. When Bophuthatswana was given its nominal independence at the end of the 1970s one of the conditions was that it included an area around Taba Nchu, traditionally occupied mainly by Tswana people.

It did and now this tiny enclave forms one of the seven separate parts of Bophuthatswana, ludicrously strung out across north-central South Africa, a geographical nonsense that a government minister once attempted to justify by comparing it to the Greek islands. Taba Nchu has all the benefits of phoney independence: Kentucky Fried Chicken and a casino where the local chief might be seen playing the one-armed bandits.

Its original inhabitants are now scattered because when this part of Bophuthatswana came into being it not only enclosed Tswana people, but in the kind of untidiness which the tidy system of the homelands creates, it also threw a cordon round thousands of Sotho people. They claimed harassment by the new Bophuthatswana administration, which had labelled them squatters, and they left.

They became the involuntary founders of Botshabelo, squatting on the white farm which gave the place its first name - a farm quickly acquired by the government in an attempt, it might have seemed, to contain the situation.

At the beginning of the 1980s there were 50,000 to 60,000 people in Botshabelo. Thousands more poured in as the abolition of the farm tenancy system and increasing mechanisation forced them off farms. At the same time Bloemfontein restricted the growth of its own black township, and many of the smaller white towns in the state 'disestablished' theirs. Botshabelo, the place of refuge, the 'dump' for all these people, was thus the grim product of social engineering.

Then in December 1987, the government, setting earlier reassurances to one side, made its overall intention clear. It announced the incorporation of Botshabelo into the tiny Sotho homeland of QwaQwa, more than 120 miles away on the other side of Lesotho. According to some reports, leaflets giving notice of incorporation were dropped on Botshabelo from security forces helicopters. The Chief Minister of QwaQwa, Kenneth Mopeli, said the people of Botshabelo danced in the streets in celebration of the news. Church observers said the scene was one of roadblocks, Casspirs of the South African Defence Force, and burning buses.

Since then there has been a long-running battle through the courts between the residents of Botshabelo, fighting to stay in South Africa, and the government, which plainly wants them out. The courts have supported the people.

The Supreme Court in Bloemfontein declared the incorporation invalid, pointing out among other things that Botshabelo included some 120,000 'foreign Blacks', non-Sotho people. Thus the kind of problem that had arisen in Bophuthatswana between the Tswanas and the Sothos could be repeated. The Appeal Court agreed with that decision.

The reasons for this long struggle, marked by petitions, marches and demonstrations, are not complicated. The people of Botshabelo fear that incorporation into QwaQwa would make their plight worse and in the long run disenfranchise them. The Chief Minister of QwaQwa wants them in because it would strengthen his own power and make the small kingdom over which he reigns a more viable unit for the sort of independence Bophuthatswana has. And the South African government wants them out because half a million black people, having been corraled in Botshabelo, in effect would be removed from the country altogether - it would be voting with their feet.

Since the Appeal Court ruling, the government has said it now accepts that Botshabelo is part of South Africa. The administration of QwaQwa says it no longer wants it. The people of Botshabelo still look nervously over their shoulders.

Joanne Yawitch, the coordinator for the National Land Committee, an umbrella organisation for a number of voluntary agencies involved in the homelands, says, "Walking through this place, this apartheid folly, a city without any infrastructure, you can't fail to become aware of all the complicated problems it poses for the future. What is going to become of all these people?"

There are examples of government activity here: the two thousand or so neat bungalows that stand amid the 'informal dwellings', the tin shanties and the mud huts. It has built supermarkets and schools. There is a small hospital and there are mobile clinics.

The government has now stopped building houses there but its agent, the South African Development Trust, in theory at least, is making sites available for people who want to build their own homes. The price has jumped dramatically. A site of 300 square metres used to cost 49 Rand. The price today is 60 Rand. The same site 'with services' is 650 Rand. No one is quite sure what 'with services' means but the question is academic. The price is wildly beyond the means of most people living there.

Around the approach to Botshabelo there is a cluster of 50 or so small factories making clothing and video equipment. Many of them are run by Taiwanese, a few by Israelis, recruited by government emissaries offering enormous subsidies which guarantee them virtually free labour. The government pays 95 per cent of the monthly wages for each worker up to a maximum of 100 Rand (£25) for seven years.

In exchange for their labour many workers earn less than a maid might get in the suburbs of Johannesburg. On occasions when they have tried to unionise they have been sacked. They are not difficult to replace.

(Source: *Guardian* 11 May 1990)

poison political opponents to assassinations such as the murder of David Webster, a lecturer at the University of Witwatersrand. Webster was shot dead in May 1989 outside his home as he was unloading his car. Sir Ronald Renwick, British Ambassador to South Africa, stated: "The Civil Cooperation Bureau are wild extremists, extremely dangerous people."

However, when the Harms Commission made its report in late 1990, no action was taken against the officers named in the newspaper disclosures. According to Allister Sparks of the *Observer* newspaper, "De Klerk is either unwilling to risk confronting the powerful security establishment or, as Mandela had suggested, he is following a 'double agenda', negotiating with the ANC while allowing his security forces to destabilise it so he can get the constitution he wants, and with his allies, win the election." More recent evidence supports Sparks' accusation. In May 1991, Sipho Alfred Madlala said in an affidavit that he was paid £1,000 by a police officer to kill Chief Mhlabunzima Maphumnlo because he was a problem to the government. The Chief, a former President of Contralesa (Congress of Traditional Leaders) was murdered in February 1991.

Threat from the Right

The activities of extreme right-wing groups have also created problems for the government, especially in the Transvaal. Despite the threats by these groups, events of 1990 seemed to suggest that they were not prepared to put their words into action by creating a white civil war. Acts of terrorism did occur: in June 1990 bombs exploded at the homes of two city councillors in Johannesburg and the offices of the newspaper *Vrye Weekblad*. Other targets have been a synagogue (ultrarightists blame Jewish money for de Klerk's 'capitulation' to the ANC) and a hotel in Johannesburg where a hand grenade attack killed two black men and injured 21. The 'White Wolves' claimed responsibility for these outrages. Their most infamous member is Barend Strydom, who murdered seven black people in Pretoria in 1988.

The weekly newspaper *Vrye Weekblad* disclosed a plot to kill Mandela and President de Klerk. In an affidavit to the newspaper, a former police spy said that he had infiltrated the AWB and discovered the plot. He also alleged that a Conservative Party politician had agreed to smuggle arms into Parliament to enable rightists to kill cabinet ministers and stage a coup. Although no charges were made by the authorities, the Conservative Party's association with terrorism has alienated some of its supporters who do not wish to follow the road to violence and chaos.

Ventersdorp

The violence which erupted in the Transvaal in August 1991, leaving three supporters of the AWB dead, had its roots in an incident on a nearby farm in May 1991, when a group of white farmers tried to evict black squatters. The farmers claimed that the squatters stole their sheep and cut down the trees for firewood. However, the squatters argued that they were born on the farm and regarded it as their home. They were moved to a black Homeland in 1978, but about 300 returned. Police opened fire on the farmers, wounding three.

When President de Klerk announced that he was going to address a Party rally in Ventersdorp (the home town of AWB leader Eugene Terre Blanche), the AWB vowed to stop him. The outcome was predictable: 2,000 exremists tried to storm the town hall where de Klerk was scheduled to speak. According to the police, several shots were fired by the extremists and the police were forced to fire back. The outcome was the death of three AWB supporters and injuries to 56 other people, including 7 policemen.

This first fatal clash between security forces and far right groups stunned the white community. At a news conference, Eugene Terre Blanche demanded that "De Klerk must give the white voters the opportunity to vote in an election. If he doesn't do that then there will be war."

'The Killing Fields of Natal'

The issue of 'black on black' violence initially in Natal where a virtual civil war is being fought between ANC/COSATU and Buthelezi's Inkatha has created dark storm clouds that threaten a peaceful future for South Africa. This 'war' began in Natal and then spread to the townships of the Transvaal. According to the ANC, 8,000 people have died in township violence since September 1984 and, despite numerous local and national truces, the killings continue. Mandela's plea "to take your guns, your knives and your pangas and throw them into the sea" has been ignored.

> "We praise all organisations which have fought to retain the dignity of our people. Although there are fundamental differences between us, we commend Inkatha for their demand over the years for the unbanning of the ANC and the release of political prisoners, as well as for their stand of refusing to participate in a negotiated settlement without the creation of the necessary climate. This stand of Inkatha has contributed in no small measure to making it difficult for the regime to implement successive schemes designed to perpetuate minority rule."
>
> Nelson Mandela, February 1990

Reasons for Escalation of Violence

1 The unbanning of black political organisations and the release of Nelson Mandela heightened black expections and sharpened rivalry between black political parties, especially Inkatha and the ANC/UDF. The conflict in the eastern Natal province was essentially a war among Zulus. Inkatha's support base was being eroded, with Zulu youth espousing the policies of the UDF and Zulu workers joining COSATU. The release of Mandela intensified the ANC campaign to destroy local government structures and organisations such as Inkatha. In February 1991, the ANC-aligned Civic Association of Southern Transvaal boasted that it had forced more than half of the remaining black town councillors in its area to resign. Although Mandela spoke in positive terms about Inkatha (see box above), he was advised not to meet with Buthelezi as this might bestow legitimacy on the Inkatha movement. An Inkatha spokesperson declared, "It must be put unequivocally to the ANC and its allies that their unwillingness to recognise the right of Inkatha to exist has become the principle factor contributing to ongoing black internecine conflict in South Africa."

2 The failure of the government and its law enforcement agencies to intervene or curtail the conflict contributed to the culture of violence. According to the ANC (and later admitted by the government), Inkatha was used as a "third force" to destabilise black opposition groups and to discredit the ANC.

The failure of the police to curb the violence in its early stages allowed the conflict to become self-generating. COSATU claims that if the security forces had prosecuted four or five of the known 'warlords' in 1988, this would have deterred their supporters. Evidence also supports the claim that the police have actively supported Inkatha's attacks. In one incident on 14 August 1990 in Thokoza, police in armoured vehicles followed a group of 1,000 armed Inkatha supporters and made no attempt to intervene as they attacked a hostel.

Moreover, the police, while pursuing a vigorous policy of searching for arms in UDF/ANC areas, failed to disarm Inkatha members. Even when 'warlords' have been taken into custody, they have been released on bail shortly afterwards to continue their orgy of destruction.

3 Criminal elements have created their own 'spheres of influence' and these 'warlords' have cloaked their criminal activities with the respectability of ideological action. Two powerful 'warlords', Shabalala and Jamile, hold or have held high office in Inkatha. Shabalala was acquitted in 1990 on charges of responsibility for the killing of several UDF youths.

THE SEARCH FOR PEACE

Numerous attempts have been made to end the carnage in Natal. On 29 January 1991, Mandela and Buthelezi signed a truce urging their supporters to lay down their arms. Nevertheless, the violence continued. In February, seventeen Inkatha supporters died in a bus ambush and in May, fifty squatters were murdered by Zulu migrant workers in the township of Kasigo.

The ANC was unimpressed by the government's show of concern. Mandela declared, "If only 100 Whites in this country had been killed through violence there would have been a revolt and the government would have been overthrown." In April 1991, the ANC issued the government with the following ultimatum (to be implemented on 9 May):

- Ban all weapons (including Zulu cultural weapons) at public rallies and marches.
- Dismiss the Minister of Law and Order and the Minister of Defence.
- Phase out single-sex migrant workers' hostels.
- Disband police counterinsurgency units.
- Ban the issuing of live ammunition to security forces assigned to crowd control.
- Establish an independent commission to investigate complaints about police conduct.

In an attempt to defuse the dispute, de Klerk met with Mandela on 9 May. The talks took place during the trial of Winnie Mandela (see box) and it was clear that the warmth established between the two leaders had decidedly cooled. The government agreed to upgrade single-sex hostels and turn some, but not all, of them into family homes. The President also favoured the setting up of a permanent Peace Commission, to be chaired by a judge, to investigate all incidents of violence and intimidation. Extra troops and police were to be drafted into the townships around Johannesburg, with all public meetings, except for religious and sporting activities, banned. However, on the issue of Zulu 'cultural weapons', the government was strangely reluctant to act. Dangerous weapons would be banned in 'unrest areas' but spears and 'ceremonial battle axes' were exempt, although the police would react immediately against any misuse of cultural weapons for criminal and noncultural purposes.

Peace Conference May 1991

The ANC was unhappy with de Klerk's limited concessions and in protest decided not to participate in a government-sponsored peace conference. The ANC boycott was supported by its allies, the SACP (Communist Party), COSATU, the South African Council of Churches, and by the militant black organisations PAC and AZAPO.

The Conference was used by the government as a valuable propaganda event. De Klerk, with the international

Viewpoints of Mangosuthu Buthelezi

on violence in Natal
"The UDF has said that it wants to destroy Inkatha. Also, the ANC has said in its broadcasts from Zambia that it wants to make this country ungovernable. It called for young people to band together and kill all those it termed 'collaborators', which included anyone who didn't accept its strategy of violence. The UDF and COSATU have also stated that they believe in making the country, the townships, ungovernable. You don't achieve that by playing marbles, but through violence. (1990)

on decentralised government
"Inkatha Freedom Party believes that government in the new South Africa should be stripped of the awesome powers that successive NP governments have built around Prime Ministers, State Presidents and Cabinets.

This implies that regional government must be made a lot stronger, either in a unitary state or in one or another form of federal or other democratic state. This means that regional government should exercise powers that are currently the sole preserve of central government." (1991)

on the state's role in the economy
"The debate in South Africa is no longer about free market capitalism versus Stalinist centralism. It is now about the correct market/state ratio within a mixed economy. This means that most parties - the NP, ANC and Inkatha Freedom Party included - recognise that the state has a central role to play in the economy of the new South Africa.

Inkatha Freedom Party places a high reliance upon the state fulfilling a number of roles. One is the classic liberal role of acting as a neutral referee, laying down the rules of the political and economic game and mediating in disputes.

The second is a more interventionist role, where the state acts to alleviate some of the worst aspects of the mass poverty that characterises this country.

The third is an active role in providing opportunities for the masses to uplift themselves. Inkatha FreedomParty believes economic policy should stress the crucial fact that without economic growth, redistributive policies are fairly meaningless. South Africa can only redistribute by growing, and to do this the state must ensure that economic opportunity is equalised for all. (1991)

(Extracts from an interview in *Leadership*, a South African publication)

Police watch from an armoured troop carrier as armed Inkatha supporters return to their hostels in Soweto - May 1991

community in mind, attacked the ANC and its supporters for their boycott. He declared, "the time has arrived for those who are dragging their feet and constantly finding excuses to come forward and make a contribution." However, de Klerk's moral ascendancy and stature as a man of integrity were about to be tarnished with the revelations about the covert actions of members of his Cabinet.

Inkathagate

In July 1991, Mandela's doubts about President de Klerk being "a man of integrity" were seemingly justified when covert activities by certain Cabinet Ministers were discovered. These proved that the government had made secret payments to Inkatha and supported Zulu violence against ANC members in the townships. De Klerk's ministers were guilty of the following underhand actions:

1. State funding of two Inkatha Freedom Party rallies in November 1989 and March 1990, which were followed by anti-ANC violence. The Foreign Minister, Pik Botha (who swore in June that his department had never financed Inkatha) had authorised payments of 250,000 Rand (£50,000).

2. Contributing 1.5 million Rand to the formation and running costs of Inkatha's United Workers' Union of South Africa (UWUSA).

3. Supporting 7 political parties during the Namibian elections in a bid to stop SWAPO winning. (See page 29.)

4. While no clear evidence of direct government involvement existed, claims were also made that a special military unit existed to carry out dirty tricks and acts of violence. This group was responsible for the September 1990 train massacre when 26 Blacks were shot and hacked to death. It was also claimed that the Army planned to manipulate the forthcoming elections in Angola to ensure victory for Jonas Savimbi. (See page 28.)

The scandal weakened President de Klerk's position and strengthened the ANC's claim that the government was carrying out a controlled campaign of violence in the townships to discredit and weaken the ANC. Moreover, the dirty tricks campaign during the Namibian election (which prevented SWAPO from winning an outright victory) was a test run for a similar operation to 'defeat' the ANC when South Africa's first post apartheid elections are held. The ANC declared that the scandal "completely rules out the government's suitability to serve as both referee and player in South Africa."

The scandal did most damage to Chief Buthelezi and his Inkatha Freedom Party. Buthelezi frantically denied that he knew of the secret payments, despite a senior policeman reporting that he was "very emotional and expressed extreme gratitude" for them. Buthelezi did not return the money and his personal assistant took the blame and resigned. Nevertheless, the government's open admission that it used Inkatha as a weapon to fight the ANC confirms Buthelezi's status as a puppet of Pretoria.

In response to the crisis, the government held a three day Cabinet conference to try to defuse the crisis. President de Klerk, in a television address to the nation, announced the following:

1. A cabinet reshuffle would take place, with the demotion of the two hardliners in his Cabinet, Adrian Volk, Minister of Law and Order and Magnus Malan, Defence Minister. (Both were replaced with committed reformers.)

2. While defending the financial support of Inkatha as being the legitimate act of a government facing a guerrilla war and international sanctions, all fundings of political organisations were to end, as would all secret projects which could be seen as being politically biased.

3. The government was not involved in fermenting violence in the townships: "We do not have a double agenda," stated de Klerk, "It is untrue that we have a strategy to disrupt our opponents ... Our hands are clean."

Mother of the Nation - Sister of Violence?

The conviction of Winnie Mandela for the kidnapping of four young people and for complicity in their brutal assault was a devastating blow for Nelson Mandela and for the integrity and unity of the ANC. In May 1991, the white judge called her "an unblushing liar" and sentenced her to a six-year jail sentence. Mrs Mandela was allowed out on bail and in July 1991 won permission to appeal against her conviction to the Appeal Court in Bloemfontein, the country's highest court. Even if she loses the appeal, it is doubtful if Winnie Mandela will ever serve her sentence, for by the time she has exhausted the legal wranglings, her husband might well be the next President of South Africa and she the First Lady.

Nevertheless, the trial highlighted the darker side of ANC activities. Significantly, Winnie Mandela displayed no remorse over the death of 14-year-old Stompie Seikei, who was killed by her chief bodyguard Jerry Richardson early in 1989, nor over the activities of her personal guard the 'Mandela United Football Team'. Her supporters argue that she is the victim of persecution for her relentless fight against white supremacy. Certainly, her record against apartheid is impressive. She married Nelson Mandela in May 1958 but they were separated in the early 1960s with Mandela's arrest and trial. With Nelson Mandela in jail, she contained her grief by continuing her husband's struggle. For this she was jailed on several occasions including a 17-month spell in detention in 1969 and 1970. She was later exiled to Brandford, a remote town in the Orange Free State, after becoming involved in the Soweto riots of 1976/77, and placed under a banning order. These restrictions were not lifted until July 1986, when Winnie Mandela returned to Soweto.

In the township unrest she firmly supported the 'Young Comrades' in their struggle to destroy the structures of apartheid and to punish those collaborating with the system. In a controversial speech she seemed to support the brutal excesses of the Young Comrades when she declared: "Together, hand in hand, with our boxes of matches and our necklaces, we shall liberate this country." The ANC leadership in exile repudiated this statement. In 1990 she was elected head of the ANC's Social Welfare Department, but she was defeated decisively in May 1991, in a secret ballot, for the leadership of the ANC Women's League.

9 The USA – A Nation of Minorities

The United States has often been referred to as a 'melting pot'. It is a nation with both black and white minorities and there are few places in the world which are not represented in America's population. America, the 'land of the free', the 'land of unlimited opportunity', has acted like a magnet to the world's poor and oppressed as well as to its adventurers and go-getters. Indeed, the vast majority of those who journeyed to America did so in an attempt to improve their lives and the prospects for their children. The 'American Dream' has given hope to countless millions over successive generations. During the latter part of the 19th and earlier part of the 20th centuries immigration rates were high - as many as 400,000 people per year flowed into the ports of America. In recent years, immigration rates have averaged 600,000 per annum.

Demands for Reform

The sheer numbers and diversity of people flocking into the USA created problems. As early as the 1920s, politicians called for restrictions to be placed on the numbers and types of immigrants coming into the country. Despite the fact that most Americans are descended from immigrants and that the country's wealth was created by them, immigration controls were introduced. Although initial immigration controls were based on legislation which tended to favour North Europeans, later legislation removed this discrimination. Since the 1960s, the pattern of immigration to the USA has changed substantially. In 1986 a total of 601,700 people were to make their new home in the United States. (see Figure 9.1)

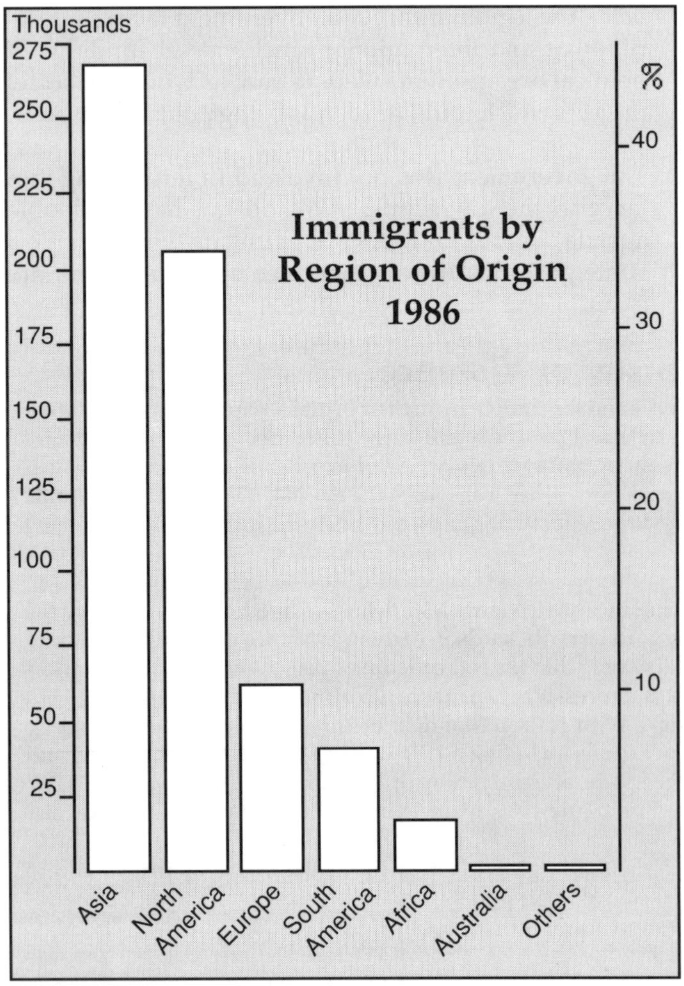

Figure 9.1

In recent years calls have been made for further reform, fuelled by developments along the American border with Mexico. For decades Mexicans moved across the border to work in the USA with very little opposition. The migrants either worked for a short time in the USA then returned to Mexico, or settled in the USA retaining Mexican citizenship or becoming naturalised Americans. The work they do is mostly in agriculture with a small number in manufacturing. By the late 1970s the authorities were becoming concerned by the increasing number of illegal immigrants crossing from Mexico. By the mid-1980s the Census Bureau estimated that as many as 500,000 'illegals' were entering the US each year, mostly over the border with Mexico. The Bureau also estimated that about 6million illegals were living in the USA in total. The social and economic impact of this massive illegal immigration was becoming increasingly evident. Racial tensions were raised as illegals pushed wage rates down and forced other minority groups onto the unemployment line.

After much debate in Congress about how to deal with the problem, agreement was finally reached and in 1986 the *Immigration and Control Act (IRCA)* was passed. This legislation attempted to gain control of the US border with Mexico by applying 'employer sanctions'. Up until 1986, employers were able to offer work to the illegals at very low wage rates. These employers had broken no law and were free from prosecution. The 1986 Act changed the position completely. The Act declared it illegal for US employers to hire people who were living in the country illegally. The Act also offered to illegal immigrants the chance to legalise their status by creating an amnesty. All illegal immigrants who had lived in the country continuously since before 31 January 1982 were given the opportunity to register for naturalisation. By 1989, 17 million illegals had registered under the Act.

Immigration and Government Policy

Immigration has been a problem for successive US governments. How were these people, coming as they did from a rich variety of cultures, customs and traditions, to be accommodated into American life? How were they to be integrated and assimilated into the mainstream? For some groups the problems would be greater than for others. While it can be said that the vast majority of immigrants deliberately set out to make the US their new home, the same cannot be said for Afro-Americans. They were an unwilling conscript slave labour force. As a result of this historical fact they have become the largest of the 'excluded' groups in American society - historically disadvantaged and oppressed.

Over the decades governments have tackled the problems associated with accommodating such a diverse mix of people in a variety of ways. Some administrations opted for a reduction in numbers through quota systems, while others used legislation on social/economic issues like education and employment as a method of harmonising the population. Sociologists have identified two main methods by which America has tried to deal with its multicultural population. These distinct approaches have become known as the Melting Pot Theory and the Salad Bowl Theory.

The Melting Pot

As the name suggests, society is likened to a great big pot containing a 'mixture' of different races, colours, religions, traditions and so on. This theory suggests that with time and government assistance, immigrant groups would be slowly 'integrated' into the pot, assimilated into the dominant culture. Given time, immigrant groups would come to see themselves as Americans rather than as Poles, Greeks or Mexicans living in America. It was argued that eventually immigrant groups would lose their differences and come to share the same hopes, expectations and values as all other Americans. This theory was put into practice by a variety of agencies promoting the American way of life - the media and the education service to name but two. The melting pot would produce American citizens.

The basics of this theory greatly influenced Ronald Reagan and his approach to race relations. On becoming President of the USA in 1980, Reagan quickly moved to create a 'colourblind society' which emphasised the virtues of fair play and equal opportunity regardless of race or colour. To Reagan, the values enshrined in the 'American Dream' should transcend all race or colour distinctions.

Critics of this approach to race relations argue that it is far too idealistic and makes too many assumptions. Indeed, it has been stated that 'colourblind' theorists have vastly overestimated the US's ability to incorporate differences. Moreover, governments should not expect or encourage people to give up their own cultures in preference to another. People would not wish to abandon their customs, culture and traditions and should not be made to feel guilty about holding on to them. A melting pot, apart from being totally unrealistic, would potentially harm the richness of society by destroying minority cultures. Integration policies would only create more problems than they could solve and would leave many people anxious and afraid, torn between their traditional and new cultures. Indeed for many, the 1980s clearly demonstrated that the theories of assimilation and incorporation failed. The tremendous upsurge in political minority interest groups, and the corresponding white backlash, signals a returning crisis in race relations in the USA. (See Chapter13)

The Salad Bowl

Unlike the melting pot which attempts to 'blend' cultures and people together, the salad bowl describes a society in which the government encourages different peoples with differing cultures, customs, language and tradition to coexist side by side in harmony, without having to sacrifice their cultural heritage. In many respects the salad bowl confronts melting pot theories. Would not minority groups, threatened by a swamping of their cultures by the dominant group in society, retreat further into their own heritage, becoming isolated and apart from the wider society? Indeed, if heritage is protected and advanced through the media and the education process, would not a sense of history, dignity and pride be instilled into young people? Social commentators argue that it was the absence of such an approach to race relations which prompted the move towards extremism and the rise of black power witnessed in the mid-1960s. (See page 64) Black youth saw in black nationalism and Black Power a vision of independence and self-identity in an antagonistic, hostile white society. Black self-assertion sloganised by 'Black is beautiful' captured the imagination of many young Blacks caught in the culture clash.

Social policies resulting from coexistence theories have caused much resentment. Many white minority groups have voiced concerns about education policy which promotes Afro-American history, or media developments which have created television channels which target a Spanish-speaking audience. Coexistence or salad bowl policies can often lead to misunderstanding between immigrant groups and the wider society. As with the melting pot policies, many people see a failure in coexistence policies. A new mood of conservatism was to emerge in America in the 1980s which had little time for policies which promoted culture or heritage other than the dominant one. This will be discussed more fully in Chapter13.

POPULATION DISTRIBUTION

In 1988 the population of the US totalled 245,110,000. The breakdown of that total is shown in table 9.1.

US Population by Race, 1988 (millions)

	1988	1980 - 1988 % Change
White	203.8	+5.7
Black	29.3	+11.4
Hispanic	19.4	+30.9
Other	7.9	+ 52.2

Table 9.1 Source: *Department of Commerce, Bureau of the Census*

The Black Population

In 1988 the black population of the USA totalled 29,333,000 - an increase of approximately 11% since 1980. The black population is growing much faster than the white population and a much higher proportion (33%) is below the age of 18.

The regional distribution of the black population is shown in Table 9.2. In 1988 the proportion of the total black population living in the South was 56% - up 3% from 1980. This reflects a change in the long term pattern of Blacks moving out of the South. It is worth remembering that 20% of the South's total population is Black.

Distribution of Population by Region and Race 1980-1988 (%)

	1980	1988
South	52.2 (18.4)	55.9 (19.9)
North & West	47.8 (8.3)	44.1 (8.2)
Northeast	18.6 (10.0)	16.5 (9.8)
Midwest	20.5 (9.2)	19.1 (9.4)
West	8.8 (5.3)	8.5 (5.0)

(Figures in brackets show Blacks as a % of total populations in each region.)

Table 9.2 Source: Department of Commerce, Bureau of the Census.

In 1980, twelve States had a black population of greater than one million; ten years later in 1990 that figure had risen to sixteen. The States with the highest proportion of Blacks are Mississippi with 36% and Louisiana with 31%; 69% of the District of Columbia's population is Black.

10 Towards Reform

In 1968 the Kerner Commission stated that American society "was moving rapidly towards two societies - one black, one white, separate and unequal." From where the Commission was standing, this was probably true. Apartheid in all its forms, social, political and economic, was very much a part of American life. However, a very brief look into American history shows us that America has *always* been two separate and unequal societies - a society for Whites and a society for Blacks. Indeed, the founding fathers, when drafting the Constitution, could not readily agree upon the status of Blacks for the purposes of population statistics or taxation.

> "Because slaves were considered property (chattels) and not persons the northern states refused to have them included in the 'population' of the South when computing representation among the states. On the other hand they insisted that they all be counted in computing the taxes for these states. The South took the opposite view whereupon both sides agreed, after a long stalemate that five slaves would be counted as three persons for both representation and taxation."
> (Milton D Morris *The Politics of Black America*)

The agreement became known as the 'Three-fifths Compromise' and inculcated into Blacks a sense of lower status, and into Whites a sense of superiority. From the very beginning, white supremacy has been deeply ingrained into the cultural heritage of white Americans. More than any other modern nation in the world, with the exception of South Africa, the United States developed with a unique social/economic structure and political system that were both racist and capitalist.

The Blacks who were not slaves, ie. the 'free Blacks' did not find themselves in a particularly advantageous position. From the 18th century onwards, free Blacks found it extremely difficult, if not impossible, to exercise the right to vote. In the 17th century a few southern states allowed some Blacks to vote, but by the end of the 18th century no southern state allowed any Black the right to vote. This discrimination was not restricted to the South. In the 19th century many northern states also passed laws preventing Blacks from voting. Indeed, some went even further, passing legislation that outlawed Blacks from certain jobs or from buying and selling property.

Contrary to popular myth, the Civil War (1861-1865) was not waged by the white North to abolish slavery, but to exert Northern Federal authority. Racism was as rampant in the North as it was in the South. Throughout the war, Blacks in the North experienced many atrocities - black homes were burned; lynchings, and looting of black property were commonplace.

During the Civil War many black Americans - approximately 190,000 - enlisted in the Union Army. They fought and died for the Union, for only half the pay of the white soldiers. Limited freedoms were given to the Blacks with the passing of the Thirteenth Amendment in 1865. In point of fact, the period following the Civil War (1863-1877) was to become known as the Reconstruction era. During this time Congress passed a series of civil rights measures, of which the last, the *Civil Rights Act* of 1875, was the strongest. The Reconstruction era witnessed a significant move forward in black social, economic and political status. The gains made by Blacks in the southern states were, to a lesser degree, mirrored in the North. However, this postwar trend towards equality for Black Americans was short-lived. In the South the modest gains made by the Blacks were deeply resented by certain sections of the white population. While Blacks were striving for their political rights a whole series of white racist vigilante groups were forming. These groups, such as the Ku Klux Klan and the Knights of the White Camelia, led organised terror campaigns in the early 1870s designed to intimidate black voters and elected officials.

The period of Reconstruction was now over. In the presidential election of 1876 the Republicans only secured a narrow victory by pledging to end civil rights measures and to restore white supremacy in the South. The Supreme Court, in 1883, overruled the Civil Rights Act of 1875, declaring it to be unconstitutional. After 1883 the atmosphere was ripe for the rise of segregation and of 'Jim Crow' laws designed to give legal recognition to discrimination. Segregation, the separation of black and white Americans by law, became the new way of life in the southern states. The principle of 'separate but equal' had arrived. 'Jim Crow' was accompanied by lynchings and terror for the Blacks. In 1896 the Supreme Court took the final step and put its seal of approval on segregation. In June 1892, Homer Adolph Plessy bought a ticket in New Orleans, boarded an East Louisiana railroad train, and took his seat - in a coach set aside for Whites. He was asked to move, refused, and was promptly arrested. Plessy was held to be in breach of Louisiana State Law which required separate but equal accommodation for black and white passengers. Plessy and his supporters took their case to the Supreme Court, arguing that Louisiana was in breach of the Fourteenth Amendment (which guaranteed Blacks civil rights). The Supreme Court did not agree and supported Louisiana State Law. The doctrine of separate but equal was now the law of the land and was to remain so until 1954. Following this ruling many states in the South began to rewrite their constitutions by excluding Blacks from the political process. Measures included:

1 Denying Blacks the right to vote. For example, in 1900 in Alabama 180,000 Blacks were eligible to vote; two years later in 1902 this figure was down to 3000.
2 Extra-legal means. Between 1882 and 1903, 2,060 Blacks were lynched in the United States. Some of the victims were children and pregnant women; many were burned at the stake.

The Move Northwards

'Jim Crow' had succeeded. The South was far too inhospitable for many Blacks. For those Blacks who dreamed of equality of opportunity the South was now a lost cause; their only hope lay in a move to the North. The great exodus from the South to the North and Northeast had started. (See Table 10.1)

The move North was dramatic. In 1940, 22% of all Blacks lived in the North compared to 10% in 1910. The migration from rural South to urban Northeast and Midwest, and the

The Black Move to the North	
Period	**Numbers Moving North**
1900 - 1910	170,000
1910 - 1920	454,000
1920 - 1930	749,000
1930 - 1940	349,000
1940 - 1950	1,599,000

Black Population in Selected States		
	1910	**1940**
New York	134,000	571,000
Illinois	109,000	387,000
Pennsylvania	194,000	470,000

Table 10.1

growth of a black urban working class brought many improvements in health care, education, economic and political life to many millions of black Americans. However, there was still a very substantial gap between the social and economic status of Whites and Blacks. Further, the move North by millions of Blacks was putting strains on the community. Further evidence of racial hatred was to emerge. In the 'Red Summer' of 1919, 70 Blacks were lynched, including 10 soldiers who had fought in Germany. In the Chicago Race Riot of the same year, 38 Blacks were killed and 537 were injured. Nearly 1,000 black families were burned out of their homes. Throughout this carnage the Federal Government did very little. State governments, meanwhile, increased segregation laws even further.

- South Carolina passed legislation that made it illegal for black and white textile workers to use the same doorways, bathrooms or canteens. Many cities passed laws prohibiting Blacks from using public parks.
- In 1926, Atlanta banned black barbers from cutting the hair of white children and women.
- In 1930 the city governors of Birmingham, Alabama, made it unlawful for Whites and Blacks to sit at the same table or to play dominoes or checkers with each other.

Segregation was entering into all parts of life. Blacks were no longer allowed to sit in the same restaurants, sit in the same theatres or use the same taxis as Whites. Segregation was inevitably backed up with force - apartheid in its fullest, most comprehensive form.

BLACK AMERICA 1945-1960

Postwar America found herself in a dilemma - she had vehemently opposed fascism in Europe but still practised apartheid at home. Blacks and an increasing number of white liberals had come back from the war in Europe and the Far East with a firm desire to change America's racist society. Three million black Americans had registered for service in World War II. They had fought against fascism (in segregated units), many had died, many were maimed for life. Those who returned had no desire to assume the role of second-class citizens. As a result of their involvement in the war and the efforts of the National Association for the Advancement of Coloured People (NAACP), Blacks began to make considerable economic gains. In addition, Blacks as a political force began to exert more leverage on both state and national affairs. By 1945 an increasing number of white Americans, especially in the North, were alerted to the fact that racial segregation would have to be modified, if not scrapped altogether.

In the years after World War II Blacks began to make decisive inroads into the political system. By 1945 there were approximately 30 Blacks serving in the state legislatures in northeastern states. Throughout the country Blacks were beginning to flex their political muscles. By 1947, 12% of all Blacks of voting age in the South had registered, up from only 2% in 1940. Segregationist legislation started to be dismantled. In many northern states racial discrimination in employment was outlawed. Gains were being made in economic status also - black membership in trade unions was rising as was the level of black incomes. This growing social and economic influence of the black working and middle classes had profound political effects. As a growing political force, they could no longer be ignored by either the Democratic or Republican Parties.

The period 1945-1954 was one of slow progress for Blacks in America. Black politics and black politicians made steady but discreet gains. It was not a period of street demonstrations, sit-ins or bus boycotts - these were soon to follow. America was gripped by another quite different phenomenon - the McCarthy 'witch hunts'. The McCarthy era was a period of tremendous anti-communist activity and so it was very difficult for black political leaders to launch a programme of radical social reform. Nevertheless, without much fuss or publicity, a whole series of black political groups began forming throughout the country. Many, taking their lead from the Congress of Racial Equality (CORE), founded a few years earlier in 1942, tested the desegregation laws in many Southern States, establishing a pattern of civil rights protest that would be repeated more effectively in the Freedom Ride movement of the 1960s.

Meanwhile, the reaction to these political gains by Blacks was surfacing once more in the South. By the early 1950s the number of registered black southern voters had risen to 1.2 million - far too high for the white racists. Brutal terror campaigns were mounted to dissuade more Blacks from registering and voting. The Senator of Mississippi publicly boasted that only 1500 out of 500,000 black potential voters were registered in his state. "The best way to keep a nigger away from a white primary is to see him the night before," the Senator declared. Southern registrars went to great lengths to devise tests to see whether Blacks were 'literate' enough to vote. One white registrar in Mississippi asked potential black voters the question: "How many bubbles are in a bar of soap?" As white racism grew more open, little was done by the Federal Government to protect the Blacks. The civil rights movement, at least in the South, had ground to a halt.

The Bus Boycotts

On a December evening in 1955, Rosa Parks, a 43-year-old black seamstress, boarded a public bus in Montgomery, Alabama, as she did every day to return from her job in a town centre department store. When several Whites got on at the next bus stop, the driver asked the black passengers near the front of the bus to give up their seats to the Whites and move to the rear. Several black passengers did as they were asked; Rosa Parks did not. The police were called and Rosa Parks was arrested and fined for sitting in the 'Whites only' section of the bus. Disgusted by this and other similar events, black civic leaders organised the black population into a 'bus boycott' - a boycott that was to catch the imagination of people all over the world. In a remarkable year-long protest, a young black doctor of divinity was to make his name, the Reverend Martin Luther King. Throughout 1956, approximately 95% of Montgomery's Blacks refused to use the buses, despite frequent attempts by police and local politicians to 'tempt' them back. During the boycott King was jailed and his home was bombed, but he persistently urged Blacks to use nonviolent protest tactics. He won. The boycott ended in November 1956 as a result of a Supreme Court ruling outlawing segregation on Montgomery buses. Bus boycotts as a tactic of direct nonviolent protest quickly spread throughout the South. Overnight, King became the charismatic moral and political leader of millions of black people. An apostle of nonviolence, he gave confidence to Blacks all over America to demand their civil rights. His group, the Southern Christian Leadership Council (SCLC), financed other nonviolent groups. A whole new movement had been started. One such group, the Student Nonviolent Coordinating Committee (SNCC), quickly organised young militant black reformers who believed that "equality was important enough to suffer for". The nonviolent movement had started to grow.

The Sit-ins

On Monday 1 February 1960, a group of young black college students went into Woolworth's in Greensboro, North Carolina. They sat down at the lunch counter and asked politely for cups of coffee. The manager told them he could not serve Blacks and asked them to leave. They refused and were eventually arrested by the police. More young Blacks came the following day and the day after that - the pattern was always the same. By the end of the week the store was filled with black and white youths. The former sat at the counter while the Whites waved Confederate flags and splattered them with ketchup and mustard. The sit-in movement was now established. By mid-April, it had spread throughout the South taking various forms: stand-ins at theatres refusing to sell tickets to Blacks, wade-ins at segregated pools and beaches and pray-ins at segregated churches. Night after night American TV viewers saw films of young Blacks being dragged out of cafes and restaurants. A major force within the larger civil rights movement was under way.

The Freedom Rides

By April 1960, over 50,000 students, both black and white, had joined the sit-in movement. By 1961 the sit-in technique had been adapted to test segregation on interstate buses, trains and at stations. Black and white 'Freedom Riders' travelled into Alabama, where they were savagely beaten, slashed with chains and knives and stoned by groups of white racists. In spite of this violence the Freedom Riders succeeded in publicising the fact that segregation on interstate transport was still a reality, despite being supposedly outlawed by the Supreme Court a year earlier.

Education

In addition to drawing attention to the segregation of public places, attention was now being focused on schools. Black parents, with the help of civil rights lawyers, were soon to make a constitutional breakthrough in challenging the legality of segregated public schooling. In 1954, after two years of legal wrangling, the Supreme Court in the 'Brown v Topeka Board of Education' hearing declared that segregated education had no place in the American educational system. (See page 67)

Civil Rights Acts, 1957 and 1960

The *Civil Rights Act* of 1957, designed to protect the existing rights of Blacks, established a Commission on Civil Rights empowered to investigate complaints by Blacks concerning voting rights infringements. The Act also gave authority to the Justice Department, enabling it to take action against any states found to be 'advancing discrimination'. The Act did little to please black people. In an effort to push it through a fairly hostile Congress, its supporters were forced to 'tone it down'. As a result it did little to protect black voters in the Deep South.

The *Civil Rights Act* of 1960 made provision for federal voting referees to enrol voters where local officials had proved to be obstructive or discriminatory. Like the 1957 Act, this one had also been modified in order to gain passage through Congress - the Southern States had fiercely opposed it .

Although both of these laws proved to be of limited practical value to Blacks, they were, nevertheless, very significant. The first such Civil Rights legislation to be passed since 1875, they were to pave the way for much more comprehensive and meaningful legislation. The legislative breakthrough had occurred at last.

'THE FRUITS OF NONVIOLENCE'

> "When the Constitution said all men are created equal, it wasn't talking about niggers."
> *JB Stoner (white racist leader)*

> "We will soon wear you down by our capacity to suffer." *Dr Martin Luther King*

The 1960s were to prove to be turbulent times for race relations - a rebirth in political awareness among Blacks; violent white reaction and violence in cities all over America. The early 1960s witnessed a tremendous increase in the number of black activist groups involved in promoting the message of equality of opportunity. The Congress of Racial Equality (CORE), almost defunct in 1959, was reconstituted and almost immediately began campaigning actively in the desegregation campaign. In addition, local groups of the SNCC and the National Association for the Advancement of Coloured People (NAACP) were attracting more and more young people to the cause. Idealism, courage and determination were evident. The SNCC was very active in promoting voter registration drives, believing that if anything was to change, the structure of power had to be altered. The successes of the black activist groups in the South gave Blacks in the North new hope and determination. Slowly but steadily CORE chapters were established in northern cities and Blacks were organised to protest over issues such as slum housing and police brutality. As its attention turned northwards CORE began to question its strategy - the question of nonviolent protest was critically assessed. The problems facing Blacks in northern cities, somewhat different from those of the South, were to encourage a completely different approach to the struggle for civil rights.

For many Blacks in northern cities the important question was economic equality with Whites. The economic position of Blacks was fairly poor; the difference in income between White and Black was increasing dramatically. As the economic situation worsened, Blacks began to demand economic reforms as part of the overall civil rights reforms. It was little comfort to Blacks to sit in formerly 'white only' seats in cafes and buses when they were still unemployed.

Birmingham, Washington and the 'Dream'

In many ways the peak of the desegregation movement was reached in 1963. Over three years the movement had grown from a small-scale demonstration at a lunch counter to the largest mass civil rights movement of the 20th century. Two events were about to take place that would have a significant influence on the direction the civil rights movement would take.

For decades, Birmingham had been recognised as the 'citadel of white supremacy'. There were few Blacks who had managed to escape the influence of white terrorism in its many shapes and forms, either racist institutions or racist 'vigilante' groups. From county hall to the sheriff's office, racism was rife. Throughout the 1950s Blacks had seen their homes, their clubs and their churches firebombed by white racist groups. Every aspect of life in Birmingham was segregated and Blacks were expected to know their place.

In the Spring of 1963, Dr King and other black leaders organised a mass campaign protesting against segregation in Birmingham, Alabama. Sit-ins were held at department stores and restaurants and marches on the town centre were planned. The Birmingham police, led by their Chief, Eugene 'Bull' Corner, attempted to stop the campaign by arresting Dr King and his associates. Weeks later, in protest at the arrests, a children's march was organised involving 6,000 black schoolchildren. As they marched, the children, fired with enthusiasm, sang 'We Shall Overcome'. Before a national television audience, the Birmingham police let loose vicious police dogs on the children as they knelt down to pray; 1,000 children were arrested and jailed. Police used fire hoses, clubs and electric cattle-prods against women and children. As these television pictures were released nationally and internationally, America and the rest of the world were repulsed by the spectacle of American racism and so-called white democracy. The events at Birmingham prompted King to write his *Letter from Birmingham Jail* in which he prompted greater nonviolent direct action to force society to examine its conscience on the issue of civil rights.

The violence in Birmingham and other southern cities continued throughout the summer. Protests were mounting across the country demanding that the President (Kennedy) deal with the racist southern cities. Protest marches were organised in cities such as San Francisco and Detroit expressing solidarity with Birmingham Blacks; thousands of telegrams demanding action were received by the President. Kennedy finally took action. He ordered desegregation, warning the State politicians that he would enforce his orders with Federal troops if necessary. In addition, Kennedy pledged that he would deliver a strong civil rights bill that would include a section outlawing discrimination in public places. Almost overnight Kennedy became a powerful friend of civil rights.

In late August 1963, Dr King gave the keynote speech to a massive biracial audience of some 200,000 in the centre of Washington DC. The nationally televised, orderly demonstration had an extremely powerful effect on the nation. However, even more powerful were the words of Dr King, who voiced the vision of what America could and might become. The speech, with its recurrent line "I have a Dream", was well received by a predominantly white television audience who thought King to be an eminently reasonable and admirable spokesperson for civil rights. King, however, was not quite so well received in many black quarters. Many black nationalists targeted King and

The Civil Rights Act, 1964

It was during the 'long hot summer' of 1963 that President Kennedy put forward his proposals for a comprehensive civil rights bill. Five days after the Kennedy assassination, President Johnson urged Congress to pass the civil rights legislation as a memorial to his predecessor. After much heated debate in which southern politicians tried to 'talk it out', the bill received the President's signature to become the *Civil Rights Act*. The main provisions of the Act were designed to:-

1 Prohibit racial or religious discrimination in public places which affected interstate commerce including hotels, motels, restaurants, cafeterias, gas stations, cinemas, theatres, and sports arenas.
2 Prohibit discrimination because of race, colour, sex, religion, or national origin by employers or labour unions.
3 Bar voting registrars from adopting different standards for white and black applicants.
4 Allow the Attorney General to take action to enforce desegregation of public places; and to allow individuals to sue for their rights under the Act.
5 Permit Federal Government to hold back the flow of funds to public or private programmes that practised discrimination.
6 Give an extension to the Civil Rights Commission; create a community relations service to settle racial disputes and an Equal Employment Opportunity Commission to enforce the fair employment section of the Act.

The Civil Rights Act, 1968

In this Act, Congress attempted to deal with segregation in housing, both public and private. It also provided criminal penalties for injuring or interfering with civil rights workers or any person lawfully exercising his or her civil rights. The Act also made it a federal offence to cross state lines with intent to incite a riot.

other nonviolent black leaders with personal and even physical abuse. Malcolm X, one of the black nationalist leaders, stated that the event at Washington was nothing but a "farce". For many black nationalists, the 'Dream' at Washington was proof that nothing would happen to advance equality for Blacks as long as their protest was nonviolent. However, 'reason' and 'right' seemed to triumph. President Johnson, in signing the 1964 Civil Rights Bill, committed his administration to "the full assimilation of Negroes into American Life".

THE URBAN RIOTS

Even as the major civil rights laws of the mid-to late-1960s were taking effect, black protest in America was entering a new phase. By 1965 population movement, the migration of Blacks from the South to the cities of the North, combined with the movement of Whites from the inner cities to the suburbs, had created numerous black urban ghettos. For many black slum dwellers the high hopes raised by the civil rights movement and the civil rights laws had brought no visible benefits. Frustration, poverty, poor housing, high infant mortality rates, disease, rat infestation and poor education continued to be the hallmarks of ghetto life. It was predicted that nonviolent direct action, a tactic of protest used effectively in the South, would have little appeal in the northern ghetto. These predictions were to prove correct. In the spring and summer months of 1964, 1965, 1966, 1967 and 1968 massive black rebellions swept across almost every major US city in the Northeast, Midwest and California.

"Burn, Baby, Burn"

On the night of 11 August 1965 Los Angeles was sweltering in a heatwave. In the Watts district of the city a white highway patrolman stopped a young black driver for speeding and arrested him. A crowd gathered, police reinforcements arrived, trouble broke out. By the time the police had left, tempers in the city's black ghetto were running high. Two days after the incident the place erupted - arson, looting and shooting on many streets. The Watts riots had begun. The Watts riots resulted in $40 million damage to private property, 34 people being killed and many hundreds injured. Watts was followed by disorders in Chicago and Cleveland in 1966 and by even more destructive riots in Newark and Detroit in 1967. Federal authorities ordered 15,000 state police and National Guardsmen into Detroit to quell the riot. However, before the order was given 43 people were killed; almost 2,000 were injured; 3,000 white-owned ghetto businesses were looted, 1,500 of which were then gutted by fire; 14 square miles of Detroit's inner city were destroyed by fire; 5,000 black people were left homeless. Outbreaks occurred in Washington and in more than one hundred other cities after the assassination of Martin Luther King in 1968. A total of 14,000 federal troops were sent to Washington, where rioters had started fires only blocks away from the White House. For twelve days armed troops occupied the capital of the USA. The totals for death and destruction were enormous. Between 1964 and 1972, 250 people died, 10,000 had serious injuries, 60,000 were arrested and damages and costs ran to billions of dollars. Politicians were at a loss to explain the scale of the revolt. During the 1967 Detroit Riot, President Johnson went on nationwide TV appealing for calm, while announcing that he was setting up a National Advisory Commission on Civil Disorders. The Kerner Commission reported in March 1968, "White racism is essentially responsible for the explosive mixture which has been accumulating in our cities since the end of World War II." To tackle these problems, the Commission recommended a huge national effort to eliminate the racial barriers in employment, education and housing. It urged a massive job creation programme setting goals for 2 million new jobs in three years. The findings and the recommendations of the Commission were extremely controversial - many Americans took exception to the statements on white racism. However, black protest had not finished. By this time black nationalism seemed a much brighter prospect to those who survived on a day-to-day basis in the northern ghettos.

The Rise of Black Power

On 5 June 1966, James Meredith, the first black student to attend the University of Mississippi, began a solo march from Memphis to Jackson protesting at the denial of civil rights in the South. Within hours of setting off, Meredith lay bleeding, the victim of a shotgun attack. On hearing news of this attack Stokely Carmichael, a former SNCC worker, and others promptly resumed the march in Meredith's place. As the march progressed and the numbers began to swell the slogan 'Black Power' was heard among the marchers - the 'movement' was born. Two years later one other event was to push the nonviolence campaign further into the background. On 4 April 1968 in Memphis, Tennessee, Martin Luther King was assassinated. Blacks across the country, even the militants, felt a tremendous loss. Martin Luther King's assassination was further proof to many black nationalists that White America had no intention of solving racial conflict nonviolently.

By 1968 Black Power had become the dominant philosophy among the majority of black youths and the black working class. Many different interpretations were offered as to what Black Power actually meant and indeed the history of black nationalism goes back into the 19th century. More recently, however, black nationalism was popularised by an extremely charismatic black spokesperson - Malcolm Little, known better as Malcolm X. He was a Black Muslim who had put forward passionate nationalist arguments a decade earlier. "We who are Muslims, followers of Elijah Muhammad," he explained, "don't think that an integrated cup of coffee is sufficient payment for 310 years of slavery."

One of the disturbing consequences of the 1964 Civil Rights Act was the alarming increase in violence against Blacks across southern states. As President Johnson and the Democratic Party threw their respective weights behind desegregation, white southern democrats left the movement in their thousands. At the same time a group of Republicans, preaching open racist policies, began to make considerable gains in both local and national elections. Those politicians who remained within the Democratic Party adopted positions on the extreme right. Two such politicians, George Wallace and Lester Maddox, moved northwards advocating anti-communist and anti-black policies thus attracting more and more support while fuelling more racial violence. Racist attacks were happening on an increasing scale in many southern states. SNCC and CORE activists continually protested that voting rights and desegregation were not enough - the violence against

Black Power

Black power had different meanings for different people, but for the Black Panthers it embraced the following:-

Politically - it suggested to some that black Americans should exercise control over their own communities, both in the urban ghettos of the North and the rural areas of the South.
Economically - Black power was linked to the creation of independent, black-owned and black-operated businesses.
Spiritually - Black power meant racial pride and dignity, giving rise to slogans such as 'Black is Beautiful' and 'Soul'.

Taking their lead from their assassinated spiritual leader, Malcolm X, the Black Panthers put forward their 'Ten Point Programme'.

- We want freedom. We want power to determine the destiny of our black community.
- We want full employment for our people.
- We want an end to the robbery of our black community by the white man.
- We want decent housing.
- We want education for our people. We want education that teaches us our true history and our role in present day society.
- We want all black men to be exempt from military service.
- We want an immediate end to police brutality and murder of black people.
- We want freedom for all black men held in American jails.
- When black people are brought to trial let them be tried in a court with a jury of black people.
- We want land, bread, housing, education, clothing, justice and peace.

Blacks had to stop. As time went by and the Federal Government showed no signs of dealing with the racist violence, the nonviolence movement began to reassess its position. Soon, the SNCC and CORE would be very close to renouncing their commitment to nonviolent protest - black nationalism was beginning to take a much firmer hold. (See Table 10.2) At this point an extremely articulate voice for black nationalism was emerging. Stokely Carmichael, along with others, had formed a much more militant, all-black political group. The group became known as the Black Panthers. Carmichael, a fiery speaker, had got into the habit of carrying a loaded gun for protection - others soon followed his example. The move from nonviolence was almost complete.

By the late 1960s, the Black Panthers had become the most influential of the nationalist organisations in the USA. The shift from nonviolent confrontation to Black Power and black militancy marked a major turning point in the civil rights movement. White liberals and black moderates stood aghast as the armed clashes between police officers and black activists increased in both frequency and intensity. In 1969 alone, 27 Black Panthers were shot dead by the police, with over 700 arrested.

The peak of black nationalist influence came in 1972. As the number of black politicians began to increase, a move was made to try and organise a "united voice for Black America". This move culminated in the Gary Convention of March 1972 - the largest black political convention in US history. At that point the nationalist voice was the loudest. However, this was not to last for long. By the mid-1970s, the black nationalist momentum had dramatically slowed down. There were various reasons for this:

- many Blacks looked towards the political process as the way in which both economic and social equality could be gained;
- most of the racist white segregationist politicians had either been removed from office or had toned down their opposition to desegregation;
- affirmative action programmes had brought tens of thousands of Blacks into middle-class jobs in both the public and private sectors;
- since Blacks were making increasing inroads into local and national politics, violence was becoming a redundant option.

The Presidential election of 1976 firmly put the lid on Black nationalism as a force in black politics. The victory of Carter (much aided by the black vote) gave Blacks new hope that federal money would be made available for inner city development, housing projects, new schools and increased social services. Blacks were now retreating from violent confrontation and instead were relying on electoral politics.

Changes in Black Attitudes toward Violent and Nonviolent Protest, 1968-71

	1968 (%)	1971 (%)
Best way to gain rights		
Laws and persuasion	33.6	41.0
Nonviolent protest	60.0	47.4
Violence	6.4	11.4
If laws, persuasion and nonviolent protest don't work, use violence?		
Yes	23.5	44.4
No	76.6	55.7

Table 10.2
Source: H Schuman and S Hatchett, *Black Racial Attitudes*, Michigan Institute for Social Research, 1974.

11 CIVIL RIGHTS IN ACTION

As has already been stated, the demise of Black Power was due in part to the development of affirmative action programmes. Extremely controversial, these programmes were to introduce tens of thousands of Blacks and other minorities into occupations and an educational system which previously had been closed to them. To many Blacks, affirmative action or positive discrimination was the real, meaningful part of civil rights legislation - words were translated into actions.

EMPLOYMENT

The Civil Rights Act of 1964 could not have been clearer: discrimination and segregation should play no part in American society, the Constitution was to be 'colour blind'. Affirmative action programmes would do just this - end discrimination in employment and segregation in education. However, there is often a difference between how a law is intended to work and how it *actually* works. It is one thing to talk about 'fair and equal opportunity', but how do you make sure that the law is carried out? How do you ensure equal opportunities for all? It was clear that the government initially seemed unsure as the law was applied in a rather haphazard fashion. During the 1970s though, the government adopted a much more consistent approach to applying and enforcing the legislation. Firms whichpreviously ignored the legislation found that they could do so no longer. Government agencies such as the Equal Opportunities Commission (EOC) and the Office of Federal Contract Compliance (OFCC) were given the authority to decide whether a firm was in breach of the law or not. These agencies now had the power to require firms to state their employment policies, the number of black people on the payroll and their employment status. If firms were found to have too few people from minority groups either on their payroll or in promoted positions, the agencies had the power to take direct action such as imposing heavy fines or taking away government contracts. It was now up to employers to demonstrate that they were providing equal opportunities.

Affirmative Action - Was It Needed?

As we have already noted, the 1964 Civil Rights Act was passed against a background of Southern hostility. Critics of affirmative action were not, however, confined to the South. Many Americans believed that to establish quotas and give preferential treatment was, in itself, discriminatory, indeed unconstitutional. Why, then, was such a controversial policy pursued - a policy which discriminated positively in favour of certain sections of society? Affirmative action was (and to an extent still is) justified on the grounds that it attempts to undo the inequality of opportunity created by generations of discrimination. Certainly, discrimination was rife in employment and it was often said that America had a 'dual' employment system with two separate job markets: one for Whites and one for non-Whites, very separate and very unequal.

Discrimination in employment was found to take many forms, some direct and some less direct. Examples of more blatant or direct discrimination included:

- employers refusing to employ suitably qualified members of ethnic minority groups for jobs advertised, because of the colour of their skin;
- employers deliberately bypassing suitably qualified employees for promotion for the same reason;
- trade unions or professional associations refusing membership to workers from ethnic minority groups where entry to a job or profession was dependent on that membership.

Examples of less obvious but equally damaging discriminatory practices were:

- financial institutions such as banks refusing to lend

Measuring Discrimination

Affirmative action programmes, pursued vigorously by administrations during the 1970s, placed employers in an entirely new situation. For the first time, employers found themselves having to monitor who they employed and who they promoted, by race. Government agencies came down hard on those firms judged to be implementing discriminatory employment policies. Firms were now involved in the business of 'quotas', 'targets' and 'preference hirings'.

Quotas: Firms were given a specific number or percentage of jobs to be filled by minorities at each skill level.

Example: In 1974, a Federal District Judge ruled that the city of Boston should in future hire one black for every white teacher until Blacks formed 20% of the teaching force.

Targets: Firms were set specific targets in terms of numbers or percentages of minorities to be employed. Failure to meet target dates would result in stiff penalties.

Example: In 1974 the city of Atlanta, Georgia, set firms minority targets of 35%. In the same year a headline in the *New York Times* read, "Truckers Pledge Minority Hirings - 7 Big Companies, Faced by Government Suit, Accept Goals of 33%-50%".

Preference Hirings: Firms were forced to change their employment policies to favour minority groups.

Example: In 1973 the Department of Labour forced building contractors in Chicago to hire and train minorities. A headline in a national newspaper at the time read, "Minority Hiring Plan Imposed on Chicago's Building Industry".

money to non-Whites who wished to set up a business;
- financial institutions charging higher rates of interest on loans to members of minority groups;
- insurance companies charging higher premiums on policies issued to businesses owned by non-Whites.

Moreover, further evidence was found by government agencies when employment patterns were studied. It was found that:

- non-Whites seemed to be overrepresented in the 'secondary' labour market, ie. those jobs which are poorly paid, offer few promotion prospects, demand little skill and offer limited security;
- Whites, on the other hand, were more likely to be found in the 'primary' labour market, ie. those jobs which are fairly well paid, demand skill, and offer promotion, authority and security;
- members of ethnic minorities tended to be concentrated in older, declining, sunset industries such as iron and steel and heavy engineering. Indeed, changes in this sector of the economy have meant that unemployment has been borne disproportionately by workers from these groups.

In effect, overrepresentation in the secondary job sector has meant that Blacks and other minorities have endured lower income levels than Whites, a greater prospect of unemployment and a higher incidence of poverty. (see Chapter 14)

EDUCATION

In 1954, a historic decision by the Supreme Court of the United States declared that the segregation of white and black children into separate schools was unconstitutional. This decision was to go a long way towards changing the whole nature of public education in the United States of America. The unanimous Court decision, summed up by Chief Justice Warren, accepted the evidence submitted that segregated schools had a detrimental effect on black children.

> "We conclude that in the field of public education the doctrine of 'separate but equal' has no place. Separate educational facilities are inherently unequal."

While the Court did not order an immediate desegregation of all schools, it added in a later ruling that school districts should desegregate with reasonable speed.

Ten years after the 1954 Supreme Court decision to desegregate schools, little actually had been done to implement this in the South. Case after case was brought to the courts by the National Association for the Advancement of Coloured People (NAACP), only to suffer defeat. The education authorities of the southern states were imaginative in the techniques they employed to thwart the Supreme Court decision and resist the desegregation of their schools. For example in Little Rock, Arkansas, the State Governor ordered the National Guard out to prevent nine black students taking their place at the local 'white' High School. It was not until 1964 with the passing of the Civil Rights Act that desegregation became more rapid, although perhaps equally important were the television pictures showing the violent lengths to which the southern states would go to preserve segregated education.

The Federal Government, taking a much closer interest in the implementation of desegregation, set up agencies to monitor its progress. After 1964 there was an astonishing acceleration in the process of desegregating the schools of the South.

However, for a short period of time during the early years (1969-70) of the Nixon presidency, it looked as if efforts were being made to slow down this process. Nixon, bowing to pressure from southern senators, made a rather weak effort to hold back the progress of desegregation. The South did not give in without a fight. Nevertheless figures released in 1970 showed that desegregation of public schools had advanced quite substantially in spite of these efforts and that desegregation in the South had progressed much further than desegregation in the North.

Desegregation - Southern Reaction

By 1956, Southern Whites' opposition to desegregation had begun to mushroom at every level. Growing numbers of politicians began to stand on blatantly racist platforms. Terror campaigns were mounted on anyone who lent support to black civil rights. Between the years 1955 and 1959 'White Citizens Councils' were founded in virtually every southern city. Composed largely of middle-class, well-to-do, white-collar professionals, they stood fiercely against desegregation. (See Table 11.1)

The further south they were, the deeper their resentment. Certain states passed laws making 'mixed' schools illegal.

Affirmative Action

The Case For

1 Affirmative action is the political action needed to undo the effects of centuries of discrimination.
2 The government has, in the past (through its inaction), been the chief oppressor of ethnic minorities, and so it should help to promote a climate of equal opportunities.
3 Affirmative action will help society as a whole. It will help heal the deep divisions within society.
4 The generation that remedies the wrongs of the past will reap the benefits of its actions.
5 Affirmative action will not eliminate poverty, but it will provide employment opportunities which were previously all but closed to members of ethnic minority groups.

The Case Against

1 Racial distinctions, for whatever reasons, are always wrong - both politically and morally.
2 Affirmative action is in itself discriminatory and therefore unconstitutional.
3 Affirmative action does not deal with the real problems facing ethnic minorities- prejudice and poverty.
4 Affirmative action increases tensions within minority groups; some gain advantages from it, others do not.
5 Quotas inevitably lead to lower standards as firms employ unqualified or semi-qualified people in order

Indeed, going completely against the Supreme Court ruling of 1954, both Mississippi and Louisiana changed their state constitutions to the effect that there would be separate schools in order that "public health and morals" be protected. Outwith the law, the Ku Klux Klan reasserted its influence by increasing its attacks on both Blacks and civil rights supporters.

After the passage of the Civil Rights Act of 1964, southern states responded to the efforts of the Federal Government to impose desegregation by pointing out the freedom of choice that existed with their dual school system - black schools and white schools. They argued that Whites could attend black schools (few did), and Blacks could attend white schools (few dared). It was not until 1968 that this 'freedom of choice' was outlawed by the Supreme Court. There were to be no identifiable black schools or white schools, only schools.

Busing

This decision of the Supreme Court created a problem for those states operating the dual school system. If there were to be no black schools and no white schools, one thing at least became obvious: massive transportation of children would be necessary to achieve properly integrated schools. Busing had arrived.

The need for busing arose from the existence of segregated living areas. Although southern cities were not as racially segregated as the cities in the North, certain racial residential patterns were emerging. Blacks were concentrated in the central city areas, whereas Whites were more likely to live in the suburbs. In a way, the segregated residential patterns had created the segregated schools

An interesting question was to emerge from the existence of segregated residential patterns. Was segregated schooling simply a consequence of these segregated living areas, ie. unintentional, or was it a product of deliberate action? At first the Supreme Court ruled that schools segregated by virtue of whether they were located in a black or white area of the city would not face desegregation by busing. It was held that this situation was not

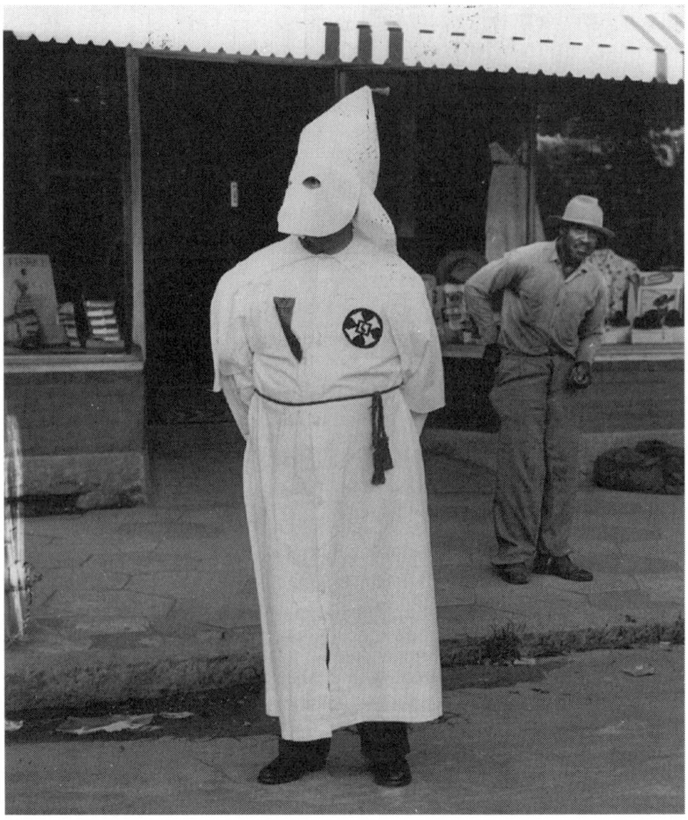

A 'white robed traffic cop' on duty for a Ku Klux Klan gathering in Georgia in 1950

unconstitutional and therefore did not warrant enforced desegregation by busing. This type of segregation was called *de facto* segregation.

It was only when *de jure* segregation was found to exist, ie. an over-concentration of either Whites or Blacks in a school created by deliberate policy, that it was declared unconstitutional and busing was imposed.

However, it was not very long before the courts found it extremely difficult to distinguish between the two. This came to a head in California in 1970 when a judge declared that there was no such thing as 'de facto' segregation, *all* racial imbalance was the result of State action, whether it had been entirely intentional or not. Finally, in 1973 the Supreme Court decreed that all segregation was illegal.

***Segregationist attitudes of Southern Politicians 1954-1973* (in percentages)**

	1954-65		1966-73	
	Peripheral South	Deep South	Peripheral South	Deep South
All Candidates				
Strong segregationists	36*	59	2	34
Moderate segregationists	42	41	15	12
Nonsegregationists	22	0	83	54
Elected Governors				
Strong segregationists	40	73	0	40
Moderate segregationists	40	27	19	10
Nonsegregationists	20	0	81	50

**Each column of three figures adds vertically to 100%*

Table 11.1
Source: *Southern Governors and Civil Rights,* E Black 1976

Busing - An Answer to the Problem?

In 1964 the Supreme Court, after listening to evidence from various educational experts, took the view that black schools in general were inferior to white schools. Black schools were deprived in terms of equipment and finance, resulting in a generally lower level of educational provision. Was busing the answer, though? Would integration close the gap between the educational achievement of white and black children? Would it improve race relations?

No aspect of positive discrimination aroused greater public outcry than busing. Its critics have come from all quarters - White and Black, working class and middle class, Catholic and Protestant, northerners and southerners. Opposition to enforced busing has been violent and undying. It has ranged from demonstrations to school bus burnings and to Whites boycotting schools. It is opposed by all shades of political opinion from extreme Democrat to extreme Republican. Busing, from its inception in the mid-1960s to the present day, has continued to be a subject of tremendous controversy. Many arguments have been put forward against it.

1 Children are unnaturally and unacceptably separated from their own communities.
2 It is an extremely costly exercise. The money spent on busing could be used to greater effect by improving inferior schools.
3 There is no hard evidence that Blacks do better in a mixed school.
4 It subjects children to needlessly long bus journeys, thus lengthening their school day.
5 It makes white parents take their children out of the public education system as they do not want their children attending inferior schools in poorer parts of the city.

There have been several studies carried out in the USA to test public opinion on the issue of busing. Table 11.2 shows some of the findings.

From the table it is obvious that Whites and Blacks had, and still have, different views on busing. However, there has been a fairly substantial change in the Blacks' position on busing. The majority of Blacks still give support to the government's efforts to ensure integration, but they also appear to be losing interest in the issue. The results shown in Figure 11.1 from a poll conducted in 1978 might help to explain this trend.

It would seem therefore that Blacks accepted, albeit reluctantly, that integration would help to achieve educational equality. Some Blacks argued that there were more important questions to consider in education, eg. the recruitment of more black teachers and the promotion of black teachers to positions of authority.

The following questions were asked of both black and white parents whose children had been involved in busing.

Q. *How did the busing of children in your family to go to school with white/black children work out - very satisfactory, or partly satisfactory, or not satisfactory?*

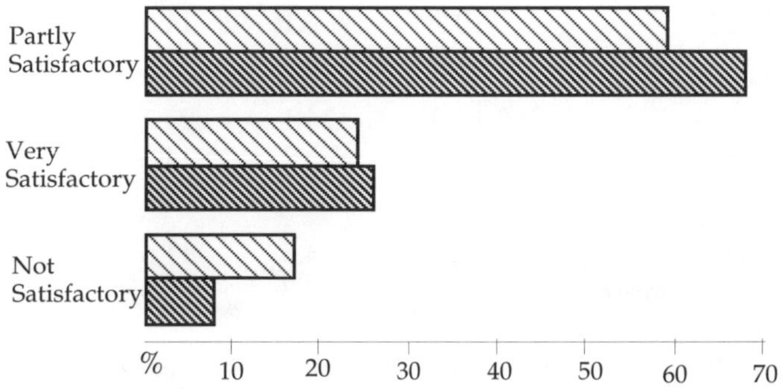

Q. *Do you favour or oppose busing children to achieve a better racial balance in the schools?*

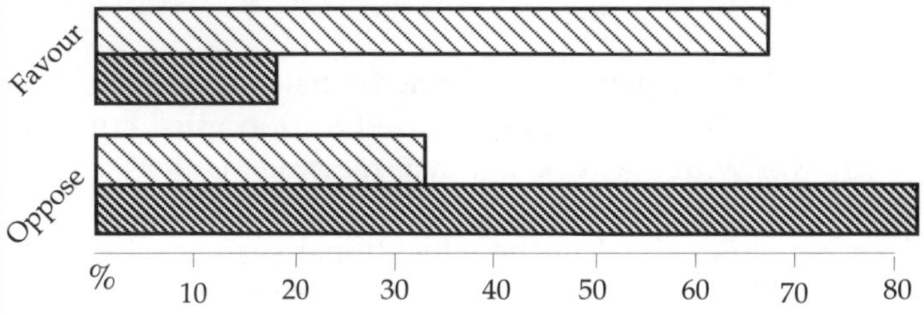

Figure 11.1

Busing - A Success?

As with the employment provisions, this is a difficult question to answer conclusively. Evidence, such as it is, is rather patchy. Certainly, as a result of past discrimination, the majority of schools with a higher intake of black children lacked both facilities and funds. It is equally certain that advances have been made in recent years. Since the 1950s, black illiteracy rates have been reduced by more than half. However, when we look at statistics relating to black education and statistics relating to black unemployment, it would appear that any advantage gained by affirmative action in education is counteracted when Blacks leave school or college to join the jobs market. (See Table 11.3)

It is interesting to note that unemployment rates for Blacks with some college education are considerably higher than those for white high school dropouts. This discrepancy in the rates of employment cannot be explained solely by a lack of education on the part of Blacks when Whites with less education are able to find employment. It would appear that discrimination is still rife. Employers, in the main being white, given two equal candidates to choose from, tend in the majority of cases to employ Whites.

The statistics above make gloomy reading when you analyse the advances made by Blacks since the 1960s in the educational field:

1 Since the 1960s black enrolment in elementary school, high school and college has increased;

Should the Federal Government Ensure School Integration? (%)

Whites only	1964	1966	1968	1970	1972	1974	1975	1976	1978
Government Ensure	37.8	42.7	33.1	41.5	32.5	29.2	27.0	19.7	23.5
Depends	7.7	7.8	7.1	10.9	6.9	12.5	14.9	8.5	-
Government Stay out	41.9	37.3	48.5	35.1	48.5	44.3	41.4	42.7	46.2
No Interest	9.8	9.6	9.9	11.5	10.8	12.5	16.7	27.6	17.9
Don't Know	2.9	2.7	1.5	1.5	1.4	1.4	-	1.5	12.4
Blacks only									
Government Ensure	74.5	74.8	83.1	83.2	74.2	74.1	79.5	61.8	60.3
Depends	4.5	4.4	3.9	1.4	6.4	4.8	4.6	9.1	-
Government Stay Out	7.2	8.9	6.3	7.1	11.2	13.0	4.6	10.3	11.4
No Interest	9.5	11.1	4.2	6.8	7.5	6.1	11.3	16.6	21.5
Don't Know	4.3	0.7	2.5	1.4	0.7	2.0	-	2.3	6.8

Table 11.2

Unemployment of Persons 16-24 years of age by Race and Years of School Completed, March 1987 % of Labour Force Unemployed			
	Hispanic	**White**	**Black**
Total	10.2	6.1	14.5
High School			
1-3 yrs	14.8	13.1	23.2
4 yrs	9.4	6.2	14.3
College			
1-3 yrs	7.2	4.5	11.6
4 yrs or more	2.6	2.3	5.3

Table 11.3 Source: US Bureau of Labour Statistics, 1988

2 The number of black students completing high school and college has increased;
3 Blacks are spending more time in education, both full-time and part-time.

If education is to play a major part in equalising opportunity between White and Black, then education must comply with the wider attack against racism. Unless equal opportunities are offered to Blacks after schooling then any benefits gained in the educational system will have been wasted. The improvement of inferior schools, the hiring of more black teachers and affirmative action (quota) programmes in universities and colleges are all helping to raise the educational levels of Blacks, but unfortunately there is no hard evidence to show whether busing is improving educational performance. All that can be concluded is that integrated education is a positive factor in helping to improve understanding between Black and White, stereotypes being replaced by realities.

AFFIRMATIVE ACTION — DESIRABLE OR SUCCESSFUL?

Without doubt these are extremely difficult questions to answer. There are differing opinions among both Blacks and Whites about the effectiveness or desirability of affirmative action. Clearly, positive discrimination helped many black people gain access to white occupations across a variety of employment sectors. However, studies have shown that those gaining most out of the programmes tended to be middle-class Blacks with a college education. Moreover, affirmative action programmes, which are aimed at those already in the employment market rather than those who seek to join it, have meant that very little has been done for the rapidly growing number of young unemployed Blacks.

There is an increasingly lively debate among black Americans about the merits or otherwise of affirmative action. On the right of the political spectrum, black conservatives argue that affirmative action demeans Blacks by making them dependent on the programmes rather than on their own efforts and hard work. Such a view is, of course, shared by the Bush administration which argues that a quota for one person is a place in the unemployment line for another. On the other hand, many civil rights activists insist that racial discrimination is so entrenched in the fabric of US society that only Federal involvement can overcome it. Indeed, a survey carried out by the Urban Institute and published in May 1991 concluded that Blacks still found more hurdles in their way in terms of career development, with equally qualified Whites progressing up the promotion ladder much faster. However, even the keenest supporters of affirmative action concede that there are imperfections. Those Blacks who have benefited from such schemes complain of being 'labelled' or of having to 'overachieve' to prove their worth to their white work colleagues.

There is, however, one thing that all agree upon. Affirmative action has not addressed the major social and economic problems facing black people - poverty and unemployment. These problems, despite government intervention, have increased in intensity and are creating misery for many millions of minority families. (See Chapter 14)

Affirmative Action - The Backlash

Of all the legislation passed by the US Congress, none has fired emotions quite so much as affirmative action laws. It is now nearly thirty years since the first affirmative action policies were implemented and in that period there has been no reduction in the controversy these policies provoke - if anything, the debate is even more heated. In the early 1960s, affirmative action meant the deliberate seeking out and preparation of minority groups for better jobs and educational opportunities. Ten years on, in the 1970s, affirmative action came to mean much more than that. It came to mean the establishment of preferential treatment in terms of quotas and targets based on race, colour and national origin. If there was resentment and opposition to the early form of affirmative action then there was active hostility and rejection for the latter. To many in the 1980s, 'affirmative action' were emotive words, meaning privilege, preference and protection for some while others were to get on, unaided, as best they could.

In voicing opposition to affirmative action, Ronald Reagan exposed a raw nerve. America is a nation of minorities, white as well as black. Many of these people came to America to escape from persecution, eg. Jewish Americans and Polish Americans. They came to a country that offered new opportunities but little in the way of a helping hand. Why should it now protect others more than it protected them? Reagan, an astute politician, had unleashed a powerful force. Nothing motivates people quite so much as the perception of unfairness. Reagan, by his words and actions, had allowed people to legitimately question the concept of affirmative action without fear of being dubbed anti-Black or racist. The white backlash was under way. (See Chapter 12)

In 1989, in a series of Supreme Court Rulings, the laws covering the employment of workers from ethnic minority groups in the public and private sectors were changed. Essentially the changes made it more difficult for such workers to prove that they had been discriminated against by their employers. The rulings also made it more difficult for employers, such as city councils, to introduce affirmative action programmes in their own establishments. Indeed, in one such case the Supreme Court, in a 5-4 decision, voted to allow Alabama's white firemen to start legal proceedings against their employers on the grounds that they had been adversely affected by affirmative action programmes introduced in their place of work.

The Civil Rights Act, 1991

In 1990 Democratic Representatives introduced a Bill which, if successful, would have returned civil rights legislation to the position it had been in prior to the 1989 Supreme Court rulings. Although the Bill set out to address 'intentional' and 'unintentional' discrimination as well as forbidding the use of 'quotas' and 'race norming', it was vetoed by President Bush on the grounds that it would ultimately introduce the "destructive force" of quotas. (see *'Quota Bill adds up votes for Bush)* The President argued that the Bill set standards so strict and allowed compensation claims so large that companies might be driven to adopt hiring quotas so that they would not be sued. In a bid to secure Republican and Presidential support, the Bill was redrafted and presented to the House in May 1991. Finally, after a considerable amount of behind the scenes bargaining, President Bush signed the *Civil Rights Act* in November, 1991. The President announced that, although deeply

Racism in the Raw in the Chicago Suburbs

Two harrowing tales show how brutal bias can still be

BY TED GUP

Last year residents of Cicero, a Chicago-area community notorious for its racism, called the police to report that a black man was impersonating a police officer, wearing a police uniform and driving a squad car. That was patrolman Wesley Scott, the town's first and only black policeman. Almost daily, he endures racial insults and humiliation, not only from the people he has sworn to protect but also from some of his fellow officers upon whom his life may depend.

Four miles away in Melrose Park, a working-class suburb of modest but tidy homes, live Donald and Stephanie Sled. This summer they packed up their few belongings and moved out of Chicago's west-side ghetto, delighted to have found an affordable apartment in Melrose Park. In their excitement to escape the squalor and fear of the ghetto, the Sleds gave little thought to what it might mean to be the first black family in their neighbourhood. "This was like heaven," recalls Donald, a 44-year-old handyman who sometimes stutters when excited. "It was so quiet and peaceful." But the Sleds have found anything but peace in Melrose Park. Instead, their new home has been under siege. Vandals have taunted them with racial slurs. They have shattered their windows, punctured their tires, torched their car and driven a blazing cross into their lawn...

In March 1987, two days after Wesley Scott graduated from the police academy and joined the force in suburban Cicero, he discovered a photo of the Ku Klux Klan pasted to his locker. "Who's going to kill Wesley?" one of the robed Klansmen in the picture asked. Another replied, "I'm going to kill Wesley." Across the bottom was written "The Ku Klux Klan is going to kill you." Recalls Scott: "A few of the guys were shaking their heads, but a lot of the guys were laughing." Scott did not report the incident to his superiors, one of whom was among those laughing. Stephen Zalas, deputy superintendent of the Cicero police, said he was unaware of the incident. "Rookies do put up with some harassment," he said. "Some of it might be in bad taste..."

Scott has problems both in the station and on the streets. One of his superior officers has called him a "stupid nigger" in front of fellow officers. On one occasion the officer asked someone he was arresting, "Do you want this nigger to see you crying?" Sometimes citizens who call for help will rebuff Scott and ask for a white officer - a request the department denies.

Scott grew up in an integrated neighbourhood in southwest Chicago. "I always believed I could go anywhere and mingle with anyone," said Scott. "It just didn't occur to me that Cicero could be so prejudiced." Still, it was impossible not to have heard of Cicero's reputation. Scott recalls how his family was appalled when Martin Luther King Jr. was forced to postpone a march through Cicero in 1966 because of the threat of violence. Scott was five years old at the time. Since then, there have been numerous assaults against Blacks who attempted to live in Cicero. "Cicero unfortunately has become synonymous with racism," says US Attorney Anton Valukas. "It is a symbol of standing tall, guarding the borders."

The city of Cicero (pop. 61,000) has given Scott - and all its municipal employees - until Sept. 30 to move within the city limits. Scott is afraid for his three young children and his wife. Reluctantly, he has joined other officers in challenging the city's residency requirement. "The people he's afraid of are the people he's here to protect," says Cicero's attorney, Dennis Both. "If he has a fear, it's not founded."

Despite the city's hate-filled past, there are signs of real change in Cicero. Even Valukas, who sued Cicero for discriminatory hiring practices in 1983, says he detects a new willingness to confront the issue of racism. Scott too is hopeful. "I am slowly making some headway with the people in the community," he says. People on the street are beginning to call him "Officer Scott". A number of fellow officers have invited him and his wife home to dinner. Even the officer who once called him a "nigger" is now supportive...

The Sleds are equally determined. When they moved into their $250-a-month apartment in Melrose Park, they were welcomed by Donna Wilbur, a widow who lives downstairs with her teenage son. But two days later, a car nearly knocked the Sleds' 14-year-old nephew off his bike. "Nigger, what are you doing around here?" the driver shouted. A week later, two wooden fence posts crashed through Wilbur's dining room window, the penalty for welcoming the Sleds to the neighbourhood. "It doesn't seem like America with people acting like this," she says.

The Sleds thought their troubles would be financial, not racial. Together they make $16,000 a year - less than Melrose Park's $22,000 median family income. Donald operates an elevator in a downtown bank. Stephanie, 35, works the midnight shift as a cashier in a filling station.

Three weeks after they arrived, arsonists set a fire beside their car. The next night Donald kept a vigil at the back-porch window. Then he dozed off. He was awakened at 1 a.m. to find their 1976 Chevy Impala in flames. Across the street four young men laughed and shouted, "Let the car burn. Niggers don't need to be in Melrose Park." One night as Stephanie set out for her cashier's job, several youths waved a rope and taunted her with threats of a lynching. Later a crude wooden cross was burned on the lawn.

The Sleds tried to laugh it off. "You know how we feel?" asks Stephanie. "Like a couple of black-eyed Susans in a field of corn." Donald sits uneasily in the kitchen, rising every few minutes to survey the street. "You have to be alert," he says. Early on he repainted the living room, but he has decided not to finish the other rooms. Too many uncertainties. Boxes are stacked against the back windows so that they might stop a fire bomb. Beside the telephone is the number of the FBI. The Sleds have warned their relatives that it is not safe to visit them. "Half of these people have more schooling than I could ever get, and yet they do this," says Donald, his eyes shaded by a Chicago Bears cap. "I can't understand."

The Sleds wonder if Melrose Park's all-white 65-member police force will protect them. The commander of operations is Lieut. John Carpino. "I don't think there is a racial problem here," he says of the Sleds' problems. "I just don't see it. We're treating it as vandalism. These are pranksters." For a couple of days the city deployed an unmarked car to watch the Sleds. Says Carpino: "Come on, this is 1988. Who's going to lynch who? This is the Midwest. This is nothing to excite anybody about."

...In 1985 the Justice Department sued Melrose Park (pop. 23,000) as well as twelve other suburbs for discriminatory employment practices. Of 217 city employees, none were black. Melrose Park contested the suit and lost in court.

White families living near the Sleds insist that they are not racists. But, they say, they are afraid that the Sleds may be followed by other black families, that white residents will move, then property values will plummet, and the neighbourhood will deteriorate. "I'm afraid of what could happen," said one 75-year-old woman. Until 1972 she and her husband lived in Austin, a Chicago suburb that went from predominantly white to predominantly black. "We had to sell our home for nothing," she said. "What happens if this whole doggone neighbourhood gets up and leaves? We're too old to move again." She does not know if she can trust her neighbours not to panic and move out. "It's all white people's fault," she said. "Blacks have a right to live where they want."

In recent weeks the incidents against the Sleds have tapered off. A neighbour across the alley has offered to keep an eye on the Sleds' car. Larry Pusateri, the son of the owner of the house, has told the Sleds, "Don't worry, I'm not going to let these bastards move you out."

From Time Magazine, 17 October 1988

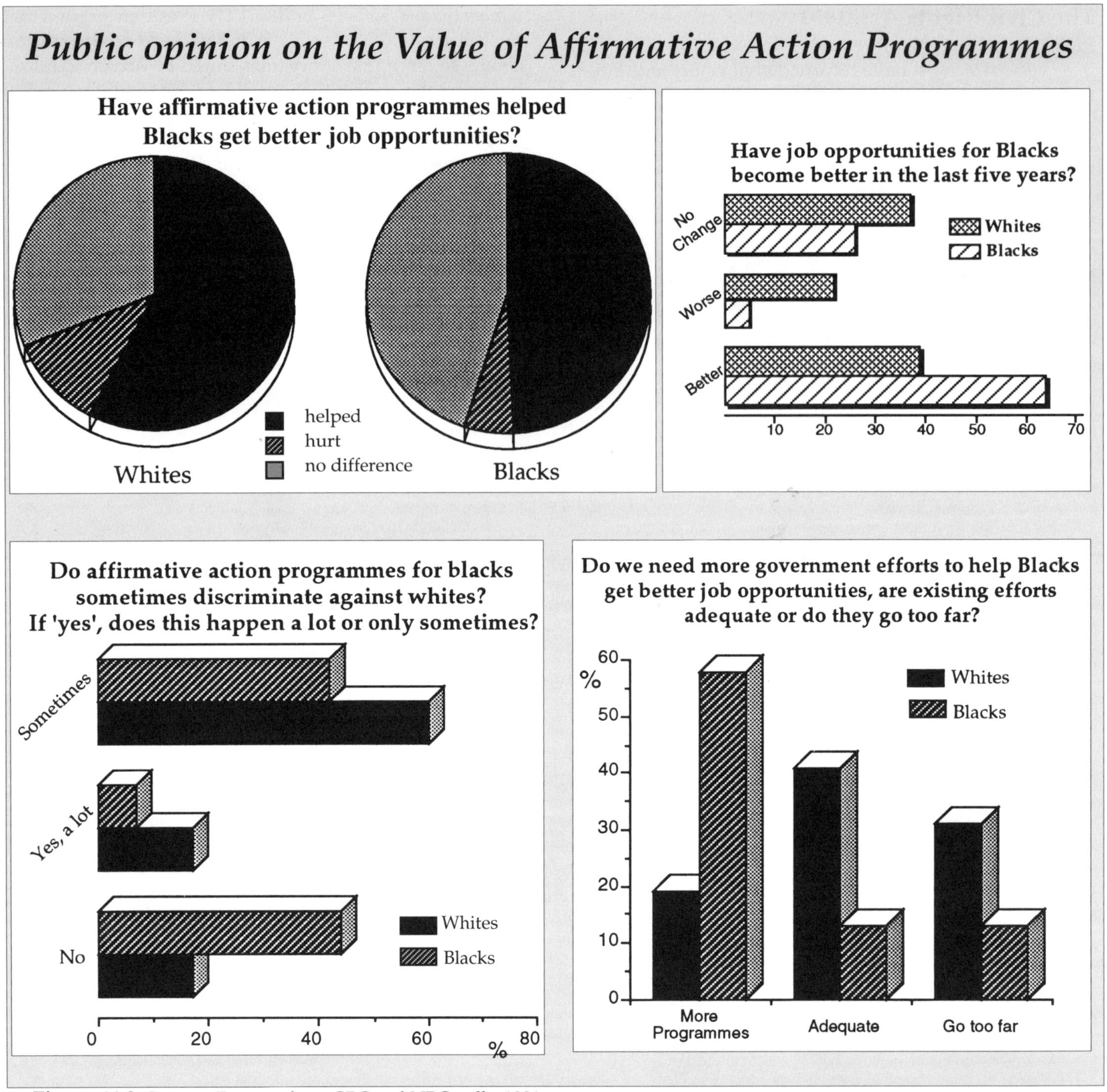

Figure 11.2 Source: Extracts from CBC and NBC polls, 1991

opposed to quotas, he supported affirmative action. Many people found this position to be rather confusing and somewhat untenable. In practice, argue many Republicans, jobs and university places are reserved for Blacks through quota systems. Nevertheless, in spite of its lengthy and tortuous passage through Congress there was one aspect of the Bill on which President Bush would not back down: the process of 'race norming' is now illegal under the terms of the new Civil Rights Act.

Race norming was one affirmative action policy which created a great deal of resentment among white workers. In a bid to employ and promote more workers from minority groups, some employers used a formula which allowed Blacks and Whites to be graded differently on an employment aptitude test. The scores from the test were ranked on different race curves. Whites' scores were usually higher on these tests than Blacks' and Hispanics'. However, to be ranked in the top 10%, a white applicant had to score a much higher mark than a Black applicant. This created a widespread view among Whites that promoted Blacks did not get to these positions on their ability but because of the colour of their skin. For many Blacks, the consequences were equally unsatisfactory, with some complaining that they felt as if they had 'Affirmative Action' stamped on their foreheads.

Civil Rights - An Issue for 1992?

The controversy which surrounded the civil rights legislation speedily turned into a 1992 election issue. Sensing that political points were to be won, the Republicans lost no time in attempting to associate the Democrats with the taboo word, 'quota'. The lesson delivered by North Carolina's Senator Jesse Helms in the November 1990 election was not lost on George Bush. Adopting an anti-affirmative action stance, Helms' final TV broadcast showed white hands holding a job rejection letter while the voice-over declared, "You needed that job, and you were the best qualified. But it had to go to a minority because of a racial quota." Senator Helms beat his black Democratic rival by 4%. However, one year later, it was events in Louisiana which were finally to persuade President Bush to accept the redrafted Civil Rights Bill.

The Duke's a Hazard

David Duke, former Nazi and grand wizard of the Ku Klux Klan, ran for Governor of Louisiana in a campaign based on an open appeal to white people who felt that they were being cheated of their American birthright by Blacks, immigrants and affirmative action programmes. In defeating President Bush's preferred Republican candidate, Buddy Roehmer, in the primary election, the threat of Duke's victory alarmed the White House so much that the President publicly advised Republicans in Louisiana to vote for Duke's Democrat opponent, Edwin Edwards. In the event it was Edwards and not Duke who won. Although defeated, Duke won 55% of the white vote, and in a post-election speech to his followers stated, "This is the beginning, not the end...I'm a civil rights militant-if that means equal rights for white folks." Initially there was not much to separate the stance of Duke and Bush on their opposition to the Civil Rights Bill-both were firmly opposed to quotas. However, the President was said to be "perplexed" about the telegenic former Klansman's obvious appeal and his dark hints that his work was not finished in stopping what he called the Bush administration's drift to the left. Certainly, as far as recent popular opinion on quotas is concerned (See Figure 11.2) it is Duke and not Bush who has the measure of the majority view.

'Quota Bill' adds up votes for Bush

From PATRICK BROGAN in Washington

The House of Representatives has passed a new civil rights Bill that will feature prominently in next year's presidential election. The Bill would outlaw racial or sexual discrimination in employment, and President Bush claims that it is a 'quota' Bill. He means that white male workers would lose their jobs to Blacks, Hispanics, and women.

Mr Bush has promised to veto the Bill and there is not much chance that the Democrats, who support it, can overturn the veto.

The Democrats insist passionately that it is not a quota Bill, and indeed there is a clause that specifically bars quotas.

Republicans argue that employers, who have a healthy dislike of lawsuits, will immediately start hiring people on the basis of their race just to keep out of trouble.

Discrimination against people on the basis of their race or sex was banned in civil rights Acts 20 years ago, but in the late 1980s the Supreme Court ruled that the law was badly drafted and that workers would have to prove that their employers actively discriminated against them.

Previously it had been up to the employer to prove that he was not discriminating. Under the new rule, workers' chances of proving their case dropped sharply. The new Bill is designed to remedy the error and to restore the conditions prevailing in the 1970s.

There is no doubt that there is still considerable discrimination in many corners of the United States but there is also no doubt that quotas have often been imposed, sometimes disguised as 'affirmative action'. Universities, for instance, routinely and openly discriminate in favour of women or coloured job applicants in the hope of correcting the large imbalance in their faculties, which remain predominantly white and male.

There is a considerable backlash against this 'reverse discrimination', even among people who admit that it is often justified. But a good liberal who accepts, for instance, that there should be more black policemen may resent it when he is himself turned down for an academic job, which is then offered to a black woman whom he considers less qualified.

The backlash is much stronger among most American workers, who are worried about their jobs anyway because of the recession. With their usual acute sense of timing, the Democrats have once again chosen an issue that is guaranteed to lose them huge numbers of votes.

Mr Bush, who has no trouble in sensing the way the wind is blowing, has been stumping the country denouncing "the quota Bill" and promising to veto it. The Bill would probably pass in the Senate, but there is no hope that the Democrats could muster the two-thirds majority they would need to defeat a presidential veto.

Their only hope is that a compromise will be worked out in the Senate. The Republicans, of course, will do their best to sabotage any compromise: they want conflict, and votes.

Glasgow Herald, 6 June 1991

12 BLACKS AND THE POLITICAL PROCESS

The 1964 Civil Rights Act, while doing a great deal to outlaw segregation and discrimination, had failed to provide voting rights for Blacks. Blacks, especially in the South, found that they would have to fight for the right to vote. Indeed, many obstacles were placed in the way of Blacks attempting to gain and exercise their democratic rights. What the Ku Klux Klan could not accomplish by intimidation and violence, a broad range of other methods did. Literacy tests and other devices were employed to keep black voters away from the polls.

Black voter registration was extremely low. In 1948, only 12% of black Americans of voting age were registered in the South. In Selma, Alabama , only 335 Blacks out of a population of over 15,000 were registered to vote in 1965. It was no accident that Martin Luther King chose Selma to dramatise the issue of voting rights. Dr King organised and led a fifty-mile march from Selma to Montgomery, the state capital, in a bid to bring attention to the plight of Blacks. However, the state military, acting under the orders of Governor Wallace, broke up the march in an extremely brutal manner using tear gas, whips and truncheons. It was during this struggle at Selma that President Johnson appeared on nationwide television promising legislation which would ensure that Blacks would be able to participate fully in the political process.

> "I pledge we will not delay or we will not hesitate, or will not turn aside until Americans of every race and colour and origin in this country have the same rights as all others to share in the progress of democracy."
> *President LB Johnson*

The Voting Rights Act, 1965

The *Voting Rights Act* (VRA), despite tremendous opposition from the politicians of the southern states, was passed by 328 votes to 74 in the House of Representatives and 79 to 18 in the Senate. The bill became law on 6 August 1965. The effects of the Act were rapid. By making illegal literacy tests, property requirements and other obstacles, black voter registration increased dramatically, particularly in the South. (see Table 12.1)

Black Registration in Southern States 1940-1988

(% of adult Blacks registered)

STATE	1940	1947	1952	1960	1966	1976	1988
Alabama	-	1	4	14	31	58	68
Georgia	2	20	23	29	46	75	57
Louisiana	-	2	25	31	39	63	77
Mississippi	-	1	4	6	14	61	74
South Carolina	-	13	20	16	38	56	57
Virginia	5	11	16	23	49	55	64
Arkansas	3	21	27	38	54	94	68
Florida	3	13	33	39	62	61	58
North Carolina	10	14	18	38	49	55	58
Tennessee	16	25	27	59	72	66	75
Texas	9	17	31	35	59	65	64

Table 12.1 Source: Various

However, despite the remarkable increases in black voter registration, many problems were to remain for Blacks, especially in the South. With the passing of the VRA a new racist mood had emerged and racist politicians, in whipping up anti-black feelings, spurred on new voter registration among poor white communities. (See Table 12.2)

Voter Registration in the South, 1964-1968

(% of voting age population registered)

	1964	1968
Black	43.3	62.0
White	73.2	78.1

Table 12.2

Nevertheless, black voter registration gathered pace and had a significant influence on other aspects of civil rights. In addition to more black candidates standing for elections, white politicians were much more likely to give their attention to issues concerning civil rights when a substantial number of potential voters were black.

Voter Registration and Political Power

The 1960s and 1970s saw the number of black Americans of voting age increase substantially. This, coupled with the effects of the VRA and the numerous registration drives organised by groups such as SNCC, CORE and NAACP, dramatically increased the number of potential black voters. However, even if Blacks were registering to vote in ever increasing numbers, it was clear that their political voice would only become relevant if their electoral power was turned into a greater share of elected representatives. Although, as Table 12.3 shows, the number of Blacks being elected to public office was increasing, the results were rather patchy with parts of the country returning few black officials.

Other political groupings were formed in a bid to increase black political participation and the number of black elected officials. In the late 1970s, Jesse Jackson's 'Operation PUSH' set out to raise black people's political awareness and alert them to the importance and power of their vote. Certainly, the power of the black vote was being clearly seen in the southern states. The former black Senator and US Ambassador to the UN, Andrew Young, when describing the power of the black vote in southern politics, noted:

"It used to be southern politics was just 'nigger' politics, who could 'outnigger' the other - then you registered 10% to 15% in the community and folks would start saying 'Nigra', and then you got 35% to 40% registered and it's amazing how quickly they learned to say 'Neegrow', and

Black Legislators 1964-1990

	1964	1968	1972	1976	1980	1984	1988	1990
House of Representatives	**5**	**9**	**15**	**15**	**17**	**20**	**24**	**26**
Senate	0	1	1	1	0	0	0	0
State Legislature	94	172	238	295	318	384	416	440
Governors	0	0	0	0	0	0	0	1

Table 12.3 Source: Various

now that we've got 50, 60, 70% of the black votes registered in the South everybody's proud to be associated with their black brothers and sisters."

While there is no doubt that black successes in politics, particularly at local level, brought to the black people a sense of pride and dignity as well as the obvious political voice, the benefits were somewhat limited. Political victories often brought with them huge political problems. Many black mayors and elected officials soon found themselves in difficult positions. The black constituents made heavy demands; they had very high expectations. Furthermore, issues that Blacks saw as important were not always seen as important by the community at large. In many respects black politicians found that in the harsh economic reality they could not deliver what was asked of them. Blacks may have grasped political power, but Whites still had a firm grip on economic power. In the cities of the North, many white people, fearing the worst from the black influx and the increasing number of black elected officials, fled to the suburbs, reducing the revenue of the cities even further. Many Blacks became disillusioned at their own people's inability to deal with their problems and, as a result, many lost faith in the electoral process and stopped voting. During the early 1970s black registration fell in many parts of the country, as did the number who actually turned up to vote. Great expectations were very quickly being replaced by mistrust, apathy and a sense of hopelessness and failure. These were the feelings which characterised black politics during much of the early 1970s and were to remain in many parts of the US until Jesse Jackson's move into national politics in the early 1980s.

BLACK POLITICS IN THE 1980s

"The most important step that a person can take is the short walk to the ballot box." *Martin Luther King Jnr*

During the 1970s, an influential white politician in New York wrote off the Blacks. He shook his head in disgust, "Forget the black vote," he said, "Blacks don't vote."

The period since the mid-1970s has destroyed the myth that "Blacks don't vote". A dramatic transformation has taken place in the political climate of America with Blacks becoming much more involved in the political process at all levels. While it is true that, in presidential elections, Blacks vote at lower rates than Whites (see Table 12.4), at local level black voting rates are as high as or sometimes higher than those for Whites. Moreover, where there is a black candidate, black turnout is extremely high.

What was the cause of this transformation, this dramatic revival in black participation? A combination of factors gives us the answer. After the assassination of Martin Luther King in 1968, Blacks were without a national figurehead or leader to give focus or direction to their activities. The emergence of Jesse Jackson onto the national political scene was soon to change that. This, coupled with the advent of Reaganomics and its impact upon race relations (see Chapter 13), helped to fuel black electoral registration and participation rates.

Jesse Jackson

"You can't plant a seed and pick the fruit the next morning." *Jesse Jackson*

Using the experiences gained and the skills developed during the civil rights era, Jackson came to national prominence in the late 1970s with his organisation PUSH (People United to Serve Humanity). The campaign, initially funded by private contribution and later by the Carter administration, attempted to instil in young Blacks a sense of dignity and pride. Jackson's strategy was to confront head on the alienation and apathy that gripped many young Blacks. Touring schools up and down the country, Jackson would address his young audiences in rhyming slogans, exhorting them to reject drugs and to work harder at school. "Down with dope, up with hope", and "Less than your best is a sin ..." : At the end of each meeting students would be encouraged to sign a pledge agreeing to study for two hours every school night, without radio or television.

PUSH was also engaged in improving the economic position of Blacks, albeit in a rather controversial manner. Boycotts or threatened boycotts of white businesses were organised in a bid to win more jobs for minorities. Since the early 1980s PUSH has had some notable successes in its endeavours. The Seven-Up agreement, for example, involved the company in a $61 million dollar commitment. The minority work force was raised to 15% of the total; minority businesses received 15% of the company's contracts and minority causes saw their charitable donations rise by 15%.

Voting and Registration by Race 1972-1988

	1972		1976		1980		1984		1988	
	Reg.	Voted	Reg.	Voted	Reg.	Voted	Reg.	Voted	Reg.	Voted
White	73.4	64.5	68.3	60.9	68.4	60.9	69.6	61.4	67.9	59.1
Black	65.5	52.1	58.5	48.7	60.0	50.5	66.3	55.8	64.5	51.5
Hispanic	44.4	37.5	37.8	31.8	36.3	29.9	40.1	32.6	35.5	28.8

Table 12.4 Source: US Department of Commerce: Bureau of the Census

Jesse Jackson

Jesse Jackson was born on 8 October 1941 in Greenville, South Carolina, the illegitimate son of a share-cropper, Noah Robinson. The young Jesse experienced at first-hand the apartheid system of the deep South. His mother, Helen Burns, eventually married Charles Jackson and the new stepfather adopted Jesse.

A talented athlete, Jackson enrolled at North Carolina Agricultural and Technical State University i n Greensboro. He became active in the civil rights movement and organised campaigns of marches and sit-ins that inevitably brought him into contact with Martin Luther King. Jackson was chosen to run the Chicago section of a regional programme, Operation Breadbasket, designed to pressurise businesses to end discriminatory hiring. Jackson later transformed the Chicago arm of Operation Breadbasket into his own organisation PUSH, much to the annoyance of other black leaders of the Southern Christian Leadership Congress (SCLC). They later accused Jackson of myth-making and personal aggrandisement, especially in his claim that he cradled the dying Martin Luther King Jnr in his arms, which they state is total fabrication.

During the 1970s Jackson became the only national black leader. Travelling the length and breadth of the country, Jackson preached the virtues of academic excellence and self-discipline to his young school-based audiences. However, it was not until the 1980s that Jackson, by now an established national figure, came to prominence as an international figure. In standing for the Democratic Presidential nomination in the 1984 and 1988 elections, Jackson successfully managed to push his populist image into white as well as black communities.

1984 PRESIDENTIAL ELECTION

The early 1980s witnessed the transformation of Jackson into a figure of national importance. One aspect of his prominence was his emphasis on black political involvement. At a 1983 rally in Washington to commemorate the twentieth anniversary of Martin Luther King's famous 'I have a dream' speech, Jackson urged the crowd to expand the dream of 1963. "We have our freedom, our civil rights, but we do not have equality," he declared. "We have moved in, now we must move up. Dream on! March on, our day has come."

It was clear to Jackson and other prominent black leaders that the first and most important step in this march was to register as voters. To this end, Jackson toured the United States speaking in an evangelical style to enthusiastic gatherings of Blacks. At meeting after meeting, Jackson converted his audience. "There is a freedom train a-coming," he boomed, "but you've got to be registered to ride. Hands that picked cotton will pick the President. From the guttermost to the uttermost! From the outhouse to the White House." In the summer of 1983 Jackson launched his 'southern campaign' to register as many as possible of the four million Blacks who were not on the electoral roll. The results were impressive. In Fulton County in Georgia alone, 11,000 new black votes were registered. Jackson was now being mentioned as a possible runner in the forthcoming Presidential election, such was his impact at local and national levels.

"Run, Jesse, Run"

In 1984 Jesse Jackson finally entered the race for the Democratic nomination for the Presidency, despite misgivings by several prominent black politicians. Jackson did not seriously expect to win the nomination; rather, he hoped to inspire black people to become more active in politics and to display to the leaders of the Democratic Party the importance of the black vote. By entering the race, Jackson was putting pressure on the Democrats in Congress and on Democratic candidates at all political levels to undertake appropriate actions and to make pledges in order that the black vote would not be taken for granted.

Jackson tried to widen the base of his political support, which was predominantly black, to include other minority groups. In creating the *Rainbow Coalition*, Jackson was making a direct appeal to Hispanics, women and poor Whites, groups who had not done particularly well under the Reagan administration. Jackson's campaign, although run on a shoestring budget, caught the imagination of the American media and public. Despite hiccups in New York where he upset the Jewish community with some anti-semitic remarks, and his association with the extremist black nationalist Louis Farrakhan, Jackson's campaign was an outstanding success. Opinion polls clearly indicated that Jackson's campaign had tempted many more voters, both black and white, to vote Democrat.

The Rainbow Coalition did not, however, find its pot of electoral gold. The results of the 1984 primaries (the elections held by the Democratic and Republican Parties to choose their candidate for the Presidential election) clearly displayed the limits of non-black support and to an extent the failure of the Rainbow Coalition. (See Table 12.5)

At the July National Convention in San Francisco, Walter Mondale became the Democratic nominee for President and Geraldine Ferraro for Vice President. The results of

Votes for Jackson in Selected Primaries 1984*	Total Vote(%)	Black Vote(%)	White Vote(%)
Alabama	19	60	1
Connecticut	12	69	4
Florida	12	62	2
Georgia	21	70	3
Illinois	21	74	4
New York	26	89	7
Pennsylvania	17	74	4

*Primaries where Jackson received 10%+ of the vote

Table 12.5 Source: NBC

this election were a setback to black political aspirations, particularly as issues of racial equality were never far from the top of the agenda throughout the primary season. Jackson won 77% of the black vote but only 5% of the white vote. It was Mondale who was consistently able to attract both black and white votes. (See Table 12.6)

Group Voting in the Democratic Primaries, 1984	% of Primary Electorate	% Vote for Mondale	% Vote for Hart	% Vote for Jackson
White	78	42	43	5
Black	18	19	3	77

Table 12.6 Source: CBS and NBC Exit Polls.

Jesse Jackson's campaign had also raised another interesting issue, white backlash. While there can be no doubt that Jackson's registration drive had been very successful, there were those who argued that it had been counter-productive in that it had resulted in a white backlash favourable to the Republicans. In the South, for example, although there

George Bush

Votes for Jackson in Selected Primaries 1988	
State	% Share of Vote
Alabama	43.6
Missouri	44.4
Virginia	45.1
Michigan	53.5
Illinois	32.3
District of Columbia	80.0

Table 12.7 Source: NBC and CBS

was a 31% increase in registration among Blacks, three times as many Whites registered, voting mainly for Reagan. Ronald Reagan in winning the Presidential race had taken 75% of the Southern white vote with him. Reagan's electoral landslide (525 electoral college votes to Mondale's 13) was a blow to black advancement and the Rainbow Coalition.

1988 PRESIDENTIAL ELECTION

The political circumstances were very interesting. For the first time in twenty years an incumbent (sitting) President would not be taking part in the nomination proceedings so there was no built-in advantage for any one candidate. The Democratic race began and ended with a clear leader. In the beginning this was Gary Hart and at the end Michael Dukakis. There was also considerable support for Jesse Jackson, who in 1984 had established himself as a national figure, a powerful speaker and for many the undisputed leader of black America. There was no doubt that in the race for the Democratic nomination Jesse Jackson spoke for the Party's core constituency, the Blacks.

In the 1988 elections Jackson attempted to establish himself in the eyes of both black and white Democrats as the champion of progressive thinking and, although he was not expected to secure the nomination, he was to give a good account of himself. As in 1984, his campaign seemed to be fuelled more by inspiration and enthusiasm than by money and no one knew what to make of a candidate who could not win but would not lose.

Jackson had an extremely strong base in the southern states and his run for nomination received a tremendous boost when he polled well in his own state of Illinois and over 50% of the vote in Michigan. (see Table 12.7) Although

Group Voting in the Democratic Primaries 1988	Proportion of Primary Vote	Dukakis	Jackson	Others
Total Vote (million)	22.7	9.7	6.6	6.4
% of Vote	100	43	29	28
White	75	54	12	34
Black	21	4	92	4
Hispanic	3	48	30	20
Catholic	30	60	18	22
White Protestant	36	43	10	47
Jewish	7	75	8	17

Table 12.8 Source: NBC and CBS

Presidential Performance by Race: 1972-1988 (%)

	1972		1976		1980		1984		1988	
	Nixon (R)	McGovern (D)	Ford (R)	Carter (D)	Reagan (R)	Carter (D)	Reagan (R)	Mondale (D)	Bush (R)	Dukakis (D)
White	70	30	53	47	55	36	66	34	59	40
Black	17	83	5	95	11	85	9	90	12	86
Hispanic	-	-	-	-	33	59	33	65	30	69

Table 12.9

Jackson was beginning to be taken more seriously as a 'real' candidate, a closer look at his support revealed that he had not been able to broaden it to any significant degree and that his core support remained among Blacks.

However, the most decisive primary election of all was yet to come, New York. Although Jackson had an extremely large support in the city, the largest in any nonsouthern state, he faced very stiff opposition from an equivalent size group of Jewish voters. New York's Jews had not forgotten nor forgiven Jackson's anti-semitic remarks made in the 1984 campaign and were still extremely suspicious of his connections with Louis Farrakhan, the extremist black Muslim leader, and his position on the State of Israel. Indeed, the Jewish mayor of New York, Ed Koch, in campaigning in support of Senator Albert Gore, Jackson's opponent, declared, "a Jew would have to be crazy to vote for Jackson". In the event, Dukakis won a clear victory, an absolute majority of the total vote and a leading position among Whites. The result in New York was the beginning of the end for Jesse Jackson. If he could not win in New York with its massive black population and liberal white population, it was unlikely that he could establish the level of support needed to win the nomination. From this point on, Dukakis would win every one of the remaining primaries, with the exception of the District of Columbia, and go on to win the Party's nomination for the Presidential race ahead. Table 12.8 summarises the results of the Democratic primaries.

Dukakis chose Senator Lloyd Bensten of Texas as his Vice Presidential running mate. Jackson and his supporters were disappointed and angered by the choice. One Jackson aide likened it to being "hit by a car bomb". Hurried moves were made to pacify Jackson and a series of meetings between Dukakis and Jackson were set up. Dukakis eventually agreed to put forward some of Jackson's policy positions such as a strengthened condemnation of Apartheid in South Africa and a massive decrease in defence spending.

Blacks and the Major Parties

Black people have established themselves as a substantial part of the Democratic Party's support. As Figure 12.1 shows, black support for the Party rose from 5% in the early 1950s to 25% in 1984.

This represents a historic shift as,until the 1930s, most Blacks had identified with the Republican Party, the party that had generated emancipation. By 1948 the Blacks favoured the Democrats by a 2 to 1 ratio and this allegiance to the Democrats has accelerated. A staggering 90% of Blacks supported Mondale in 1984 with 86% supporting Dukakis in 1988. (see Table 12.9) The figures for selected southern states also indicate the strength of black allegiance to the Democrats.

Black support for the Democratic Party 1950 - 1984 *(as a percentage of total support)*

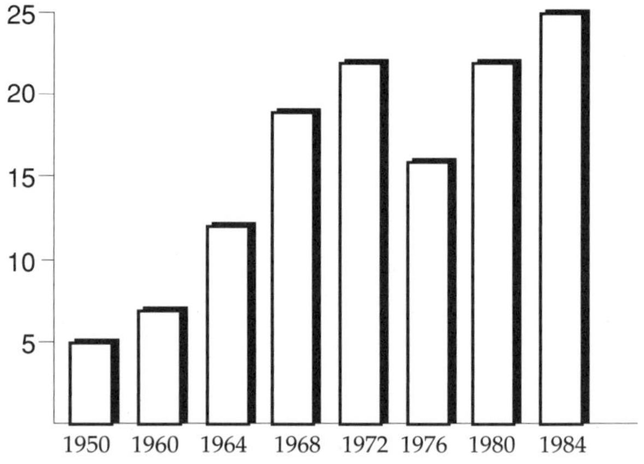

Figure 12.1

The 1988 Election - Was Race an Issue?

On 24 July 1988, the influential *Washington Post* published a story which indicated how the Republican candidate, George Bush, planned to attack the Democratic candidate, Michael Dukakis, on his attitudes towards and policies on crime. The attack was to focus on Dukakis's support for a scheme which gave weekend release to prison inmates, a scheme the Massachusetts Governor had inherited from his predecessor. One of the participants in this programme, a black man named Willie Horton who had been convicted of first-degree murder, had assaulted and raped a white woman while on a weekend pass. Bush used Willie Horton as a symbol of Dukakis's lack of toughness on crime. By election day on 8 November, Willie Horton had become as much of a household name as Michael Dukakis, thanks to a slick media campaign fought by the Republicans. In particular, one TV advert showed zombie-like prisoners moving through revolving doors, the voice-over making the point that Dukakis's policy was to allow weekend passes to first -degree murderers.

It was to prove an extremely successful attack, gaining Bush a substantial amount of support. While ostensibly criticising Dukakis's policies on crime, it also jarred the racial prejudice in numerous white people. Nothing is quite as abhorrent to a great number of white people as the thought of a black man raping a white woman. Bush may have been talking crime, but many were thinking race.

Presidential Preference by Race in Selected States, 1988 (%)						
	Whites		Blacks		Hispanics	
	Bush	Dukakis	Bush	Dukakis	Bush	Dukakis
Alabama	72	24	7	93	-	-
Florida	63	37	8	92	63	32
N Carolina	67	33	8	92	-	-
Texas	65	35	10	90	21	79
Louisiana	75	25	10	90	-	-
Mississippi	80	20	13	87	-	-
S Carolina	78	22	10	90	-	-

Table 12.10 Source: NBC

Since the 1970s the Republicans have made repeated efforts to woo the Blacks. Millions of dollars have been spent at state and national elections in a bid to attract the black voter to the Republican cause. As Table 12.10 illustrates, nationally these campaigns have had little success. Clarence Pendleton, Chairperson of the Civil Rights Commission, blamed his fellow Blacks for their lack of influence within the Republican Party. Their identification with the Democrats and with figures such as Jesse Jackson and Douglas Wilder has left them in the political wilderness. In Pendleton's opinion, black dependence on welfare schemes and affirmative action programmes has emasculated the Blacks and drained them of initiative and self-respect.

While Republican Party leaders would very much like greater black support, the policy preferences of black leaders for higher Federal spending on social welfare conflict with the minimal government stance of the Party. It would appear that there are two possible routes the Republicans can take to gain black support. They can either moderate their position on public welfare spending or attempt to convince the black electorate that they will benefit from policies which emphasise growth in the private sector. At the time of writing it is unclear which path George Bush and the Republicans will take.

Whichever path the Republicans take, it is clear that the Black community is not impressed with the language and action of the Bush administration. Surveys carried out into voter opinion after the 1990 mid-term elections make the point clearly. (see Table 12.11)

Interestingly, compared to Whites and Blacks, Hispanics seemed to be more positive about the direction in which the country was moving and the job George Bush was doing.

	Whites	Blacks	Hispanics
Voters Approve of Bush's Job	59%	31%	61%
Disapprove	38%	65%	37%
The Country is on:			
Right Track	40%	23%	50%
Wrong Track	56%	73%	44%

Table 12.11

Douglas Wilder

The grandson of slaves, Lawrence Douglas Wilder became the nation's first black Governor when he was elected to office in Virginia in November 1989. A lawyer by profession and a product of segregated education, Wilder, a Democrat, began his political career in the late 1960s when he secured a seat in the State Senate. Wilder does not consider himself to be an activist. Indeed, during the civil rights era Wilder was more likely to be found in a courtroom than on a freedom march. More concerned with making money than making headlines, Wilder very quickly amassed personal wealth - he is now a millionaire.

Although his victory in 1989 was by a whisker, it was, nevertheless, significant. Wilder attracted almost 60% of the white vote, a major feat in itself in a country where, for many voters, the colour of a person's skin is more important than the issues on which he or she stands.

13 THE IMPACT OF THE NEW RIGHT

When Ronald Reagan was elected President of the United States in November 1980, it was to herald a completely different approach to race relations and was to be the start of a series of policy decisions which were to have substantial direct and indirect effects on the lives of black Americans. Unlike the 1960s when race occupied centre stage in US politics in an almost unprecedented manner, and the 1970s when affirmative action programmes sprang up all over the country, the 1980s saw race removed from this prominent position in US social affairs. An ideological backlash to the political gains made by minority groups was taking place. Prime position had now been taken over by 'Reaganomics' - or more precisely the effects which Reagan's policies had on various social issues, race relations being but one. Many people felt that a counterrevolution in civil rights was under way in America. During the Reagan years (1980-1988), Federal Government spending on projects designed to help end racial segregation and to promote opportunities for disadvantaged minorities was drastically reduced. This new, more conservative economic climate gave support to those who had always regarded civil or group rights with distaste. Indeed, Reagan put forward the view that government aid to minorities was economically useless and socially divisive.

Reagan's position with regard to affirmative action programmes became very clear in the speech made at his first press conference after taking office in 1981, when he stated that some affirmative action programmes had been distorted into quota systems. The former President went on to say, "I'm old enough to remember when quotas existed in the US for the purpose of discrimination, and I don't want to see that happen again." Following these words from its leader, the administration attempted, through its various agencies, to reverse affirmative action programmes by attacking the concept of 'preference' in hiring and promotion. An influential member of Reagan's administration argued that positive discrimination does more harm than good when he stated, "It's demeaning because it says people are going to get ahead not because of what they can do, but because of their race." Indeed, in 1985 the Chairperson of the US Commission on Civil Rights informed Reagan that the Commission was "working on a colourblind society that has opportunities for all and guarantees success for none." This approach fitted in very neatly with Reagan's own view of society where no special privileges or rights should attach to one's race or colour. Reagan's record on racial policy was consistent with that view; he opposed every major civil rights measure considered by Congress as well as voicing opposition to the 1964 Civil Rights Act and the 1965 Voting Rights Act.

In March 1985, at a gathering in Alabama commemorating the march led by Martin Luther King from Selma to Montgomery some twenty years before, the Reverend JE Lowery, President of the Southern Christian Leadership Congress (SCLC), told the crowd, "We have kept the faith but the nation has not kept its promise." To many people involved in the civil rights movement, political forces, including the Reagan administration itself, were trying to "turn back the clock of racial history". Lowery's comments painted an accurate picture of the state of black America during the 1980s. The position of Blacks, when measured by indicators such as employment rates, number of families falling below the poverty line, and the widening gap between black and white infant mortality, showed a worsening situation. Yet, with the advent of freemarket Reaganomics, many people detected a new mood of 'social meanness' in the country with many Americans resenting having to provide for the 'underprivileged'. If, under Reagan, civil rights and affirmative action programmes were "under attack", this attack had the support of an increasing number of Americans.

Employment

It was not long before the Reagan administration began to chip away at that aspect of employment legislation which was most disliked by the President - affirmative action programmes. In particular, Reagan changed the regulations controlling the withdrawal of government contracts from firms deemed not to be complying with affirmative action targets. As a result, many more firms, particularly smaller ones, were released from their statutory requirement to employ a certain number of minorities. The emphasis was now on voluntary participation in such schemes.

To the Reagan administration, compulsory affirmative action programmes could be considered to discriminate against Whites and it was not long before this stance was to be tested in the courts. The city of Indianapolis had eagerly embraced the affirmative action legislation and had set quotas of 25% for Blacks in the police and fire services. In 1985, more than 13% of the city's firemen were black compared with 8% in 1978 and 14% of its policemen were black compared with 11% in 1978. Although city officials wished to increase these figures, in an important 1985 Supreme Court case, the Justice Department successfully opposed the city's efforts to use hiring quotas to help minorities get jobs in local government. In the same year, the Department urged states, counties and cities to

Ronald Reagan

voluntarily modify their affirmative action plans by removing numerical goals and quotas. There was a strong hint that failure to comply 'voluntarily' might result in court action. The hint was taken and nationwide many affirmative action schemes were modified or dismantled. According to the then Chief of the Justice Department, "The Law requires equal opportunities but not equal results; it encourages attempts to recruit women and Blacks through special programmes but it does not entitle any groups to jobs or promotion; these must be won by merit. Compensation for past discrimination is to be confined to individuals who have personally suffered and should not be extended to cover a whole class of people."

Education

As with employment, it was not long before the Reagan administration's free market philosophies began to be felt in the educational world. President Reagan, firmly opposed to busing, offered a much more low-key approach to enforced desegregation. Reagan's opposition did not stem from a belief in segregated schools. Rather it was derived from a belief that school integration means that the state takes away the decision making powers which should be with the parents: deciding in what kind of communities their children will be raised and what kind of education their children will receive. Reagan also believed that busing would lead to the loss of neighbourhood schools, resulting in a weaker community and family instability. As a consequence of this low-key approach to enforced desegregation, many cities are now going their own way, with the result that desegregation policies vary greatly from city to city.

The Reagan administration encouraged education authorities and establishments to get around enforced desegregation in other ways. Since 1970 the Inland Revenue Service (IRS) had refused tax exemption to any private school that practised discrimination. However, in January 1982 President Reagan announced that the IRS policy was illegal and should therefore be reversed. Many private educational establishments were delighted that they had regained their original tax-exempt status and two in particular had cause to celebrate. Two southern evangelical private colleges, the Goldsboro Christian Schools in North Carolina, admitted no black children and the Bob Jones University in Greenville, South Carolina admitted black students but expelled them if they dated Whites. These establishments argued that since they were educational and their discriminatory practices sprang from their religious beliefs, they should be tax-exempt. The Reagan administration agreed with them. However, in the now famous Supreme Court case and in an embarrassing rebuff to President Reagan, the Supreme Court judges ruled by an overwhelming 8 -1 that racially discriminatory private schools should be ineligible for tax exemption.

THE NEW RIGHT

During the 1970s and 1980s the United States underwent a great transformation. Economically, the country was at its most vulnerable since the 1930s, with inflation and business collapses surging to unprecedented levels. Americans, used to ever-increasing standards of living, were at a loss to understand what was happening to their country. Socially, problems were intensifying. Unemployment and poverty rates were reaching an all-time high. The flood of immigrants and refugees from Latin America and the Far East only added to the problem. Many white Americans blamed the seemingly endless stream of 'illegal aliens' as the cause of their misfortune.

On the international scene the country had suffered the humiliating 'losses' of Vietnam and Nicaragua, the final straw coming at the end of the 1970s with the humiliation of the Iranian hostage crisis. As the country ran deeper into debt with no prospect of relief in sight, people in the US began to contemplate the idea that perhaps they were no longer 'Number One'.

Mainstream America had seen its perpetual prosperity and military invincibility shaken to its foundations. Traditional conservatism seemed to have little to offer people reeling from the shock of the previous decades. It was against this background that the new right was to emerge and develop. The new right is not a political party; rather it is a well-organised movement of politicians, pressure groups and fundamentalist Protestant sects, bonded together by a common philosophy and shared objectives.

The new right, bound together by the following ideological themes, found its support growing considerably during the 1980s. At the heart of the new right philosophy is:

- the respect for authority;
- the mistrust of Federal Government programmes;
- the defence of traditional moral values;
- the opposition to special privileges for minority groups.

Although the new right does not display overt racism, the pursuit of the above objectives can, and often does, lead to race becoming an issue in its own right. Ronald Reagan and his successor George Bush, while distancing themselves from significant aspects of the new right agenda, have, nevertheless, found themselves in agreement with new right racial positions, affirmative action programmes being a case in point.

The grumblings of white ethnic discontent were first heard in the southern states of the USA but it was not long before it had developed into a national roar. In 1964 when George Wallace started to move out of the South with his widely publicised resistance to school desegregation, he found to his surprise an eager and enthusiastic support in the northern states. Indeed white reaction to affirmative action could be witnessed in various parts of the USA - California, Seattle, Washington, New York, Boston. Issues ranging from housing to school desegregation had aroused the deeply rooted prejudices in many white people.

Interestingly enough, the reaction was not confined to white Protestant southerners or northerners - White Anglo Saxon Protestants (WASP). Studies were to show that support for politicians like Wallace was to come from traditional European immigrants, eg. Poles, Irish, Italians - groups that had only recently dragged themselves up from poverty and powerlessness.

Another factor which was to help increase white reaction to affirmative action was the growth of black consciousness movements. During the 1960s the attitudes of politically active Blacks had undergone quite a rapid transformation. Attitudes such as "we are like everyone else and want only integration" had changed to "we are of course different from anyone else and want our proper share of power and wealth". The Negroes had become 'Blacks'. This hardening of attitude was mirrored by a changing attitude from various white ethnic groups. Reactions such as "we are like all other Americans - even more so" ... "We work harder" ... "We are more patriotic - we are more anti-communist" were much more common. White ethnic groups that had had to give up much of their cultural background to be "more American than most" were filled with resentment when they saw their schools and colleges offer courses in Black Studies, Puerto-Rican Studies and the like. This resentment was often fuelled by the extreme right-wing groups such as the John Birch Society, the Ku Klux Klan and the American Nazis. This rise in right-wing extremism took place against a background of economic recession. Many poor unemployed Whites saw the gains made by Blacks during the 1960s and 1970s as being achieved at their expense. The decline of traditional industries in northern cities accompanied by rising unemployment provided a fertile breeding ground for racist philosophies. Certainly the 1970s-1990s has seen the spread of groups such as the Ku Klux Klan into northern and urban areas. Violent reaction to affirmative action was fiercest among the poorer working-class Whites - "We have to live beside them, work beside them and send our children to school in the same bus."

The Revival of White Supremacy

As we have already noted, the passing of civil rights legislation in the 1960s and the effects of the affirmative action programmes in the 1970s fuelled a revival of anti-black feeling. Between 1971 and 1980, the Ku Klux Klan almost tripled its national membership to approximately 20,000. As the ranks swelled, Klan intimidation and violence became much more open and much more outrageous. Across the country newspapers carried reports of Klan atrocities-lynchings, shootings and fire-bombings. However, these same newspapers rarely reported that the perpetrators of these crimes had been brought to justice. Federal response to these atrocities was very muted. Public feeling towards Blacks was changing rapidly. So much so, that Jesse Jackson, speaking in November 1980, noted, "Racism has become fashionable again and feelings of guilt towards Blacks have turned to feelings of hostility." Many Whites accused the government of racism in reverse and looked in anguish as their economic status was eroded by the recession and unemployment.

The Extreme Right

However, unlike the early 1960s when extreme right-wing groups targeted individual Blacks, it is now the Federal Government which attracts their wrath. "... To go out and shoot a negro is foolish," stated Klansman Thomas Robb. "It is not the negro in the alley who's responsible for what's wrong with this country. It's the traitors in Washington." To many people on the extreme right, society has become polluted by the Federal Government and its increasing impact upon day-to-day life. A feeling of anxiety in some Whites, engendered by the supposed over-attention given by politicians to minority interests has led to the view being increasingly voiced that "It's nice to have someone that represents white people ...". (see page 72)

14 ECONOMIC SITUATION OF BLACKS

During the years of the Reagan administration there was a general feeling of isolation and neglect among the black population of America. Reagan, elected to office in 1980 and re-elected in 1984 on a manifesto which appealed to the vast majority of (white) American voters - lower taxation, a reduction in inflation, a reduction in bureaucratic waste and inefficiency, a balanced budget, a strengthened military - was hailed as the man who would get the US off its knees. However, as the President's policies were implemented, it became clear that to achieve his aims a drastic cut in public welfare spending would take place. Very soon many social welfare programmes were cut or disbanded. The cutbacks in public spending hit hardest at the minorities and disadvantaged in the country. Reagan's policies were criticised as being socially divisive as they took from the poor and gave more to the rich.

UNEMPLOYMENT

In 1968 the Kerner Report put forward the view that the majority of Blacks were living in a "state of crisis". Black unemployment levels were nearly double those for Whites. Despite the implementation of affirmative action programmes during the 1970s and 1980s, there was no significant improvement in this ratio. In 1990 under George Bush, the most popular Republican president with Blacks for two decades, there was no improvement, with the unemployment rate for Blacks at 13% compared to 5.3% for Whites.

Perhaps the most worrying aspect of black unemployment is the unemployment rate for black teenagers. In the post-recession period of 1983, black youth unemployment reached a staggering 48.5% - a full 29% higher than that for white teenagers. (See Figure 14.1)

These extremely high levels of youth unemployment have created tensions in inner city areas. Many city officials are concerned that, unless finance is made available to reduce unemployment, civil disorder similar to that which devastated Los Angeles and Detroit in the late 1960s and Miami in 1980 may be repeated. During the 1980s the government's response to these high levels of youth unemployment was to encourage 'work yourself off welfare' schemes. President Reagan, a great exponent of the Workfare concept, believed that they would free the unemployed from the "spider's web of dependence on government handouts". President Bush, like his predecessor, is extremely suspicious of 'big' government intervention and argues that the solution to unemployment and other social problems lies with the people themselves. In 1990 President Bush set up a special cabinet committee to examine the ways in which Federal Government could 'empower' local agencies to deal with their problems.

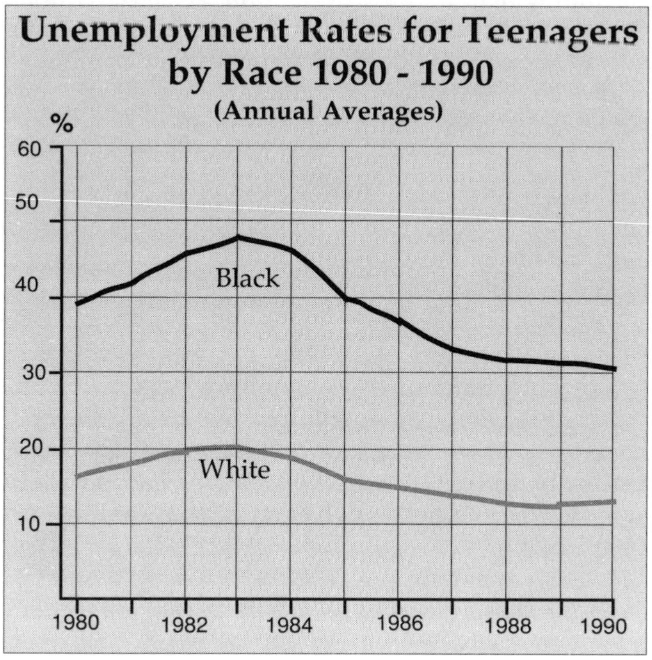

Figure 14.1 Source: US Department of Commerce, Bureae of the Census

Despite the fears of many city officials, no serious outbursts have occurred in American cities, with the exception of Miami. Although poverty and unemployment levels are higher now than they were in the 1960s, things are relatively calm. If economic conditions are the acid test for social unrest, then should there not be serious inner city upheaval? Several theories have been put forward as possible explanations. Firstly, it has been argued that the social and economic effects of Reagan's policies were not felt by Blacks alone. Secondly, many Blacks have channelled their energies and aggressions into the political process rather than on the streets. Although Blacks may be in a worse position economically than they were in the 1960s, politically they are much stronger, with far more local and national representation. Thirdly, it is all too evident that the mounting frustration and dejection among black youth has given rise to personal rather than group protest. The rising levels of black gang violence and increasing use of drugs signal self-destruction as opposed to inner city destruction.

As Table 14.1 illustrates, although unemployment rates in

Unemployment Rates by Sex and Race: 1983 and 1988 (%)
Annual Averages

	White		Black	
	1983	1988	1983	1988
Persons, 16 years & over				
Total	8.4	4.7	19.5	11.7
Male	8.8	4.7	20.3	11.7
Female	7.9	4.7	18.6	11.7
Persons, 16-19 years old				
Total	19.3	13.1	48.5	32.4
Male	20.2	13.9	48.8	32.7
Female	18.3	12.3	48.2	32.0

Table 14.1
Source: US Department of Commerce, Bureau of the Census

general have fallen over the period 1983-1988, the unemployment rate for black teenagers remains two and a half times higher than the figure for white teenagers. However, unlike the 1960s when black youth, filled with a sense of anger and bitterness, lashed out against the symbols of white property, power and privilege, the 1980s have seen the ghetto's black rage unleashed against itself. Black crime rates have soared. About half of the American prison population is Black. As the *Economist* on 30 March 1991 noted, "The average black boy is more likely to go to prison than university. His life expectancy is falling and he is seven times as likely to be murdered as a white boy. In parts of the country, a black man between the ages of 15 and 25 is more likely to be killed than was an American soldier in Vietnam ...". Table 14.2 illustrates the alarming figures.

Death Rates from Homicide, by Race 1970-1988
(Rates per 100,000 of population)

		1970	1980	1985	1988
White	Male	6.8	10.9	8.2	8.0
	Female	2.1	3.2	2.9	3.0
Black	Male	67.6	66.6	48.4	58.0
	Female	13.3	13.5	11.0	13.0

Table 14.2
Source: US Department of Commerce, Bureau of the Census

In June 1986 over 1,700 people were held in US jails awaiting execution - 43.5% of this group were Black. (See Table 14.3)

Prisoners Under Sentence of Death 1980 and 1986

	1980	1986
Total	714	1781
Black	287	775
White	427	1006

Table 14.3
Source: US Department of Commerce, Bureau of the Census

Drug abuse has reached unprecedented levels among the young. Drugs such as cocaine, heroin and crack are now being pushed fairly openly in the inner city high schools. Not unexpectedly, drug related crime is also on the increase. Juvenile gangs are much more evident in many cities, resulting from unemployed black teenagers having nothing better to do with their time. For those who drop out of school and for those unemployed, the Federal Government has little to offer. Since the 1980s, Federal employment and training programmes have been cut by about 50%.

The massive increase in drug abuse by Blacks can now be

Drug Overdose Deaths, by Race: 1979-1988
(per 100,000 of population)

	1981	1982	1983	1984	1985	1986	1987	1988
Blacks	4.6	4.7	4.5	5.5	5.8	6.8	7.4	8.2
Whites	2.9	2.9	2.9	3.0	3.2	3.7	3.4	3.8

Table 14.4
Source: US National Centre for Health Statistics Data

seen to be affecting the black population in other ways. Blacks have been particularly hard hit by a rapidly growing share of drug-related deaths and incidence of AIDS. (See Tables 14.4 and 14.5)

Incidence of AIDS, by Race: 1990
(per 100,000 of population)

Black	Males	2,378
	Females	514
White	Males	785
	Females	39

Table 14.5
Source: US National Centre for Health Statistics Data

BLACK POVERTY IN THE 1990s

"Children grow up without fathers in an atmosphere of poverty and deprivation which is increased as mothers are forced to work to provide support."
Kerner Report, 1968

In a speech to the NAACP in July 1981 Ronald Reagan outlined his views on why poverty persisted and the ways in which he intended to deal with it. "Many in Washington over the years have been more dedicated to making needy people government-dependent rather than independent. They've created a new kind of bondage. Just as the Emancipation Proclamation freed black people one hundred and eighteen years ago, today we need to declare an economic emancipation ... Rebuilding America's economy is an absolute moral imperative if we're to avoid splitting society in two, with class against class. We must bring more Blacks into the mainstream and we must do it now." The message was clear - the poor would benefit only when the entire economy improved. Blacks should put their faith in private enterprise and not public welfare.

However, statistics taken from the 1990 census would seem to indicate that little has changed for black America since the Kerner Commission reported in 1968. Unemployment and a deteriorating social environment have continued to have a destructive effect on black families. In 1989 about 2.1 million or 30% of all black families were below the poverty line, an increase of two per cent on the 1979 figure. (See Figures 14.2 and 14.3)

The past two decades have witnessed an unprecedented deterioration of the two-parent family across all groups, but it has been most striking among Blacks. (See Table 14.6)

Approximately 50% of all black children, as opposed to 16% of white children, live in families headed by a woman, and two-thirds of these children live below the official poverty line. Moreover, the average income of households headed by a black woman is only about a third as high as in those where there are two parents. (See Tables 14.7 and 14.8)

Even for those Blacks who are in employment, the last twenty years have seen the gap between their average income and the average income for Whites widen. (See *My colleague not my neighbour*, page 87))

The Statistics demonstrating a Black Underclass

Families below the Poverty Level by Race 1979 - 1987 (%)

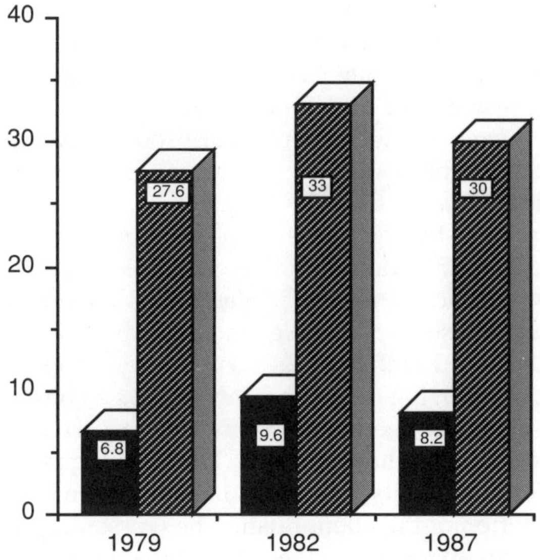

Figure 14.2

White Black

Persons below the Poverty Level by Race 1979 - 1987 (%)

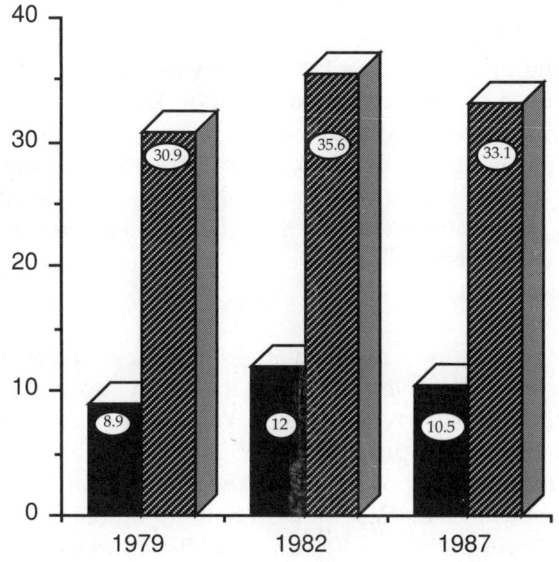

Figure 14.3

White Black

Changing Family Patterns, by Race: 1970-1990 (%)

	1970			1980			1990		
	Black	**All**	**White**	**Black**	**All**	**White**	**Black**	**All**	**White**
Two-parent families	64	87	90	48	79	83	39	72	77
One-parent families:	36	13	10	52	22	17	61	28	23
- headed by mother	33	12	9	49	19	15	56	24	19
- headed by father	3	1	1	3	2	2	4	4	4

Table 14.6

Poverty Levels for Female Headed Families by Race (% Below Poverty Line)

	1979	1982	1987
White	22.3	27.9	26.7
Black	49.2	56.2	51.8

Table 14.7

Average Family Income, by Type of Family and Race of Householder: 1979 and 1987 ($)

	Married Couple		*Female Householder*	
	White	**Black**	**White**	**Black**
1979	34,050	26,300	17,890	10,750
1987	35,300	27,180	17,020	9,710
1989	35,975	27,750	18,946	10,630

Table 14.8

Expectation of Life at Birth, by Race (Years): 1970-1986

		1970	1980	1986
White	(Male)	68.0	70.7	72.0
	(Female)	75.6	78.1	78.9
Black	(Male)	60.0	63.8	65.5
	(Female)	68.3	72.5	73.6

Table 14.9

Infant Mortality Rates, by Race: 1970-1985

(Deaths per 1,000 Live Births)

	1970	1980	1985
White	17.8	11.0	9.3
Black	32.6	21.4	18.2

Table 14.10

Health Insurance Coverage Status, by Race:

(% Covered by Private or Government Health Insurance 1985)

	Total	Private	Medicaid	Not Covered
White	87.6	79.6	5.0	12.4
Black	80.7	55.7	21.6	19.3
Hispanic	73.0	55.2	15.9	27.0

Table 14.11

Source for Figures 14.2 & 14.3 and Tables 14.6, 14.7, 14.8 and 14.9 : US Department of Commerce, Bureau of the Census

Source for Tables 14.9, 14.10 & 14.11: US National Centre for Health Statistics Data

Other indicators paint an equally gloomy picture. Not only are there now more Blacks below the official poverty line than there were in the late 1970s, but many are dying sooner. Health statistics, another indicator of lifestyle and life chance, point out the wide gap that still exists between black and white America. (See Tables 14.9, 14.10 and 14.11)

GHETTO LIFE

During the period 1960 to 1988 there was a tremendous movement of population into and out of American cities. Basically, Whites were moving out of city centres and Blacks were moving in. By 1988, 57% of all black Americans lived in central city areas, and only 25% lived in the suburbs. By contrast, only 27% of the white population lived in city centres while almost 50% lived in the suburbs. (See Table 14.12)

According to figures released in 1988, Blacks living in cities, regardless of their poverty status, were more likely to be living in poverty areas than Whites or persons of Hispanic origin. Approximately 55% of Blacks living in central areas lived in poverty areas and 71% of poor Blacks were concentrated in these areas. The comparable figures for Whites were 17% and 40% and for Hispanics 45% and 62% respectively. Evidence would seem to suggest that segregation, not integration, is on the increase. Studies of the 1980 and 1990 censuses have revealed startling patterns. In Chicago, St Louis, Detroit and Philadelphia, more than half of the black residents lived in segregated neighbourhoods in 1990. Detroit actually had more Blacks living in segregation at the end of the 1980s than at the beginning. For poor Blacks, without the money to move, living in an inner city ghetto can mean going for days without seeing a white face. Such segregation inevitably breeds resentment and fuels prejudice. Young Blacks, isolated from the wider world, are soon drawn into the destructive spiral of their social condition. (See *North Lawndale: Middle Class To Underclass*) The situation is made worse by the expanding phenomenon of 'black flight'. The past decade has seen a 50% increase in the number of black managers, professionals and government officials. These black people who have made a success of their lives and could act as positive role models to the young are moving out of the ghettos. As a consequence, the status of the ghetto poor, sometimes referred to as the underclass, is further reduced. The growing isolation of America's inner city minorities has now been brought to the attention of President Bush. The worsening situation of inner city Blacks is now seen to be affecting the whole of America. The cost of the welfare system has risen dramatically: spending on all federal programmes more than tripled over the period 1965 to 1987. In 1965 the American taxpayer poured $141 billion into federal programmes; in 1987 the figure was $520 billion. Despite this, poverty still exists and America's Blacks still seem to be destined to fail in the land of opportunity.

Residence of Population, by Race: 1988 (%)

White		Black
27.0	City Centres	57.0
49.8	Suburbs	25.0
23.4	Non-Metropolitan	18.0

Table 14.12
Source: US Department of Commerce, Bureau of the Census

NORTH LAWNDALE: Middle Class to Underclass

In early 1966, Martin Luther King rented a small apartment in North Lawndale, a middle-class Jewish district in West Chicago, to launch his 'fair housing' drive. A fairly prosperous district, North Lawndale was able to provide ample employment opportunities for its citizens by way of a Western Electric factory, an International Harvester plant and Sears world headquarters.

Today, however, things are very different. The house which Martin Luther King and his team rented is gone, replaced by dereliction, broken bottles and weeds. The Jews have long gone, to be replaced by Arab shopkeepers working from behind bullet-proof shields and carrying guns in their belts. In terms of employment, all that is left is a slimmed down Western Electric Company employing only 1,000, a bank, a supermarket, some shops, bars and off-licences. The resulting high level of unemployment has been compounded by the flight of the well-educated black middle class, the beneficiaries of the civil rights gains. Today North Lawndale is a typical underclass ghetto.

It is a dangerous and violent place to live. Although each day the city spends more than $40,000 policing the district's streets, a violent crime will occur on average every three hours. With a population of 61,500, two per cent of Chicago's total, North Lawndale accounts for 10% of the city's ambulance and fire brigade call-outs. Inevitably, nearly all the cars stolen from the suburbs end up in North Lawndale and nearby ghettos. The cars are stolen by organised gangs whose members are aged between 10 and 19. For these young school drop-outs it is the drug dealers with their heavy gold bracelets, neck chains and Nike trainers who are the role models.

Born into the underclass, very few will escape from it. The inevitability of this process can be seen in the life of Dorothy Sanders, a pleasant woman of 32 who lives in North Lawndale. Dorothy's mother, pregnant with Dorothy at 15, left her home in Mississippi to live in a small apartment in Chicago. When Dorothy was 15, she too became pregnant and left school to have her baby, Barbara. To Dorothy's great dismay, Barbara followed her mother's and grandmother's example. Now Barbara, single, unemployed and with child, waits eagerly every month for 'mother's day' to arrive, for that is the day when the welfare cheque will arrive and perhaps, more than likely, a visit from the absent father.

My colleague, not my neighbour

A visitor who flies between America's larger cities, and who elects to stay, probably against his hosts' advice, in hotels in the centre of town, may leave with the impression that the United States is a predominantly black nation. By day, office-workers and shoppers bring the usual mix of colours to inner city streets; at sunset the people, as well as the sky, turn darker.

A single-family suburban home is the American dream and, with America's blessing of space, often an attainable one. Middle-class white families are much less likely than their counterparts in Europe to live near the centre of town. City-dwelling white middle-class families already had their eyes on the suburbs before the post war migration of black families from country to town, from south to north, hastened their flight.

In the early 1940s, three-quarters of all Blacks lived in the southern states; by the 1970s no more than half of them were still there. Black families had left pell-mell, like the children of Israel fleeing Egypt for the promised land. The south-north railway lines, as much as anything, dictated their destination, leading them to Chicago, St Louis, Philadelphia and New York.

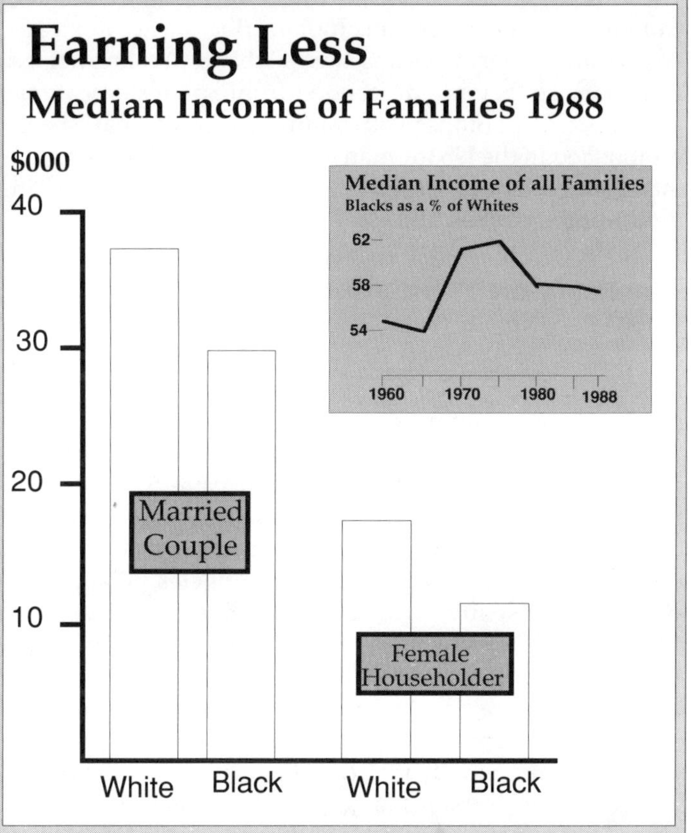

The 1980s saw a small net migration of Blacks back southward, as black families, like white ones, set off for the promising sun-belt cities. But black migration to the cities, and white flight to the suburbs, have radically changed many of America's largest cities. Chicago grew from 8% black in 1940 to 40% black in 1980; Detroit from 9% to 63%; Cleveland from 10% to 44%; Washington from 28% to 70%. By 1988 roughly the same large proportion of Blacks as of Whites lived in metropolitan areas; but, within those areas, more than half of the Blacks, compared with a quarter of the Whites, were living in the cities themselves.

Gradually, as the black migrants saved their money, they too set off for the suburbs - but with difficulty, and not, as a rule, to the same suburbs as the Whites. Although the proportion of white Americans who live in an all-white neighbourhood declined in the 1980s from 75% to 35%, black-white segregation in housing has survived the death of legal discrimination. Well-off, well-educated Blacks who want to move out of the inner city will encounter difficulties. Other things being equal, Blacks may find it harder to get a mortgage than Whites would. And black house-hunters, whatever their income or education, tend to be steered toward black areas rather than to an integrated neighbourhood.

The cities where they are left behind are of every sort. Many, like the curate's egg, are good in parts, but pretty bad overall. They have desolate centres, lonely and dangerous by night. They have mean slums, dangerous by day or night. Black families in the cities, whatever their income, are exposed to far more ugliness, crime and bad education than white families in the suburbs.

Source: Adapted from *Economist*, 3 March, 1990

15 The Hispanics

Most Americans can claim that, at some time in their family history, they were members of a minority group which struggled to establish itself in American society. As we have already seen, some groups were able to establish themselves better than others. Non-European immigrants and their descendants have always found it much more difficult to get a foothold on the American ladder of progress. This is well illustrated by the failure of the black community to prosper in American society to the same extent as European groups. However, there are a number of other minority groups of non-European descent who have found it equally difficult to prosper in America. These include the Mexican-Americans, Puerto Ricans, Cubans and the indigenous Indian tribes. The Mexican-Americans, Puerto Ricans and Cubans are known as Hispanics as they are descended from Spanish-speaking ancestors. Most of these other minority groups have been established in the US for many years but they have gained increasing attention in recent years due to the increase in their numbers. (See Table 9.1 page 58)

The Hispanic Population

In 1989 the Hispanic population of the United States totalled 20,100,000, an increase of over 34% since 1980. It is interesting to note that approximately half of this growth resulted from net migration and half from natural increase. The rate of increase has been extremely rapid and, as is the case with the black community (see page 59), this has resulted in a very youthful population with 35% under the age of 18. This has caused severe problems for certain cities. In the school district of Los Angeles, 62% of the pupils are Hispanic, with a drop-out rate approaching 40%. The 'Hispanisation' of the city is being quickly followed throughout the state. In 1985 one Californian in five was a Hispanic. On present trends this figure will increase in the early 21st century to one in two. If school drop-out rates remain as high as they are today, the social and economic problems facing the cities will be immense. One social commentator likened the prospect to the "Third World re-conquering the heartland of the American Dream".

The Hispanic population is composed of people from various countries and these Subgroups are shown in Figure15.1. Unlike the Blacks, however, Hispanics are not so widely spread over the USA. In 1989, nine states accounted for 89% of the Hispanic population. Three states alone - California, Texas and New York - were home to 65% of the Hispanic population. Figure 15.2 shows the full breakdown.

SOCIAL & ECONOMIC CHARACTERISTICS

Educational Attainment: Although there has been a considerable improvement in educational attainment, Hispanics still have a fair amount of catching up to do when compared to other groups. (See Figure 15.3)

Indeed, there are differences in attainment levels among the Hispanic Subgroups. Young Mexicans, for example, are least likely to complete 4 years of high school education. (See Table 15.1)

Income and Employment: Very little has changed for Hispanic people in terms of income and employment. For those Hispanics in employment low wages are the norm, with a great many (40%) earning less than $10,000 per year. (See Table 15.2) What has changed, though, is the thriving black economy to be found in the Hispanic 'barrios' where illegal immigrants work at such jobs as maids and gardeners. With the massive influx of illegal immigrants over the last decade, the black economy is booming. Occupational distribution has not changed much either. Hispanic men tend to be employed more in blue-collar jobs such as factory workers or drivers. Hispanic women, on the other hand, are more likely to be found in administrative employment. However, 24% of Hispanic women are

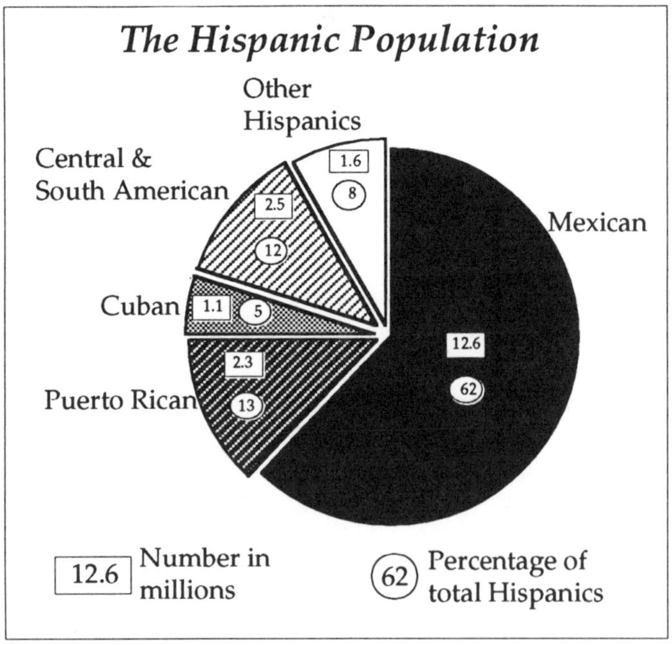

Figure 15.1

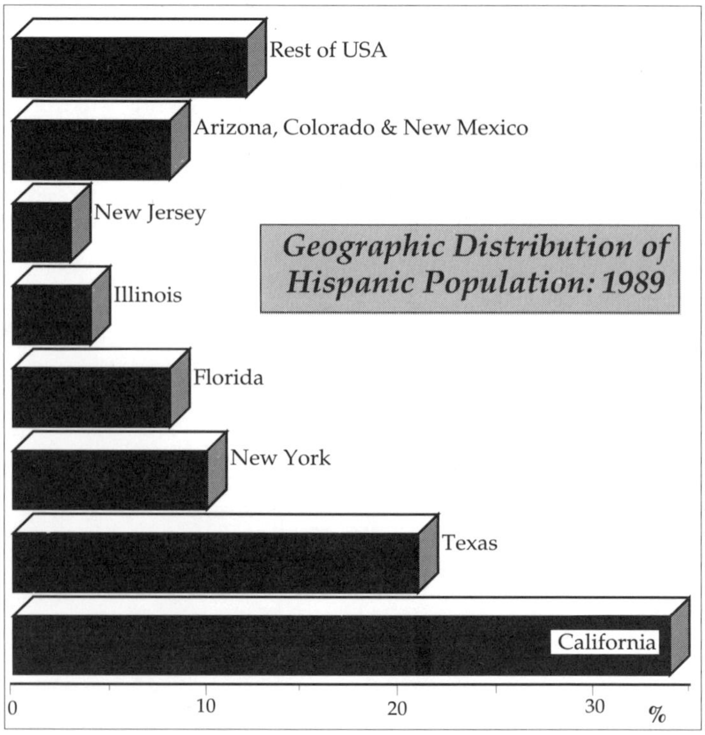

Figure 15.2

A Statistical Picture of the Hispanic Population of the USA

Educational Attainment by Race: 1988

Those completing four or more years of high school

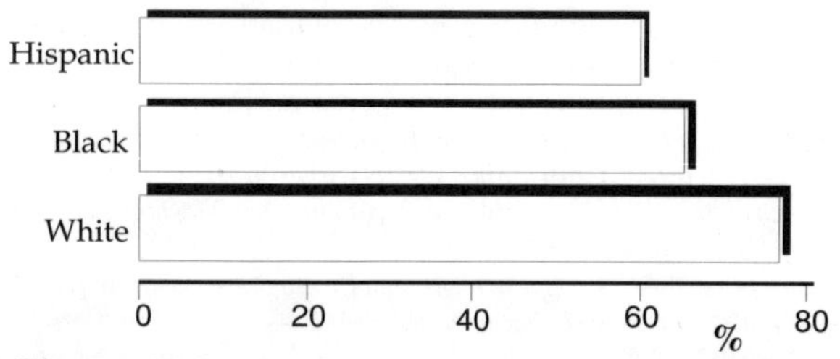

Figure 15.3
Source: US Department of Commerce, Bureau of the Census

Unemployment by Subgroup, 1989

Total Population	5.4%
Total Hispanic Population	7.8%
Mexican	8.5%
Puerto Rican	9.1%
Cuban	6.1%
Central & Southern American	6.2%
Other Hispanic	6.0%

Table 15.3

Hispanics who completed 4 or more years of High School by Subgroup, 1989

	25-34 Yrs	35+ Yrs
Total Hispanic	60%	45%
Mexican	50%	38%
Puerto Rican	76%	42%
Cuban	84%	58%
Central & Southern American	70%	63%
Other Hispanic	77%	56%

Table 15.1
Source: US Department of Commerce, Bureau of the Census

Those Living Below Poverty Level by Subgroup, 1988

Total Population	13.9%
Total Hispanic Population	26.7%
Mexican	28.5%
Puerto Rican	33.7%
Cuban	16.5%
Central & Southern American	17.9%
Other Hispanic	22.8%

Table 15.4
Source: US Department of Commerce, Bureau of the Census

Male Earnings by Subgroup, 1988 (%)

	Total Population	Total Hispanic	Mexican	Puerto Rican	Cuban	Central & Southern American	Other
Less than $10,000	25.9	35.3	39.7	27.4	27.4	27.7	29.5
$10,000 - $24,999	33.2	43.3	41.9	48.0	36.6	47.8	45.7
$25,000 - $49,999	31.4	18.7	16.6	21.2	26.9	20.9	21.3
$50,000 or more	9.6	2.8	1.8	3.5	9.2	3.6	3.5

Table 15.2
Source: US Department of Commerce, Bureau of the Census

employed as service workers, mainly in the catering industry.

Hispanics are still more likely to be unemployed than non-Hispanics. In 1989 the unemployment rate for Hispanic males over 16 years of age was almost 8%. Table 15.3 gives the figures in more detail. Linked to unemployment is, of course, poverty.

In 1988, 26.7% or some 5.4 million persons of Hispanic origin were living in poverty and half of this total were children under 18 years old. (See Table 15.4)

Political Activity

Generally, the Hispanics have had a very low level of participation in elections for all public offices. (See Table 15.5) A number of possible explanations have been put forward to explain why Hispanics do not vote. Firstly, there is a high proportion (37%) of the Hispanic population who are not American citizens and so do not qualify for a vote. Secondly, younger people are less likely to vote than older people and since the Hispanic population is a particularly youthful population, we might expect a lower voting rate. Thirdly, studies have shown that there seems to be a link between educational achievement and political participation. The more education an individual has received, the more likely he or she is to vote. The language barrier is another factor. With many Hispanics maintaining that the Spanish language is inseparable from their ethnic and cultural identity, many remain primarily Spanish-speaking. This, of course, makes participating in the election process difficult. The low voting rates among Hispanics has also been evident in their lack of

Mario Vargas Llosa on the economic miracle that a colony of Cuban exiles created in the US.

Miami's tale of two cities

Señora Evita is Bolivian and she came to Miami 10 years ago, on a tourist visa that she obtained in La Paz. She stayed there illegally, looking after children, cleaning houses and ironing, until the police caught up with her seven years later because of a traffic accident. The State of Florida started deportation proceedings against her and she was obliged to turn to a specialised lawyer who was able to delay her expulsion by one year at a cost of $1,000.

When it seemed inevitable that she would be deported, the same lawyer put Señora Evita in touch with an agency that rented her a husband - a Cuban with a US passport - who agreed to marry and then divorce her as soon as she was naturalised (that cost $2,000).

The legal proceedings take a minimum of two years. However, Doña Evita's husband turned out to be an inveterate drunkard who died after one year of marriage. With the threat of deportation hanging over her once more, she was saved last year by the amnesty on long-term illegal immigrants. Now she is a fully legal resident, ironing clothes 10 hours a day in the elegant residences around Key Biscayne.

She told me her story, among bundles of shirts and trousers, in the house of a Columbian industrialist and landowner, Don Cesar P., whom the reign of violence in his country has obliged to move to the US from where he runs his businesses. His wife, Esther, misses her family and friends in Cali, but she already has a circle of new friends, all Latin Americans.

Neither Doña Evita nor Doña Esther feel the least bit handicapped by not being able to speak English. To tell you the truth, they do not really need to in Miami. Two newspapers are published daily in Spanish; two television channels broadcast in Spanish; innumerable radio stations transmit only Latin programmes and music. There are no famous singers from Spain or Latin America who don't appear frequently in Miami. The city holds an Hispanic Theatre Festival, and there is a Latin Carnival in which, every year, a million people dance rumbas and huarachas, sing cumbias and merengues, and parade dressed as gauchos or guajiras.

Exile can render people almost religiously attached to their own cultures. In some places they've celebrated, for instance, the 80th anniversary of the famous bolero Quiereme Mucho by the Cuban composer Roig. Nearly 2,000 spectators crowded into the municipal theatre in Dade County to listen to two young singers, Orlando and Mara, brought up in exile. They brought the audience to its feet singing, with reverence bordering on ecstasy.

I'm amazed by the way Latin American customs and language - 'the Hispanics' as they're known in the States - have become firmly rooted in Miami, to the extent of giving it a truly unique character. A rich mythology has been built up around the city, particularly its negative aspects. Supposedly all South American villains turn up there, sooner or later: drug barons to ex-dictators, not to mention crooked politicians and the dubious nouveaux riches. Which is no doubt an accurate picture.

Equally, Miami has a growing and varied cultural life, with two symphony orchestras, a ballet company, dozens of art galleries, and a vast complex of museums and theatres under construction. Many writers, artists, composers, and academics of Latin American origin work in their disciplines.
It is the first time in US history that a wave of immigrants has not been absorbed and dispersed by the melting pot (the putrid pot): the Cubans have retained their cultural identity, at the same time participating in the US economy. This Latin touch has been the incentive for tens of thousands of Columbians, Nicaraguans, Salvadoreans, Panamanians, Peruvians, Ecuadorians.

It is quite likely that the Spanish-speaking population has overtaken the English-speaking population. It is certainly not a passive community. It is well organised with its own mayors, aldermen, deputies, and it knows how to lobby Congress. Many immigrants have to start off at the bottom, second-class citizens discriminated against, exploited by the establishment. But in Miami this is not the norm, it is the exception.

When the first big wave of Cubans arrived three decades ago it was still a small and lethargic southern city. In the space of a generation, that wave has transformed the place into a bustling metropolis. Today it is one of the big financial centres on the continent. Miami is an instructive example of how, in the right surroundings, Hispanics can be as tenacious, disciplined, and equally good in enterprise as the Anglo-Saxons and the Japanese.

One afternoon, as I came out of the Florida International University - its rector, Modesto Maldique, is the only rector of Latin American origin in the US - I bumped into a young Peruvian engineer whom I knew from Lima. He had come to stay. He showed me his hands: "I only managed to get work as a labourer," he explained, "but I'm earning a lot and I'm sure that, with a bit of hard work and luck, I will be able to get ahead."

From The Guardian 11 June 1991

representation in Congress. Even in those areas where there are high concentrations of Hispanics, very few Hispanic candidates are to be found.

MIAMI - THE BROKEN MOSAIC

Florida is one of the sunbelt states which prospered during the 1970s and 1980s. This prosperity is also reflected in Miami, which is the principal city of South Florida. Her prosperity is partly attributable to her geographic position, being well placed for trade with Central and South America and the Caribbean. The growing importance of these markets has attracted commerce and industry into the city and to Dade County.

This accelerating prosperity also turned Miami into a magnet for many different groups wishing to escape economic or political repression in the numerous poverty-stricken countries of the Caribbean and Latin America. Since the early 1960s the city has been the main point of entry to the USA for many immigrants from these areas with Cubans, Puerto Ricans and Haitians dominating at the beginning. Today, though, it is from Nicaragua that the new surge of immigration is coming. During the period 1989 to mid-1991 as many as 200 refugees a day were flooding into the city. This has had a major impact on the population of Miami, with an estimated 150,000 more Nicaraguans seeking refuge in the city.

However, unlike the 1960s when the flood of Cuban immigrants brought economic benefits to Miami, the immigrants of today bring only economic and social problems.

Voting in Presidential & Congressional Elections by Race (%)

	Presidential Elections			Congressional Elections		
	1988	**1984**	**1980**	**1986**	**1982**	**1978**
White	59.1	61.4	60.9	47.0	49.9	47.3
Black	51.5	55.8	50.5	43.2	43.0	37.2
Hispanic	28.8	32.6	29.9	24.2	25.3	23.5

Table 15.5
Source: US Department of Commerce, Bureau of the Census

Population Change in Dade County, 1950-1985

	White (%)	Black (%)	Hispanic (%)
1950	80	13	4
1960	80	15	5
1970	61	15	24
1980	44	17	39
1985	42	15	43

Table 15.6

White Reaction

As Table 15.6 shows, until the 1970s Miami and Dade County were populated mainly by white Americans. As a result, Miami's politics, economy and culture reflected the dominant population.

This was to change rapidly. Since the 1970s the Hispanics have introduced their own language, traditions and culture. The changes to which this inevitably led in Miami society were accepted by many Whites. White businessmen, especially, recognised that their future prosperity required them to accept a bilingual and bicultural society. Consequently, Spanish and English are now spoken in most banks and offices, with Hispanics and non-Hispanics working alongside each other. Nevertheless, integration rarely goes beyond the workplace with the English and Spanish-speaking communities going their own ways at the end of the working day. This situation was summed up by the *Economist* in 1982 when it said that Miami "is not a melting pot of cultures. It is a mosaic."

For many Whites, however, this 'Latinisation' was unacceptable. They felt that their own 'traditional' way of life was under threat from alien cultures and that they were foreigners in their own country. Many Whites simply decided to leave Dade County, describing the Miami they left behind as 'Little Cuba'. The extent of this white flight is indicated in Table 15.6 and by the changes in the political scene in the city. Cubans have now become the dominant political force in the city and in 1985 Xavier Suarez was elected the city's first Cuban-born mayor.

Black Reaction

In 1962, an article in the *Economist* noted that "Miami is not a good city in which to be black." The article went on to document the high incidence of black poverty, the absence of a black business class and the virtual collapse of the black political establishment. It would seem that Miami is still not a good city in which to be black. In 1989 *Time* magazine, in describing the increasing tensions between Hispanic immigrants and native-born Blacks, described the city as "A Brightly Coloured Tinderbox". Unlike the Hispanics, Blacks have made few economic or political gains since the 1960s. Since 1980 black unemployment in Dade County has risen to almost 11%, while the rate for Hispanics has dropped to under 6%. While Hispanics in general and Cubans in particular have expanded their ownership of small businesses, the already small black professional class is contracting further. As one black social commentator noted, "A larger and larger segment of the black community is falling further and further behind the rest of us in income and in quality of life."

The waves of Hispanic immigrants and more recently the influx from Central America has led to considerable resentment among the black community. For many decades Miami's Blacks have competed unsuccessfully with the incoming Hispanics for jobs, housing and other opportunities. While the power structure of the Hispanic people has grown, the ability of Miami's Blacks to influence city policy has diminished. Indeed, many Blacks now openly accuse the city administration of favouring Hispanics at their expense. Further resentment is fuelled by the richer Hispanics buying up property in the ghettos and replacing the Whites as the absentee landlords. On four separate occasions during the 1980s, this resentment boiled up into violence. The most recent riots in January 1989 saw several nights of arson, looting and random shootings in the ghettos of Overtown and Liberty City. When the rioting subsided, one person had been killed, 22 people had been wounded and property was damaged to the value of $1 million. Less serious than the 1980 Race Riots when 18 people were killed, 400 wounded and $100 million of property was damaged, the 1989 disturbances brought into sharp focus the increasing divide that exists between Blacks and Hispanics.

INDEX

Abolition of Discriminatory Laws, *19*
Affirmative Action, *66-72, 79-81*
African National Congress, *9, 21, 25-27, 30, 39-41, 43, 45, 52, 55-56*
Afrikaner Resistance Movement, *20, 40, 42, 55*
Apartheid
-application, *10-14*
-dismantling, *36-45*
-legacy, *46-57*
-modernising, *15-22*
-structures, *6-9*
-United States of America, *61*
Asians (Indians), *6, 16, 36-37, 49*

Bantu Authorities Act, *7*
Bantu Homelands Citizenship Act, *7*
Bensten Lloyd, *77*
Biko Steve, *15, 23-24*
Birmingham (Alabama), *61, 63*
Black Consciousness Movement, *23-24*
Black Nationalism, *59*
Black Panthers, *65*
Black Power, *59, 64-65*
Black Poverty, *84-85*
Black (Urban Areas) Consolidation Act, *10*
Boesack Allan, *26*
Bophuthatswana, *7, 12-14*
Botha PW, *15-22, 36, 39*
Botshabelo, *54*
Broederbond, *4, 39*
Bus Boycotts, *61-62*
Bush George, *71, 78, 80*
Busing, *68-69*
Buthelezi M, *18, 25-26, 56*

Carter Jimmy, *65*
Ciskei, *7*
Citizens Councils (White), *67*
Civil Cooperation Bureau, *53*
Civil Rights Act
-1875, *60*
-1957, *62*
-1960, *62*
-1964, *63-64, 66-67, 68, 73*
-1968, *63*
-1991, *71-72*
Civil Rights Commission, *78-79*
Civil Rights Movement, *61-63*
CODESA, *45*
Coloureds, *6, 10, 36, 37*
Community Councils (Act), *11, 18-19*
Congress of Racial Equality, *61-62, 73*
Conservative Party, *18, 20, 22, 36-39, 40, 42*
Corner Eugene 'Bull', *63*

de Klerk FW, *36-38, 54-57*
Democratic Party
-South Africa, *36-37, 40*
-USA, *61, 72, 75-78*

Discrimination
-Education, *46-50, 67-70*
-Employment, *66-70*
Dukakis Michael, *76-77*
Duke David, *72*

Elections (Presidential), *75-78*
Equal Opportunities Commission, *66*
Extreme Right, *81*

Farrakhan Louis, *75, 77*
Ferraro Geraldine, *75*
Freedom Charter, *23, 27*
Freedom Rides, *61-62*

Gary Convention, *65*
Ghettos, *86-87*
Grand Apartheid, *4, 7, 17, 42*
Group Areas Act, *10, 20*

Harms Louis, *53-54*
Hart Gary, *76*
Healthcare, *51-52*
Helms Jesse, *72*
Herstigte Nasionale Party, *18, 20, 42*
Hispanics, *88-91*
Homelands, *6-7, 10-14, 52-53*

Immigration and Control Act, *58*
Immigrants (Illegals), *88*
Immorality Act, *6, 16*
Inkathagate, *57*
Internal Security Act, *8*

Jackson Jesse, *73-78, 81*
Johnston Lyndon B, *64, 73*

Kennedy John F, *63*
Kerner Report, *83*
King Martin Luther, *62-63, 73*
Knights of the White Camelia, *60*
Ku Klux Klan, *60, 68, 72, 81*
Kwazulu, *7, 13*

Land (Distribution), *52-54*
Luthuli Chief Albert, *23*

Magus Malan, *53, 57*
Mandela Nelson, *20, 22-23, 26, 35, 38-45*
Mandela Winnie, *41, 57*
McCarthy Joseph, *61*
Mass Democratic Movement, *36*
Melting Pot (Theory), *58-59*
Miami (Florida), *90-91*
Migrant Labour, *12-13*

Mineral Resources, *4-5*
Mixed Marriages Act, *6, 16*
Mondale Walter, *75*

National Advisory Committee on Civil Disorders, *60, 64*
National Association for the Advancement of Coloured People, *61, 67, 73*
National Party, *4, 6, 18, 36-37, 39-41, 45*
National Security Management Systems, *20-22, 39*
National Union of Mineworkers, *25*
(Native) Lands Act, *6, 40*
Nonviolent Movement, *62-63*
New Right, *79-81*

Office of Federal Contract Compliance, *66*

Pan Africanist Congress, *22-23, 39-40*
Pass Laws, *8, 16*
Petty Apartheid, *15-16, 22*
Population Registration Act, *6, 40*
Preference Hirings, *66*
PUSH, *73*

Race Riots, *60, 64*
Rainbow Coalition, *75*
Ramaphosa Cyril, *25, 44*
Reagan Ronald, *70, 76*
 -Reaganomics, *79-80*
Reconstruction, *60*
Reikert Commission, *17*
Republican Party, *61, 72, 75-78*

Salad Bowl (Theory), *59*
Section 10 Rights, *7, 11, 17*
Segregation
 -de facto, *68*
 -de jure, *68*
Separate Amenities Act, *38*
Shanty Towns, *12*
Sisulu Walter, *39, 41, 44*
Sit-ins, *62*
South Africa (Foreign Relations), *28-35*
 -Angola, *28, 30*
 -British Commonwealth, *20, 32-33*
 -European Community, *34*
 -Namibia, *29-30*
 -Olympic Games, *32*
 -Sanctions, *32-35, 43*
 -SADDC, *28*
South African Communist Party, *40-41, 44-45*
Southern Christian Leadership Congress, *62*
State of Emergency, *15, 19-21, 39*
Student National Coordinating Committee, *62*
Strydom Barend, *42, 45*
Suppression of Communism Act, *8*
Supreme Court Rulings, *60, 62, 67-68, 70-71, 79*
Suzman Helen, *10*

Tambo Oliver, *25-26, 41*
Targets, *66*
Terre Blanche Eugene, *42, 55*
Terrorism Act, *8*
Tomlinson Commission, *12*
Townships, *10-12, 17-19, 21, 54*
Trade Unions, *16, 24-25*
Transkei, *7, 12-14*
Treurnicht Andries Dr, *18, 40*
Tricameral Parliament, *17-18, 36*
Tutu Archbishop Desmond, *15, 19-20, 39*

Uitenhage, *19*
Underclass, *86*
Union of South Africa, *4*
Union of Soviet Socialist Republics, *30-31*
United Democratic Front, *18, 21, 26, 44*
United Nations, *29, 55*
United States of America, *16, 31-32*
 -Constructive Engagement, *20, 31*
 -Free South Africa Movement, *31*
 -Sullivan Principles, *24, 31-32*
Unlawful Organisation Act, *8*

Venda, *7, 12*
Ventersdorp, *55*
Verwoerd VH, *4, 15*
Vorster John, *15*
Voting Rights Act, *73*
Voting Patterns
 -Blacks, *73-78*
 -Hispanics, *89-90*
 -Registration, *73*

Wiehahn Commission, *16*
Wilder Douglas, *78*
White Liberation Movement, *42*
White Supremacy, *81*

X Malcolm, *64*

Young Andrew, *73*